I0866292

DRAWING CLIMATE

Daniel J. Ryan
Jennifer Ferng
Erik G. L'Heureux
(Eds.)

Visualising
Invisible Elements
of Architecture

DRAWING CLIMATE

Birkhäuser Basel

DRY WET

COOL

HOT

CODA

Introduction: redirecting the arrows of climatic design

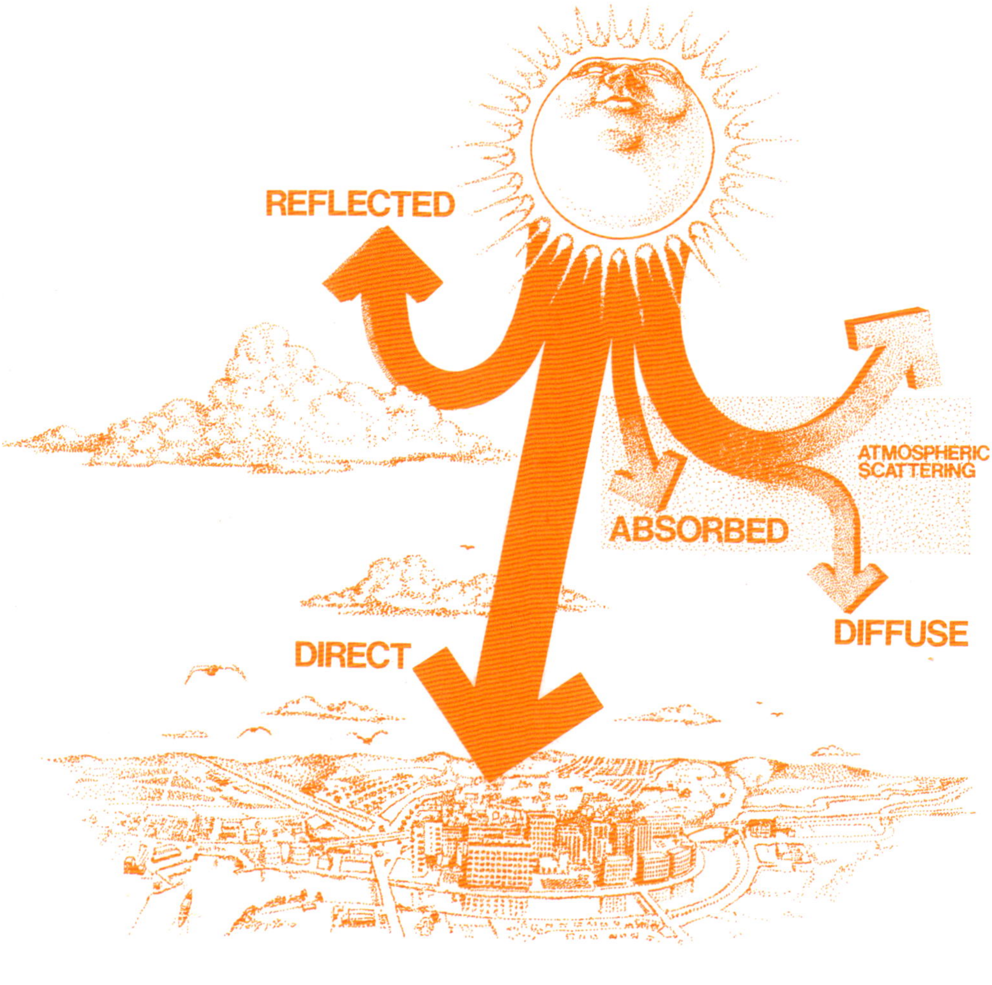

1 Russel Ball, What happens to solar radiation intercepted by the earth's atmosphere, from Edward Mazria, *The passive solar energy book,* 1979, p. 13.

Climate change has reinvigorated architecture's purpose in the realm of sustainable design. However, its drawings have not adapted to contemporary demands. Open any book about climatic design from the 1950s to today, and the chances are the drawings will have changed very little. The same graphic techniques prevail throughout architectural practice and are transferred into the curriculum of architecture schools. The same obsessions about sunlight, wind and air also persist in the standardised architectural sections that depict sunshine as a smiling yellow circle. Amid an ongoing planetary crisis, architects seem to be stuck.

As visual thinking about climate has become reductive, architects have limited their repertoire of environmental drawings. The drawings that are used, such as site plans, summer and winter environmental sections and heat flow diagrams, have become so banal that few consider their potential beyond explaining comfort and energy. Mostly they remind us that the sun exists and that on a good day wind flows through the building. Even when lacking in content, environmental drawings, particularly those showing climate, give a design some moral authority—they suggest the architect is sensitive to the natural world, even if the design does little to ameliorate conditions.[1] Such drawings touch on how architects position their work, how they leverage the moral weight of environmentalism, but they can give a false assurance that climatic issues are important.[2]

Some of the stagnation in how architects draw climate comes from the uncritical acceptance of the initial premises of mid-century climatic design. Many of the key texts from this period, such as Victor Olgyay's

Design with climate (1963), Baruch Givoni's *Man, climate and architecture* (1969) and Koenigsberger, Ingersoll, Mayhew and Szokolay's *Manual of tropical housing and building* (1974) still hold sway.[3] Today's books on climatic design continue to adapt and re-use their drawings and frameworks.[4] While still useful, the frameworks have many blindspots. For example, Olgyay noted that his book *Design with climate* was based on the provision of thermal comfort, and therefore the effects of moisture received far less consideration.[5] It is little surprise then that while today's architects still emphasise thermal comfort, few environmental architecture books include any mention of rain, snow, frost or fog.

Climate is not just averaged weather conditions but also includes weather events and predictable phenomena. The German meteorologist Rudolf Geiger pointed out that 'the climate of a given site is comprised of the average conditions, the regular sequence of weather events, and the repeatedly observed special phenomena such as tornadoes, dust storms and late frosts.'[6] We might add wildfires into that definition.

So how can we reconsider the way architects draw climate? One option is to be more inclusive, to give greater weight to moisture and weather events. This is the approach that this book takes. It is based on our conviction that we need a broader understanding of climate to address current environmental challenges. While we still see benefits in representing sun, wind and air, we believe that portraying more facets of climate, such as fire, dust or monsoons, creates richer drawings and allows for more thoughtful architecture. Another is to better consider the social effects of climate, as the justifications we offer for moderating climates have political and cultural histories and consequences.[7]

Thirdly, we wish to expand the geographical range of examples. This book brings drawings by Australian and Asian architects into discussion with those from Europe and the USA. It is not that architects have failed to show fire or ice or monsoons in their drawings. It is more that such considerations often happen at the margins. We believe that the long experience of architects in Australia with fire and of those in Southeast Asia with monsoon can highlight productive ways of engaging with climate. We hope furthermore that the range of images and critical analysis will provoke current and future practitioners to reframe how they think and draw climate.

Drawing climate into architecture

Drawings have many lives, as the following examples show. But like people, they can have a midlife crisis. Looking at drawings depicting heat exchange may serve to explore how this crisis came about.

Scientific phenomena are not always easily understood by a lay audience. It takes skill to break down complex concepts for novice students. Although mathematical equations elegantly explain the relationships of various phenomena, they rarely appeal to uninitiated members of the public. Visual aids can be more effective. We might expect architects trained in science or visual communication to do this well, but this is not always the case. When German meteorologist and climatologist Rudolf Geiger published his ground-breaking textbook on microclimatology, *The climate near the ground* (1927), he filled it with graphs and diagrams explaining key concepts to those entering the field. First published in English in 1950, it introduced generations of students to the environmental sciences. Geiger's text clearly spelt out the concepts and terms needed to understand the field, but it is the afterlife of a small drawing in the book, and its translation into architecture, that is of interest here.

Geiger wanted to explain the earth's radiation energy balance to an American audience; as a result, he created a Sankey diagram filling an entire page (Figure 2). Energy balance is defined as the amount of energy coming from the sun, directly and via the atmosphere, reaching towards the ground and bouncing back again. It assumes that during the day the ground will be warmed by the sun and at night some of that energy is released back to the sky. These drawings were illustrated with directional arrows of various thicknesses, moving to and from the ground. Each arrow represented a different type of heat transport—for example, short-wave radiation, long-wave radiation, eddy diffusion, conduction and evaporation.

For Geiger, the drawings explained the relative importance of radiation compared to other forms of heat exchange.[8] The thickest arrow symbolised the combined effects of short-wave radiation from the sun and the atmosphere. Two more arrows indicated atmospheric long-wave radiation and ground radiation. The other arrows expressed the remaining forms of heat exchange but were much thinner in width, demonstrating that conduction and convection held less impact on the heat balance.

Since its introduction in the late nineteenth century, engineers have used Sankey diagrams to explain material and resource flows.[9] In these diagrams all flows are proportionately scaled and drawn as a stream connecting one process with another. The stream branches out further as it loses energy. The viewer can understand how energy flows by following the arrows at the end of each branch. Geiger carefully grouped different forms of heat transportation together. He introduced hatching for each kind of heat transfer, alternating between curved and straight lines to indicate how energy branched off the main flow. This made it easy to understand how radiant energy was transformed.

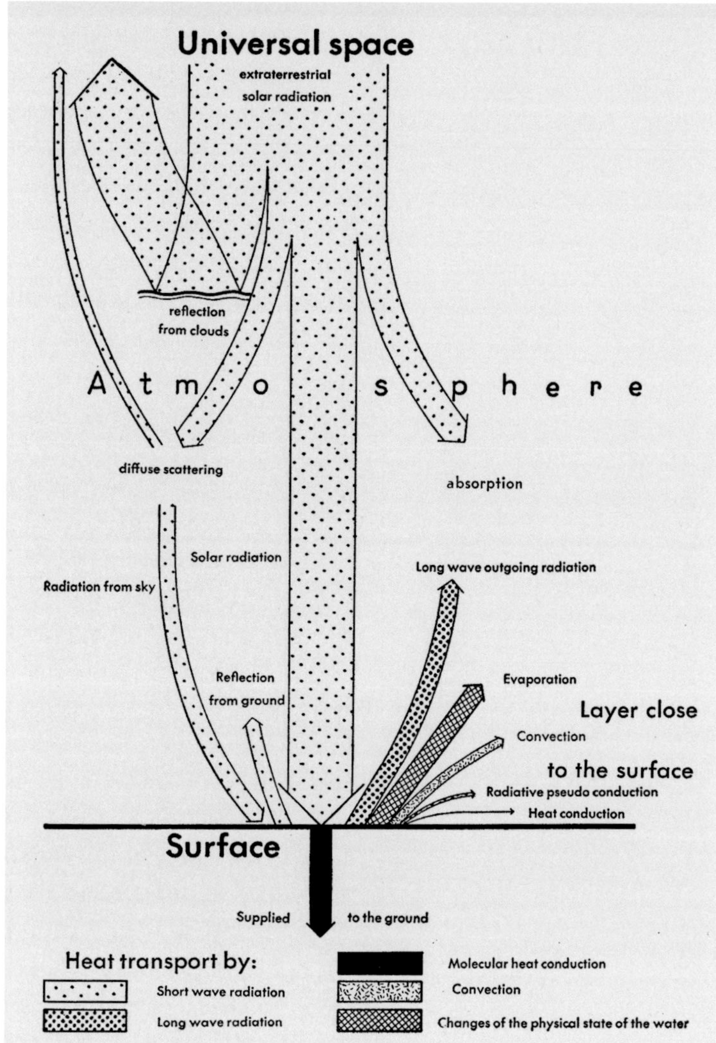

Geiger's energy balance drawing experienced multiple lives and was reproduced in 1963 by Victor Olgyay in *Design with climate*, the book that introduced architects and students to the practices of bio-climatic design.[10] In this book, Olgyay developed his own representations of climate, emphasising how people, buildings and climate could be in balance. He also redrew and reprinted other geographers', architects' and physiologists' drawings, giving the impression of a unified visual style. In most cases he improved on the original diagram(s), foregrounding how to understand climate and buildings in terms of people's needs, in a kind of climatic humanism for architects.[11]

Design with climate was both a project of visual curation and a showcase of design methods. It was Olgyay who, in fact, introduced

Geiger's concepts to architects. Few would realise that the diagram on solar radiation flows belonged first to Geiger, not Olgyay — such was the consistency of this image with the rest of Olgyay's drawings.

The diagram (Figure 2) seemed customised for an architectural audience, narrating the story of how radiation travelled from 'Universal space' to 'surface' through an intermediary, the 'atmosphere.' The prominence of these three terms seemed to position the discussion of heat exchange as one concerned with modernist ideals about world-making. After all, 'Universal space' was a term more familiar to adherents of the Bauhaus and de Stijl than those working in climatology.[12] It was this term that Mies van der Rohe used for his indeterminate and flexible long-span spaces. And yet here it was in the middle of an energy balance diagram. It seemed like meteorology was just another branch of modernism.

The drawing reappeared in architecture books throughout the 1970s and 1980s, as the sun gained importance as a solution to the energy crisis. However, Geiger's diagram was simplified as climatic design advocates feared that people were turned off by anything too technical. As Ed Mazria noted about passive solar design at the end of the 1970s, presentations up to then were 'too technical, cumbersome and time-consuming in application.' Instead he argued that 'to be useful, information must lead to the necessary degree of accuracy at each stage of a building's design.'[13]

2 Rudolf Geiger, Heat exchange at noon for a summer day, from *The climate near the ground*, 1950, p. 3.

Mazria's *Passive solar energy book* from 1979 tried to change this. Addressing architects, builders and owner-builders, the book was filled with graphs, tables and perspectives by Russel Ball, who used visual analogies and humour to explain the science behind the information. The solar energy balance diagram in the book shows a tarot sun's floating above a city (Figure 1). Tentacles of radiant energy twist from its smiling face. The point that there are different kinds of solar radiation is clearly made, but the diagram has lost its association with the ground. In making the ideas accessible, the diagram tries to balance between presenting facts and engaging an audience through appealing to their experiential knowledge. These quasi-technical images, as Daniel Barber notes, did this to suggest a 'universal validity, and to produce a new image of the world to influence new kinds of expertise.'[14] While not quite scientifically accurate, at least, such drawings added a touch of humour.

Retro-climate

Where Olgyay curated Geiger's ideas for architects, expanding their relevance, recent revisions by architects miss the opportunity to question how the current climate crisis requires a broader and more

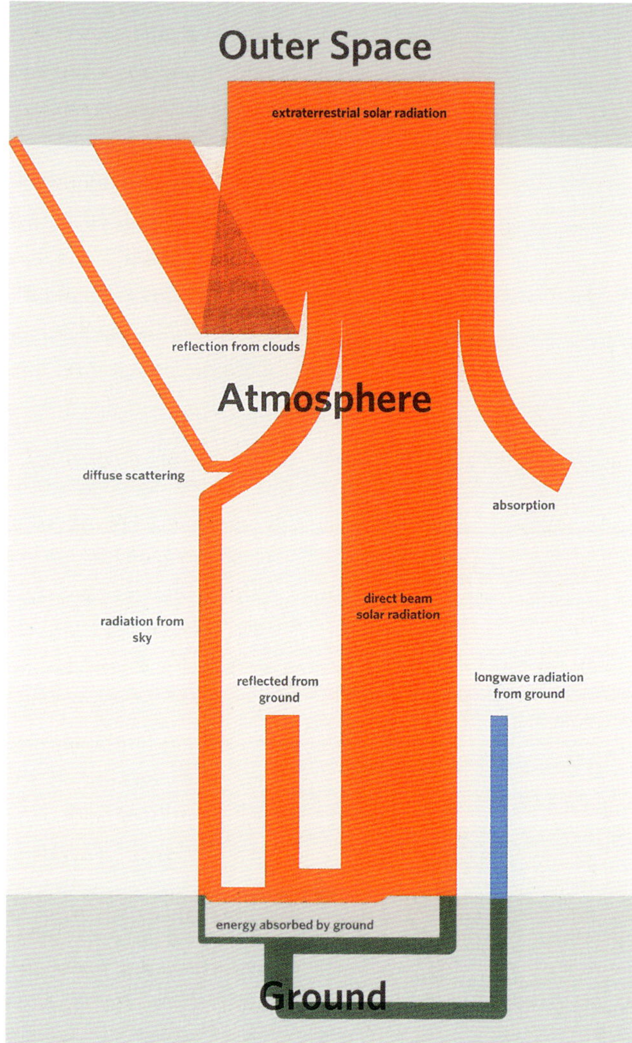

considered range of drawings. Instead, as noted earlier, today's drawings pay homage to some golden era of mid-century modernism. In the twenty-first century, environmental drawings lack the humour of their counterparts from the 1970s, as they fight fears of future catastrophe. Faced with a climate crisis of such proportions, architects have returned to more tried and trusted methods. In a recent book, *Architectural Science and the Sun*, Geiger's drawing of heat exchange reappears (Figure 3). However, Geiger is not credited, and the drawing is no longer at noon but, instead, titled 'solar radiation flows.' 'Universal space' has become 'outer space' and 'surface' has become 'ground.' Otherwise, the labelling remains the same, but the drawing has been stripped of any other kinds of heat exchange, which are vital components of Geiger's

3 Greg Arcangeli, Solar radiation flows, from Matt Fajkus and Dason Whitsett, *Architectural science and the sun: the poetics and pragmatics of solar design*, 2018, p. 79.

interpretation. Gone, too, are the directional arrows, leaving the reader a little unclear where the flows start and end. So, what at first sight seems a careful replica has lost both the detail and clarity of Geiger's original synthesis.

This retroactive approach to climatic drawings seems to pine for both an age of technical certainty and novelty. It suggests that, by recovering mid-century methods of climatic design and updating drawing styles, today's architecture students will be able to find a way out of our current predicament. This is only partly plausible, as the challenge of climate change goes beyond comfort and low-energy design.

Structure of the book

This book has been conceived from a sense that architecture needs to take a more expansive interest in climate. The book plays with the history of defining places climatically. Rather than classifying the world into temperate, tropical or extreme, we split the book into four sections—*Dry, Wet, Cool* and *Hot*. Doing so creates new adjacencies between climatic events and climatic elements and how they inform architecture. The selection of images is not meant to be comprehensive or definitive. Instead, it is hoped that each chapter will draw attention to the breadth of imagery available for each theme and some of the representational issues that each phenomenon raises.

In many cases, authors explore climatic representation at multiple scales. The first section, *Dry*, includes chapters on dust and wind. Moving through scales allows us to see climate from below, as Jennifer Ferng shows in her study of dust, linking the microscopic to the global. For every scale at which we examine a phenomenon, there is often a corresponding drawing in circulation. Designers are expected to understand a phenomenon at multiple scales, from global to local, but often intervene at a much more local level. In some cases, as Christhina Candido suggests, the advent of newer and more accurate forms of visualisations has not always improved outcomes. Instead, she argues for greater awareness of how best to intervene.

Many of the chapters deal with the difficulty of representing climatic phenomena and the questions these raise. This is particularly true of wet climates. Lilian Chee considers how our own body can be a register of the weather and how phenomena like monsoons are experienced relationally, as lived experiences. For Nathan Etherington, drawing water is a challenge as it is unpredictable. He shows how attitudes to rainfall's unpredictability have shifted over the past century. Etherington traces how architects once emphasised hydraulics in drawings but today emphasise atmospheric effects. On the other hand, Erik L'Heureux questions how the cloudless, blue sky has come to dominate architectural imagery, even in the tropics. He argues for architects to shed their 'cumulus prejudices.' He shows how, by embracing the dynamics of local cloud formations, architects can more carefully frame a building's setting.

Other chapters address questions related to climate change and risk, particularly in the third and fourth sections on *Cool* and *Hot*. Johanna Sluiter considers how the occupation of the Arctic has fascinated a number of modernist architects and how climate change has opened up the possibility of occupying the vast icefields of the Arctic. In other cases, climate can be read in terms of gendered anxieties surrounding race and temperature, as Nicole Sully and Deborah van der Plaat show in the case of the Queensland bush house. The uncertainty surrounding the future and how this informs representational strategies is the theme of Daniel Ryan's chapter 'Revealing fire.' Ryan connects some of the aesthetic themes about climate change with a longer history of the sublime, drawing parallels between early-nineteenth-century paintings of the apocalypse and recent designs for bushfire-sensitive buildings.

The Coda of the book showcases a range of experimental projects that look at how climatic design can be implemented and visualised in practice. Featuring work by students from Sydney and Singapore, 'Explorations' shows how some of the climatic phenomena explored throughout the book can inform architectural design and representation.

Seeing unseen futures

Architectural drawings allow us to see the unseen, to filter and aggregate past experiences into a projected future. They order space and materials and give weight to an architectural idea. Indeed, they also give weight to a particular aspect of climate, to certain kinds of weather. Air is ordered to flow through openings. Shade is given a predictable pattern. Water is channelled out of spouts. If climate is mediatised weather, then architecture mediates the weather and its events. It can make the weather seem hotter or cooler, drier, more humid. It can also make climate seem predictable, as if the building were tuned to every possible weather occurrence. Architecture gives the impression of taming climate, making even the most inhospitable places seem tolerable.

This is a representational challenge as much as a design challenge. If architects seem stuck, in that the same drawings are being repeated *ad infinitum*, then perhaps architects need to rethink what aspects of climate they are drawing and designing for. It is time to redirect climatic design's arrows. We hope this book starts the process.

1 I treat technical drawings as analogous to advertising. See Michael B. Beverland, Adam Lindgreen and Michiel W. Vink, 'Projecting authenticity through advertising: consumer judgments of advertisers' claims,' *Journal of Advertising*, 37:1 (2008): 5–15, https://doi.org/10.2753/JOA0091-3367370101.
2 For a broader discussion of environmentalism, capitalism and marketing, see Peter Dauvergne, *Environmentalism of the rich* (Cambridge: MIT Press, 2016), 139–152.
3 Victor Olgyay, *Design with climate: bioclimatic approach to architectural regionalism* (Princeton: Princeton University Press, 1963); Baruch Givoni, *Man, climate and architecture* (Amsterdam: Elsevier, 1969); O. H. Koenigsberger, T. G. Ingersoll, Alan Mayhew and S.V. Szokolay, *Manual of tropical housing and building* (London: Longman, 1974).
4 Vivienne Brophy and J. Owen Lewis, *A green Vitruvius: principles and practice of sustainable architectural design* (London: Routledge, 2nd ed. 2011), and Richard Hyde, *Climate responsive design: a study of buildings in moderate and hot humid climates* (London: Taylor & Francis, 2000).
5 Victor Olgyay, *Design with climate*, 32.
6 Rudolf Geiger, Robert H. Aron and Paul Todhunter, *The climate near the ground* (Braunschweig: Vieweg, 5th ed. 1995), 3.
7 On climatic design's downplaying of the social role of architecture, see Jiat-Hwee Chang, *A genealogy of tropical architecture: colonial networks, nature and technoscience* (Abingdon, Oxon: Routledge, 2016).
8 Rudolf Geiger, *The climate near the ground,* 13.
9 For a history of Sankey diagrams see Mario Schmidt, 'The Sankey diagram in energy and material flow management: part 1 history,' *Journal of Industrial Ecology,* 12:1 (2008): 82–94, https://doi.org/10.1111/j.1530-9290.2008.00004.x.
10 Victor Olgyay, *Design with climate,* 33.
11 See Daniel A. Barber, 'The nature of the image: Olgyay And Olgyay's architectural-climatic diagrams in the 1950s,' *Public Culture,* 29:1 (1 January 2017): 129–164, https://doi.org/10.1215/08992363-3644433.
12 Universal space, or *Allraum* in German architectural theory, was an idea promoted by modernists such as Walter Gropius and, later, Mies van der Rohe. For Gropius it suggested the exterior into which modern architecture dissolved, while for Mies it was a lightly structured interior space or flexible open plan. For a detailed discussion of Gropius' concept of *Allraum,* see Tim Steffen Altenhof, 'Breathing space: the architecture of pneumatic beings,' PhD diss. (Yale University, 2018), 177–181. Available from ProQuest One Academic (2070918889).
13 Edward Mazria, *The passive solar energy book* (Emmaus: Rodale Press, 1979), 2.
14 Daniel A. Barber, 'The nature of the image,' 131.

DRY

Particles to dust storms: seeing climates from below

1 Aerial photography of dust storms over East Asia and pre-monsoon storms moving over India, 2008.

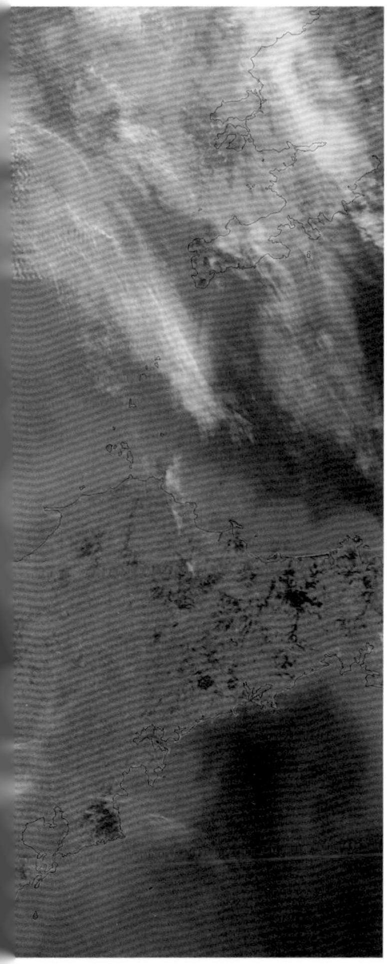

Not surprisingly, dust is defined by its passive nature. Dust particles can be caught in gusts of wind, and lacking any type of agency, they take flight where the air leads them.[1] Dust particles have remained invisible to the human eye, and as a result, over the centuries, their evolving incarnations—film, grime, grit, haze, patina, pollen and pollution—have never been considered a part of climatic design. They belonged instead to the scientific discourse on meteorological phenomena. Architects, in executing climatic design, have openly acknowledged that sunlight, rain and fire are critical elements that architecture must address. However, what about the role of dust? Swirls of dust blowing off desert dunes and sandy clouds billowing from a single road in an abandoned town evoke romantic images of dust as being atmospheric in nature. But buildings, in fact, are designed to keep out dust; dust moving from outdoors to indoors signals an everyday, if not, banal occurrence. Dust represents a part of the natural environment that is more of a hindrance than contemporary architects would like to admit. The accumulation of dust becomes a nuisance for those who must regularly clean built surfaces, wiping the film of dirt from exterior façades. Dust becomes bothersome in its ability to aggregate in every corner.

Dust is also classified as a type of irritant, causing human beings to sneeze, cough and gasp when the air is filled with too many particles.[2] Architectural historian Robin Evans referred to the role of architecture as that of a container excluding foreign matter. For Evans, the 'logic of containment' between private and public spaces was embodied within discrete systems of doors, windows and corridors.[3] Foreign matter, however, tends to spread everywhere—dust always finds a way to seep into a building. It emerges from windowsills, air ducts and laundry vents, blown inside from balconies.

Architectural historians John Ruskin and Jorge Otero-Pailos have explored how dust remains a source of historical fascination for antiquarians, architects and artists.[4] Surface pollution, or what Ruskin called 'the golden stain of time,' remains a challenging problem for experts in heritage conservation.[5] Following developments from the eighteenth century into the present day, this chapter analyses a brief series of visual images from the microscopic level to the scale of a building—from plates of micro-animals and living organisms to nationwide dust storms. Specifically, I argue that dust in itself embodies a type of 'climate from below'—a term I use to explain how meteorological elements engage with the built environment at the microscopic scale and simultaneously, at the broader scales of geographic regions and nations. Dust as a climate from below consists of invisible particles that aggregate into larger masses, impacting how buildings must cope with external forces. The intrusive character of dust remains unstoppable. Dust particles and dust storms are constituted from the same matter; nonetheless, when transformed at an urban scale, their behaviour reflects the way in which architects should address dust. Moving from the microscopic tardigrade to the red dawn that plagued Sydney in 2009, this chapter contends that dust, like many of its elemental counterparts, plays a significant role in twenty-first century climate change. Connected to greater ecological patterns like desertification, industrial pollution and soil erosion, it epitomises one of many meteorological elements that will impact how cities will adopt sustainable measures over the next few decades.

Kleine Wasserbären

Before contemporary concerns around climates were articulated, the eighteenth century remained a rich source of scientific information about the animate nature of dust. Micro-animals, in fact, constituted some of these discoveries made by Protestant pastor Johann August Ephraim Goeze, who stumbled upon a specimen that looked like a little 'water bear' (*Wasserbär*) in 1773 (Figure 2). When examined under a microscope, the water bear resembled an inflated, segmented body with four pairs of legs ending in matching claws (or sucking disks). Water bears lacked a face or any eyes, but only possessed a single mouth-like protuberance. Goeze was thus credited with the first sighting of the tardigrade or water bear, one of many micro-animals who lived in the mountains, deep oceans, volcanoes, tropical rain forests and even

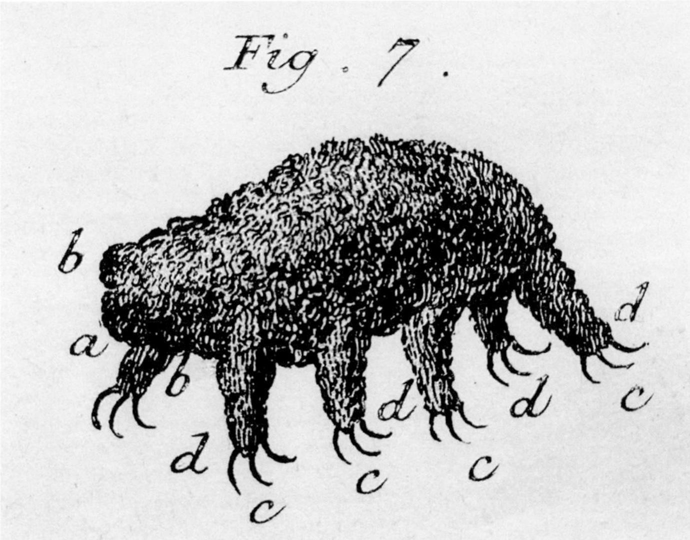

2 Johann August Ephraim Goeze, Tardigrade, from *Über den kleinen Wasserbär, Herrn Karl Bonnets Abhandlungen aus der Insektologie*, 1773.

Antarctica. Today, they have been tested as some of the most resilient animals on the planet. Tardigrades are catalogued as a 'pioneer species,' which are able to introduce other species into new environments.[6] Observed by Goeze as well as modern-day scientists, tardigrades are particularly sluggish walkers; their gait is akin to that of a slow-moving bear. Tardigrades have survived long periods of time in extreme climates including outer space; they have been exposed to radiation, dehydration, starvation, air deprivation and extreme pressures and temperatures. Tardigrades are able to subsist on a diet of moss and algae and often prey upon other, smaller species of tardigrade.[7] Yet, despite the extreme characteristics of these environmental conditions, tardigrades have managed to thrive as a species.

Tardigrades were among some of the first discoveries where scientific pioneers were able to detect the presence of microorganisms within air (and consequently, dust). This animate nature of dust runs contrary to its public image of something that is devoid of substances. Practices of modern architecture, in fact, have forgotten about these complexities of the external environment, and dust, like air, has been defined only as a passive occurence within climatic design.

Given this precedent, biological and environmental references from the microscopic world have influenced built design in strange and wonderful ways. Eugene Tssui's Ojo del Sol or Sun's Eye in Berkeley, California, for example, combines the formal aspects of the tardigrade's anatomy and incorporates them into the structure of a family residence. Tssui conducted some zoological research on the tardigrade, discovering

its reputation as the most indestructible creature on the planet. The house was constructed for Tssui's parents, who were worried about the possibility of earthquakes. The architecture of the house revolved around the biology of the tardigrade—Tssui as 'polymath nonpareil' tried to make the house impermeable to fires, earthquakes, flooding and pests (Figure 3). The ovular shell of the house possesses no hard edges or angles, modelled after the tardigrade's ability to diffuse external stress through its body. The gently sloping walls are angled at 4°–5° to create a low centre of gravity in case of an earthquake (while minimising wind and water resistance).[8] Tssui had formerly worked with architects Victor Prus in Montreal, Bruce Goff in Tyler, Texas, and Frei Otto in Germany. The central feature of the house revolves around 4.5 metre oculus window generated from Tssui's 'ethic-biologic' design, finished with stucco mixed with crumbled abalone shell.[9] The Ojo del Sol has never been tested in an earthquake emergency, but Tssui assures sceptics that the house performs in terms of energy conservation, maintaining 18–21°C within its interiors all year round. Tssui has constructed 16 projects in the San Francisco area, with seven residential buildings underway in the USA, another in Portugal. In this extraordinary example, the tardigrade personifies both a formal template for architecture and a structural diagram for the construction of the house.

3 Tssui Design and Research, Ojo del Sol, 1994–1995, Berkeley, California.

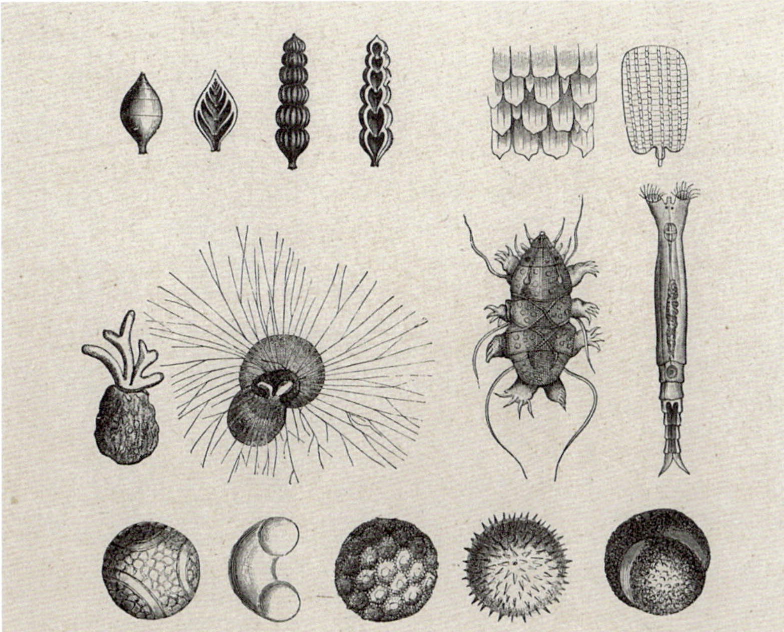

Fig. 27. — Ce que nous respirons. Corpuscules en suspension dans l'air.

4 Camille Flammarion, What we breathe: airborne corpuscules, 1873, from *L'Atmosphère: Météorologie populaire.*

Des microzoaires vivants

Almost one hundred years later, nineteenth-century French astronomer Camille Flammarion wrote a number of popular books on the nature of science, including science fiction and research on the potential of psychic powers. Flammarion was obsessed with the biological philosophies of Charles Darwin and Jean-Baptiste Lamarck as well as the growing spiritualism associated with mystics and storytellers. In his book *L'Atmosphère: description des grands phénomènes de la nature* (1873),[10] Flammarion trained his gaze upon the invisible dust mite (Figure 4). Substances contained within air represented a relatively new discovery at the turn of the nineteenth century—even the idea of oxygenated air, or what we know now as the ozone and ammonium nitrate, heralded new knowledge related to oxygen's role in combustion. Flammarion described mundane appearances such as a single cloud of dust floating away from a building site:

> When we pass close by a house that is being pulled down, or one in the course of construction, and find ourselves enveloped in a cloud of dust that penetrates down our throats, we, often, beyond a doubt, inhale hundreds of these tiny atoms.[11]

5 Anonymous, Trombes de sable dans la Steppe, from Marie de Ujfalvy-Bourdon, *De Paris* à *Samarkand [...], impressions de voyage d'une parisienne,* 1863.

But he was clear to point out that minute particles or even living, breathing microorganisms (*des microzoaires vivants*) were alive, calling them 'the fish of our blood.' Even from this point in the nineteenth century, dust and air seemed to go hand in hand. In fact, it was impossible to have dust without the presence of air. Despite his tendencies for spiritual science, Flammarion's examination of microorganisms was rather rational, based solely on visual observations and tangible evidence.

In a diagram entitled 'Ce que nous respirons,' Flammarion lists the different types of particles unseen to the human eye contained in the air we breathe—*foraminifères, écailles d'ailes de papillon, milioles, le tardigrade, le rotifère*. He mentions that millions of petite grains of pollen are held suspended in midair; as a result, all of these particles grow in size, and consequently, human beings are able to inhale these substances.[12] Flammarion's particles are not unlike the tardigrade seen by Goeze under the microscope. Many of these invisible germs could be dissolved into soluble matter. Even the sheer number of particles that could be squeezed into a single drop of water was impressive—almost 32,000 dust particles could fit into the area of one square centimetre.

Dust devils, or dust storms, were visualised in the nineteenth century by European travellers who witnessed dust channelled into tall funnels moving across Central Asian cities like Samarkand. Atmospheric changes, including fluctuations in temperature, generated sand and waterspouts when air rising upward would assume a 'rotative movement'[13] (Figure 5). Dust devils drew up bodies and liquids over which they travelled, moving forward while maintaining a longitudinal directional axis. Sand spouts destroyed everything in their path—uprooting trees and destroying buildings, carrying debris and distributing it over large areas of land. Sand spouts appeared simultaneously as thunderstorms and were often associated with thunder.

Tiny, minute particles of dust that suffuse buildings symbolise the enemies of modern architecture; dirt, mould, spores and waste are associated with dust particles as well. Thus, any cultural history of dust becomes quickly measured against rituals of purity and contamination. Represented by its white walls, modern architecture, according to Rodolphe el-Khoury, embodied the absence of visual stimuli, marked by its odourlessness and cleanliness.[14] Dust—or fine dry powder consisting of tiny particles of earth or waste matter—could be found lying on the ground or moving through the air. Even in the midst of the 9-11 attacks on the World Trade Center in 2001, dust as a by-product of the violence of commercial airplanes crashing into the Twin Towers forcefully reminded

spectators of the power of accumulation. Legal assistant Marcy Borders, who unfortunately passed away from stomach cancer in 2015, was known in New York City's popular press as the 'Dust Lady' (Figure 6). An iconic photograph taken by Stan Honda emerging from the 9-11 attacks captured Borders fleeing a building completely covered in layers of yellowish dust. Only a portion of her face remained visible.

6 Stan Honda, Photograph of Marcy Borders covered in dust as she takes refuge in an office building after one of the World Trade Center towers collapsed in New York, 2001.

Referring to ancient tropes addressing hygiene, anthropologist and cultural theorist Mary Douglas argued that the themes of pollution and taboo revealed the meaning of dirt throughout diverse contexts. Ritual, religion and lifestyles all played a role in defining how dirt was

7 E. H. Dixon, *King's Cross, London: the great dust-heap, next to Battle Bridge and the Smallpox Hospital*, water-colour painting, 1837.

understood by societies around the world. Dirt could generally be defined as 'matter out of place.'[15] Douglas' influence upon philosopher and psychoanalyst Julia Kristeva and her concept of abjection typified feelings of horror when confronted with defilement, sewage and muck.[16] These feelings of filth were equally resurrected in the 'great dust-heap' that lay next to Battle Bridge and the Smallpox Hospital in nineteenth-century London (Figure 7). In this context, dust men and cinder sifters were considered to be 'pariahs of the metropolis.' Such dust heaps were generated from years of filthy accumulation becoming a local haunt for innumerable pigs.[17]

Megan Born, Helene Furján and Lily Jencks' *Dirt* (2012) presents a selection of architectural works that examine dirt not as filth but as 'a metaphor, material, process, design tool, narrative, design system.'[18] They include Robert Smithson's *Spiral Jetty* and live models of the Arctic ice caps as examples of the intersection between dirt and design. Dirt and dust as interchangeable elements retain a sensibility of matter being out of place. Such lessons in design and nature remind architects to accept dust as part of the natural environment, and that its presence remains inescapable.

'Asian dust'

Landscapes and the expression of geological forms can be viewed from the air, and dust storms as visual phenomena can be tracked as they drift across nations. In fact, dust plays a major role in landscape development and processes in Asia and Oceania. Dr Richard Greene, at the ANU Fenner School, insists that 'layers of dust up to three metres thick form across many parts of the Australian landscape. Loose sediments from the Lake Eyre and Murray Darling basins are the likely source of much of the fine grained dust that the wind transports across the nation.'[19] Dust in Australia traverses predominantly in a west-to-east direction, settling in the Eastern Highlands. Greene's research also focuses on the nature and composition of dust particles, which can significantly influence environmental degradation processes such as salination and soil erosion. Within a distribution model of dust deposits across Australia, Greene refers to *aeolian dust*—characterised as a 'player and recorder of environmental change.'[20] As a form of visual evidence, aeolian dust is intimately tied to the processes of formation, transport and deposition, all of which are ecological patterns key for predicting global climate change. Greene confirms that 'records from continental ice sheets, loess, lacustrine and deep-sea sediments can show the timing of aeolian dust deposits. Aeolian processes pertain to wind activity in the study of geology and weather (specifically, the wind's ability to shape the surface of the Earth).'

> High accumulation rates during full glacial conditions for instance have been taken to signify aridity and postulated fertilization of oceanic regions. Desertification and associated dust storms possess forthcoming threats for public health, habitation and agriculture in many parts of the world. Overgrazing and poor land use policy may be the cause of these environmental problems, but they may as well be caused by changes in the climate system. The impact of climate variability on desertification at frequencies relevant to human societies (decades, centuries, millennia) is not well documented and understood.[21]

Dust represents an ageless element of climate. As an ancient phenomenon in Asia, dust was recorded as part of China's national heritage, documented as part of classical literature. Dating back to the Shang dynasty, Zhushu jinian 竹书纪年 documents that in the fifth year of Di Xin, it rained dust at Bo, located in the Henan Province, China.[22] Northwestern China, for example, has experienced dust storms ever since 300 CE and until 1949, with storms averaging at least every 31 years.

8 Aerial photography of dust storms over East Asia and pre-monsoon storms moving over India, 2008.

For example, an aerial photograph taken by NASA depicts brownish, yellow clouds moving across the Asian continent (Figures 1 and 8). The dust storms materialise as a miasma hanging over patches of land and sea. Moving towards East Asia, this so-called plague of yellow dust—yellow sand, yellow wind or Asian dust—remains endemic to this continent. Large quantities of dust, originating in China as well as the deserts of Mongolia and Kazakhstan, are funnelled into high-speed surface winds and as a result, dust storms generate dense clouds of fine, dry soil particles. Asian dust clouds are comprised of a mixture of chemical elements: silicon, aluminium, calcium and iron, as well as a few poisonous substances like mercury and cadmium. Fine dust particles, if inhaled as a large quantity, can trigger long-term scarring of lung tissue as well as induce cancer and lung disease.

In March 2008, yellow dust from the Gobi Desert blew over Beijing, China.[23] During the 2008 Olympics in Beijing, nations that had sent athletes to compete in the games ensured that their athletes were outfitted with face masks on the advice of leading exercise physiologists.

The incoming American cycling squad, for instance, was photographed wearing their face masks.[24] This press image upset Chinese officials, a reaction predicted by the International Olympic Committee (IOC). Other international teams were training in nearby towns like Dalian, located at least 1 hour and 15 minutes away from Beijing. Chinese officials had tried to control Beijing's natural environment before the commencement of the Olympic games. Factories in the city and the surrounding provinces were shut down or moved in order to reduce air pollution. Major construction projects were halted, and cars were taken off the road on alternate days. Yet, the skies over Beijing remained hazy.

Thailand, India and Hong Kong are also experiencing high levels of industrial pollution, as weather patterns, coal heating and carbon emissions continue to contribute to the acceleration of climate change. Bangkok officials have started using cloud-seeding techniques (rain-making) in order to ease pollution in given districts. Cloud-seeding involves injecting clouds with a modest amount of inert chemicals, such as silver iodide, in order to increase rainfall. Firefighters have even used high-pressure water cannons to clean dust from Bangkok's City Hall.[25] In India, Delhi's pollution ranks among the highest in the world. After the Diwali Hindu festival of lights, parts of the city reached hazardous levels exceeding AQI 300 (the US Embassy reported pollution levels measuring 999). Rickshaw drivers are particularly prone to health problems such as breathing difficulties, chest pain and coughing. The Indian National Clean Air Programme began in 2017, with the aim of reducing levels of air pollution by 30% by 2024.

Hwang Sa or yellow dust in Korea remains much maligned since it carries several industrial pollutants—viruses, fungi, bacteria and even heavy metals. There is a direct correlation between yellow dust and the quality of a person's respiratory health. At 400 micrograms per cubic metre, people are recommended to limit their heavy exercise and outdoor sports.[26] Yellow dust corresponds to increased asthma attacks and frequency of doctors' visits. To counter the gradual processes of desertification, planting trees as government policy has assisted with slowing down soil erosion.

Korea absorbs its fair share of dust from neighbouring China—upon which it blames its health problems and industrial pollution. The geopolitics of dust travelling from China into Korea indicates the significance of climatic design; China's pollution, according to the region's journalists, is severely choking South Korea.[27] This influx of dust pollution from China has been proven to cause increased mortality from respiratory and cardiovascular diseases in South Korean districts.[28] Given these high levels of dust particles in the air, South Korean cities have resorted to using digital media to monitor breathing levels for their population. Known as *misae misae*, this app, like others, measures the amount of fine dust in the air, particularly during the spring months. Digital sensors distributed around Seoul, for example, collect data on dust levels and send this information back to the app. The 'social disaster'[29] triggered by China has inspired the Korean government to pass emergency laws to address dust pollution. Since seven major cities in Korea suffer from dangerous PM 2.5 particles, this legislation has prompted politicians to limit the use of private vehicles and coal-fired power stations as well as reduce the amount of dust generated by building sites. But these measures have had little success; almost 50%–70% of fine dust in Korea still continues to originate in China.[30]

Red dawn

If the particle embodies the singular component of dust, dust storms represent the aggregate accumulation of these same particles. In 2009, Sydney residents awoke to an apocalyptic red haze that had settled over the city (Figure 9). Accompanied by gale force winds of 1,400 km/h, the dust reduced visibility, and public commentators openly declared that it looked like Armageddon, a 'scene from the end of the world.'[31] Red dust infiltrated Australians' homes and even birds were blown out of their nests. A woman from Dulwich Hill looked out from her kitchen and claimed that there was an intense red glow emanating from outside. Another resident contacted the ABC saying they went outdoors for a bicycle ride and returned looking like a 'red panda.'[32] Dust had begun to infiltrate alarm systems, wreaking havoc for local fire brigades. Over 500 callouts signalled an extraordinary event. Dust particles were getting into the electrical circuitry and setting off alarms designed to pick up dust matter in smoke. The orange, crimson light, as another resident put it, was quite 'eerie.' Transportation proved to be problematic—car headlights were incapable of illuminating anything in the red dust so it was impossible to see.

For about three days, thousands of tons of dirt and soil were lifted into the air and dumped into Sydney Harbour and the Tasman Sea. The dust clouds at this point were quite visible from outer space. Even on international television channels like the Weather Channel, journalist Richard Whitaker commented: 'This is unprecedented. We are seeing earth, wind, and fire together' (calling it the mother of all dust storms).[33] Almost immediately, the sale of face masks surged quickly as residents struggled to protect themselves against dust. The 2009 dust storm deposited a great amount of phytoplankton biomass directly into ocean waters.

In this case, even though it was the largest on-record dust storm in terms of soil loss, the staging and delivery of iron nutrients was quite timely: it caused plankton to bloom and gave them the ability to absorb greater amounts of carbon.[34]

Dust storms summon the worst manifestations of soil erosion. According to Community Dust Watch, the 2009 dust storm cost New South Wales approximately AUD 300 million.[35] Begun in 2002, Community Dust Watch is one of Australia's longest running citizen science programmes. Volunteers across Australia collect data about dust in their local neighbourhoods and send this information to the Department of Planning, Industry and Environment. Around 40 monitoring stations across Australia have contributed data that has directly led to agency instigated projects—among them test models of wind erosion and dust transport, confirmation of dust storms measured by satellite imagery, and the conversion of visibility records from the Bureau of Meteorology into dust concentrations.[36]

Even mining dust—classified as such—signifies an understandable concern for local residents. Dust emissions from local sites are graded by the size of particle. Even though particulate matter (PM) is microscopic and invisible to the human eye, the scale of the type of particle causes different effects on the human body. The NSW Department of Health uses a visual analogy that compares marbles with basketballs. Total Suspended Particulate Matter (TSP) refers to the total amount of particles suspended in the air: 'even the largest of these particles is barely half the width of a human hair.'[37] Measuring between the grades of PM 10 and PM 2.5, these sizes are still smaller than 2.5 millionths of a metre. Human activities like shoveling, bulldozing, blasting and vehicles on dirt roads contribute annually to the number of dust particles in the air.

The particulate character of dust, magnified hundreds of millions of times, remains capable of generating large-scale effects on the natural and built environment. Industrial pollution and soil erosion are among a few of the large-scale issues faced by countries like Australia, China, Korea and Mongolia. Dust storms do not respect the conventional borders of nations, leaving behind problems for a country's neighbours. Geopolitics of dust are embedded now within pollution governance and transnational agreements on sustainable measures for international cities. Thus, the ubiquitous presence of dust on every continent transforms it from being a local nuisance to a universal responsibility. Beyond scientists and meteorologists, architects too must contend with dust as a force of nature, allowing animate matter to co-exist alongside buildings as part of their deliberate approaches to environmental management.

9 Sydney covered in a blanket of dust during an extreme dust storm, 2009.

1 The Bureau of Meteorology in Australia defines a dust storm as 'an area of raised dust that moves with the prevailing wind system. The size of the dust particles can range from 0–1000 micrometres. Dust storms have been known to [move] dust particles as high as 4.5 km into the atmosphere with the average height of a dust storm being 1–2 km. Dust storms can move particles halfway across the Earth and can move as fast as the prevailing weather system.' http://www.bom.gov.au/nsw/sevwx/facts/dust.shtml.

2 Dust allergies are common to all human beings—sneezing, known as sternutation, is defined as a semi-autonomous reflex and allows the body to expel unwanted germs.

3 Robin Evans, 'Figures, doors and passages,' in *Translations from drawing to building and other essays* (Cambridge: MIT Press, 1997), 75.

4 Jorge Otero-Pailos, Scraping Ruskin, lecture as part of the exhibition *Unto this last: two hundred years of John Ruskin*, Yale Center for British Art, Yale University (5 September–8 December 2019). See also Jorge Otero-Pailos, 'The ethics of dust: Carthago Nova' at the *Dirt, dust, and ruins* exhibition, curated by Zanny Begg and Jennifer Ferng, Tin Sheds Gallery, The University of Sydney (2013).

5 John Ruskin, *The seven lamps of architecture* (Cornhill: Smith, Elder, & Co., 1912), 234.

6 Tardigrades are nicknamed 'moss piglets'—this moniker reflects a visual description of their rotund bodies and tendency to be found in locations like moss and lichen. Thousands of tardigrades were sent to the moon in an Israeli lunar probe in April 2019, and it is predicted that they will be able to survive in a suspended state of animation. See https://nypost.com/2019/08/07/tiny-bears-likely-survived-crash-of-israeli-probe-on-moon/.

7 Almost 1,150 species of tardigrade can be found in Australia alone, under the classification of water-dwelling, eight-legged animals.

8 For more information on the architect Eugene Tssui see https://baynature.org/article/an-architect-and-a-tardigrade/ and http://www.telosmovie.com/.

9 On Ojo del Sol, refer to https://www.berkeleyside.com/2015/11/30/how-quirky-is-berkeley-eugene-tssuis-fish-house-part-1. Tssui wrote an article on China's first zero-energy housing complex located in Guangzhou, developed for the State Key Laboratory of Subtropical Building Science. Positioned 30 metres below ground, the building is based on the design of an African termite's nest. Suspended ceiling plates for humidity evaporation and underground water pools are used as cooling mechanisms.

10 Camille Flammarion, *L'atmosphère: description des grands phénomènes de la nature* (Paris: Librarie Hachette, 1911).

11 Flammarion, *The atmosphere*, trans. James Glaisher (New York: Harper, 1873), 70.

12 Flammarion, *L'atmosphère*, 50–51.

13 Dust devils are also known colloquially as 'dirt devils' or 'dancing devils.' See scientific papers on the behaviour of dust, Ralph D. Lorenz and Jani Radebaugh, 'Dust devils in thin air: vortex observations at a high-elevation Mars analog site in the Argentinian Puma,' *Geophysical research letters*, 43 (8) (28 April 2016): 4010–4016.

14 Rodolphe el-Khoury, 'Polish and deodorize: paving the city in late-eighteenth-century France,' *Assemblage*, 31 (December 1996): 6–15. Thanks to Nicole Sully for this reference.

15 Mary Douglas, *Purity and danger: An analysis of pollution and taboo* (New York: Routledge, 1966). Refer also to Julia Kristeva, *Powers of horror: an essay on abjection* (New York: Columbia University Press, 1980).

16 Robbie Duschinsky, 'Abjection and self-identity: towards a revised account of purity and impurity,' *The sociological review*, 61 (2013): 709–727.

17 E. H. Dixon, 'King's Cross, London: the great dust-heap, next to Battle Bridge and the Smallpox Hospital' (1837), https://wellcomecollection.org/works/ssu37wcd.

18 Megan Born, Helene Furján, and Lily Jencks, eds., *Dirt* (Cambridge: MIT Press, 2012). See also Ben Campkin and Paul Dobraszczyk, 'Architecture and dirt,' *Journal of architecture*, 12.4 (2007): 347–351.

19 On aeolian dust, refer to https://fennerschool.anu.edu.au/research/research-stories/dust-storms-and-eroding-landscapes. See also: Richard Greene, Robyn Gatehouse et al., 'Aeolian dust—implications for Australian mineral exploration and environmental management,' *Australian journal of soil research*, 39.1 (January 2001): 1–6.

20 Refer to the themed papers on aeolian dust at https://agupubs.onlinelibrary.wiley.com/doi/toc/10.1002/(ISSN)1525-2027.EDUST1. See Stephen Cattle, Richard Greene et al., 'The role of climate and local regolith-landscape processes in determining the pedological characteristics of Aeolian dust deposits across south-eastern Australia,' *Quaternary international*, 209.1 (2009): 95–106.

21 'Eolian dust as a player and recorder of environmental change' (5 February 2018), https://agupubs.onlinelibrary.wiley.com/doi/toc/10.1002/(ISSN)1525-2027.EDUST1.

22 Hui Sun, Zaitao Pan and Xiaodong Liu, 'Numerical simulation of spatial-temporal distribution of dust aerosol and its direct radiative effects on East Asian climate,' *Journal of geophysical research: atmospheres*, 117 (D13) (16 July 2012): 1–14.

23 Refer to https://earthobservatory.nasa.gov/images/8477/dust-storm-over-east-asia. Asian dust was documented travelling over Death Valley, California on 14 and 15 April 2001, tracked by NASA's earth observatory. See https://earthobservatory.nasa.gov/images/1352/asian-dust-arrives-over-california.

24 Refer to https://www.nytimes.com/2008/08/06/sports/olympics/06masks.html. See also 'Air quality at the 2008 Beijing Olympics,' USC US China Institute.

25 World Health Organization, *Global Urban Ambient Air Pollution Database* (2016), https://edition.cnn.com/2019/01/15/asia/asia-smog-pollution-intl/index.html.
26 See https://asiasociety.org/korea/hwang-sa-yellow-dust. Duha Altindag, Deokrye Baek and Naci Mocan, 'Chinese yellow dust and Korean infant health,' *Social science & medicine*, 186 (August 2017): 78–86; Zhan Guo, Ning Ai and Karen Polenske, 'Evaluating environmental and economic benefits of yellow dust storm-related policies in north China,' *International journal of sustainable development and world ecology*, 15.5 (1 October 2008): 457–470.
27 Ruixue Jia and Hyejin Ku, 'Is China's pollution the culprit for the choking of South Korea? Evidence from the Asian dust,' *The economic journal*, vol. 129, issue 624 (November 2019): 3154–3188.
28 Jin-Ok Park, Sanghoo Yoon, Myung Hwan Na and Ho-Chun Song, 'The effects of air pollution on mortality in South Korea,' *Procedia environmental sciences*, 26 (2015): 62–65.
29 Justin McCurry, 'Social disaster: South Korea brings in emergency laws to tackle dust pollution,' *The Guardian* (13 March 2019), see https://www.theguardian.com/environment/2019/mar/13/social-disaster-south-korea-brings-in-emergency-laws-to-tackle-dust-pollution.
30 Refer to South Korea's Special act on particulate matter reduction and management (2019): http://www.koreaherald.com/view.php?ud=20190215000521.
31 On popular accounts in the press about the 2009 dust storm in Sydney, refer to https://www.abc.net.au/news/2009-09-23/dust-storm-chokes-sydney/1438510.
32 Ibid.
33 Ibid. See also https://en.wikipedia.org/wiki/2009_Australian_dust_storm#/media/File:2009_Dust_Storm_-_Australia_and_New_Zealand_Map.png.
34 A.J. Gabric, R. Cropp et al., 'Tasman Sea biological response to dust storm events during the austral spring of 2009,' *Marine and freshwater research* 67(8) (2015): 1090–1102.
35 See https://www.environment.nsw.gov.au/topics/land-and-soil/soil-degradation/wind-erosion/community-dustwatch.
36 On the role of dust and erosion, refer to the government literature on soil degradation in Australia. See https://www.environment.nsw.gov.au/topics/land-and-soil/soil-degradation/wind-erosion/community-dustwatch.
37 On mine dust in NSW, refer to https://www.health.nsw.gov.au/environment/factsheets/Pages/mine-dust.aspx. On the health risks posed by the 2009 dust storm in Sydney see Alistair Merrifield, Suzanne Schindeler, Bin Jalaludin and Wayne Smith, 'Health effects of the September 2009 dust storm in Sydney, Australia: did emergency department visits and hospital admissions increase?' *Environmental health* (2013): 12–32.

Wind, making the invisible visible: design for and with natural ventilation

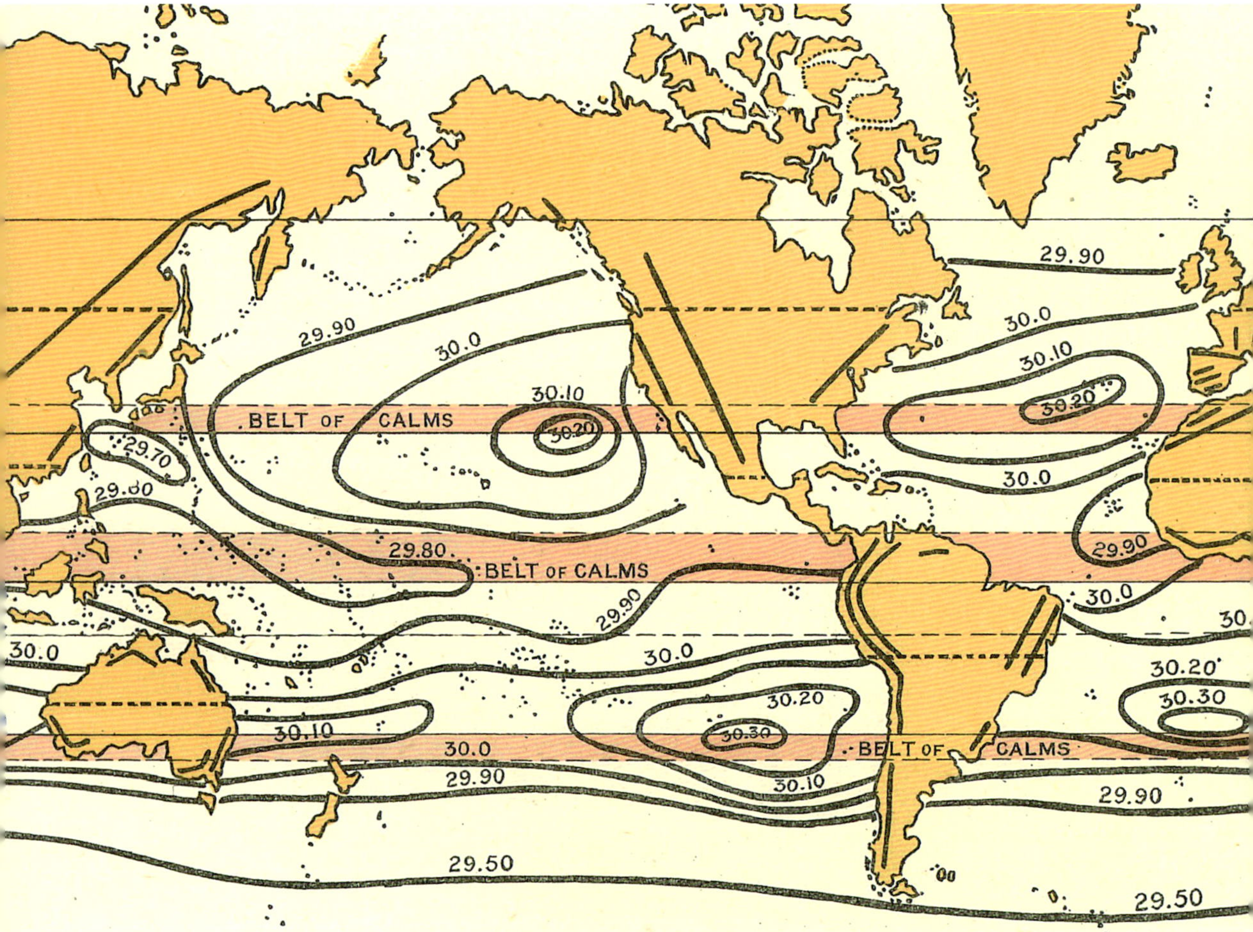

1 Belt of calms, from: John James Wild, *Thalassa, An essay on the depth, temperature, and currents of the ocean*, 1877.

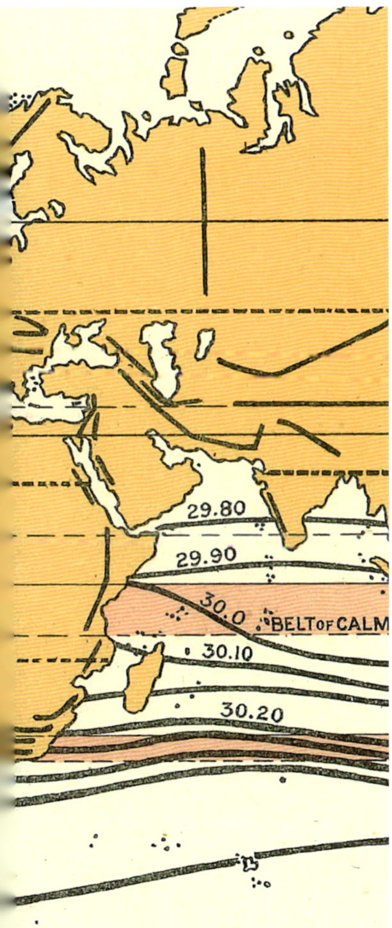

The rise of sustainable and low-carbon architecture has rekindled interest in natural ventilation. Once again, airflow appears as whimsical ribbons on architects' drawings. As extreme weather events increase in frequency and intensity, designing with climate is imperative. In warm and hot climates, prioritising natural ventilation becomes essential to reduce our dependency on air-conditioning use. Considering that much of the world's population can be found there, it is essential to look into ways to naturally cool buildings to curb carbon emissions.

While wind is one of the most important climatic elements for architects, representing it has proven challenging. Unlike shade, wind is a non-visual phenomenon and is typically represented as a vector—a force with direction. This chapter looks at diverse tactics for representing airflow in buildings. From the supposed accuracy of Computational Fluid Dynamics (CFD) to whimsical ribbons, designers remain optimistic about how airflow is transformed into systems of ventilation in buildings. Yet rather than argue for the power of the computer over the suggestiveness of a sketch, the chapter looks at how key analogue studies are still relevant.

Airflow can be increased indoors by mechanical means or passive means. Mechanical measures include ceiling fans and exhaust fans, while passive means includes natural ventilation. Natural ventilation is the result of air moving through a space due to pressure differences between inlets and outlets. It can also be due to significant temperature differences between indoors and outdoors, a phenomenon known as the stack effect.

Natural ventilation can be used for three complementary purposes. The first relates to maintaining appropriate indoor air quality. This may be achieved through the adequate renewal of air in such spaces. Doing so removes impurities and maintains appropriate oxygen levels. Good air quality can be achieved with proper air change rates in buildings, as determined by international standards such as ASHRAE 55.[1]

The second purpose of ventilation is to cool the building itself. This reduces thermal loads that result from the exposure of the building to solar radiation. It also reduces thermal gains produced inside the buildings by occupants, electrical equipment and artificial lighting. In these cases, high ventilation rates can ameliorate indoor temperatures.

The third purpose is related to the physiological cooling of occupants and, consequently, aspects of thermal comfort. This refers to the cooling effect caused by the evaporation of sweat from the skin and by heat exchanges by convection, which occurs when airflow comes in contact with the human body. The intensity of this cooling is a function of air speed and temperature, but it also depends on the turbulence of the airflow and the relative humidity. Physiological cooling is particularly important in regions with high humidity, as sweaty skin is often identified as the main cause of discomfort. In places where the wind availability is stable in direction and frequency and a reasonable average speed (above 3 m/s) can be found, natural ventilation is the simplest and most efficient cooling strategy.

Wind circulation and gradient

Out of all classic building design strategies that enable comfort, ventilation is perhaps the one that designers struggle with the most. Wind, after all, is a troublesome beast. It varies seasonally due to a complex and dynamic system ignited by the earth's rotation and inclination. Rising warm equatorial air later meets cold polar winds, but not before it moves around north and south. It also varies daily, due to the earth-ocean dynamics of warming up and cooling down, thereby generating breezes that may move towards or away from land. The so-called thermal equator is not a straight line, it oscillates according to seasonal variations and the presence of large bodies of water, geographic circumstances or natural vegetation. These factors affect the temperature distribution on the earth's surface and, consequently, the global configuration of wind circulation.

Added to this permanent airflow fluctuation are conditions specific to the natural and built environment. They in turn influence the direction and availability of free-flowing air at various scales found within the built environment. It is quite a complex phenomenon that is often simplified in drawings. For instance, the globe is subdivided by belts of calm winds in Figure 1. These types of representation are commonly used to introduce many climatic design guides, especially those that claim global relevance. At first sight, these appear to subdivide the world into clearly defined zones, but what is actually going on?

The circulation of air in the atmosphere can be classified into vertical and horizontal movements. The vertical circulation is generated by the heating of the air around the equator, due to the greater intensity of solar radiation reaching this part of the earth. The heated air expands, becomes less dense and rises vertically, creating areas of low pressure. The air currents from the subtropical regions are displaced towards these low-pressure zones, generating horizontal circulation. The heated air rises to a certain point, then cools and descends around the subtropics, producing high-pressure zones, and propagates in north and south directions.

The simple diagram of warm and cold currents can tell us something about global circulation but it can only tell us so much. If we wish to zoom in to urban and suburban conditions, wind patterns are best explained in section as force diagrams. From the simple arrows at global scale to the force diagrams at a more local scale, we next move to swirls and whirls of microclimatic airflow. This is most often shown as free-flowing arrows through a building.

However, it is worth taking a step backwards to consider how general site conditions affect wind speed. The increase in wind speed along a vertical axis varies from zero, on the earth's surface, to a speed equal to that of the free flow of obstructions, generating what we call the wind speed gradient. The altitude at which the wind speed is free from the influence of the earth's friction is known as the height of the gradient. It is a function of the roughness of the earth's surface. There are different heights of wind gradients for open fields, suburban areas and cities, since the roughness of these areas is quite different. Consequently, the wind speed at the time of construction will depend on the environment in which the building is located. Understanding the wind speed gradient diagram can inform design choices about the height of a building and whether we wish to profit from increased levels of airflow or by contrast minimise them (Figure 2).

At a site level, data from meteorological stations provide wind-related information. This includes wind direction, frequency and speed. For use in building design, these data are collected on an hourly basis, as they inform the behaviour of the wind throughout the day, in addition to seasonal variations. Information is depicted graphically. These types of information are extremely relevant to designers when studying natural ventilation options for a specific location. This microclimatic-level analysis

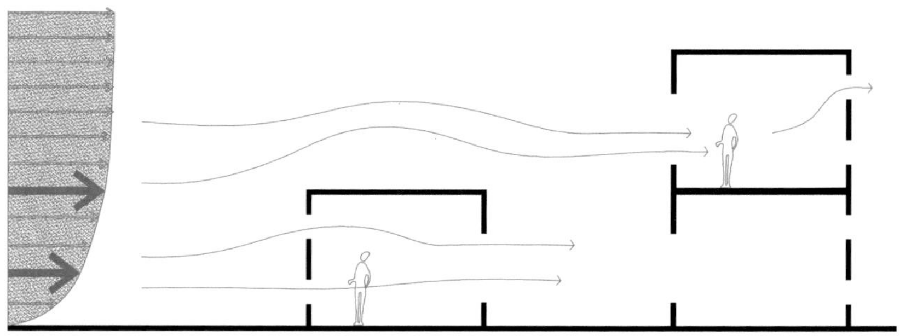

can be further advanced by simplified calculations for wind gradient at specific heights and for different terrains. Further, site observations can consider surrounding obstacles to prevailing winds and their impact on direction and speed. Once put together, this provides a full picture of wind availability and frequency. It may even be too much to take in as at early design stages buildings tend to be designed towards one, maybe two prevailing orientations.

2 The speed of prevailing wind changes depending on the gradient.

Designing for natural ventilation

While we have reviewed some of the typical ways in which airflow has been represented, it is worth considering the implicit knowledge found in traditional architecture. In many cases, ideas about shade and ventilation can be found working together. To represent these means considering the building's porosity. For buildings, airflow distribution and speed can be shown in relation to the size, location, types and overall configurations of inlets and outlets. Other architectural elements that feature include shading devices, pergolas and perforated blocks. Drawings typically show blacked-in walls and blank openings, with flow paths inside and around the building. The overall airflow distribution may be uniform or not, depending on the intended use of the space, interior layout and location of occupied zones. Further, much has also been documented about changes in indoor airflow distribution and speed as a function of changes in specific design features of windows, windcatchers and other types of architectural elements adopted with the intention to enhance opportunities for natural ventilation.

The degree of architectural porosity in the design of buildings and human settlements in general indicates not only the prevailing passive design strategy but also the amplitude of seasonal and daily variability in terms of temperature, humidity, solar radiation and air speed. In hot and dry climates, buildings try to damp down the significant temperature amplitude, creating more stable conditions indoors by embracing thermal mass. Traditional vernacular architecture in such climatic regions produces buildings with thick walls with small openings, wrapped around courtyards featuring vegetation and water, to create microclimates that are more humid and cooler than the conditions found outdoors during the day due to excessive solar radiation. Within this context, airflow is normally not welcomed indoors within occupied zones as it may cause thermal discomfort to occupants. Airflows are redirected indoors by windcatchers and at the same time humidified and cooled down by wet fabric and/or pots inside the towers (Figure 3). Perforated blocks and other types of filters, such as *mashrabiyas*, are in use on building façades to help filter excessive solar radiation, provide privacy and protect indoors against unwanted ventilation. In hot and humid climates, by contrast, vernacular architecture welcomes ventilation to the highest possible degree, while avoiding excessive heat gains from solar radiation. Natural ventilation is the main bioclimatic design strategy recommended in hot and humid climates for the purpose of indoor thermal comfort and cooling down the building itself.[2] Vernacular architecture in such climatic regions maximises porosity. Buildings make extensive use of lightweight construction, large openings, perforated blocks and other architectural elements that allow constant indoor airflow indoors. For example, perforated blocks are commonly found in Brazilian architecture.

Further, in hot and humid climates, buildings make use of verandahs and pergolas to physically and visually integrate indoor and outdoor spaces. These spaces of transition are used throughout the year. They help maximise shading of the façade yet still allow filtered light and airflow to reach indoors. These types of architectural elements can be found in traditional architecture in hot and humid regions in India, Brazil, Portugal, Spain and other countries around the globe.

Designing with climate and for natural ventilation can be a powerful influence on the overall architectural design of buildings. We see this in much Brazilian architecture, particularly in the work of João Filgueiras Lima, commonly known as *Lelé* (1931–2014). Lelé's landmark work, the Sarah Kubitschek Hospital in Salvador, shows that understanding of building physics and overall climatic demands can result in architectural designs that have low overall energy consumption while at the same time providing thermal comfort indoors.[3] By making the most of principles of shading and ventilation, Lelé managed to develop a distinct architectural aesthetic that allowed the building fabric to breathe, also protecting against excessive solar radiation.

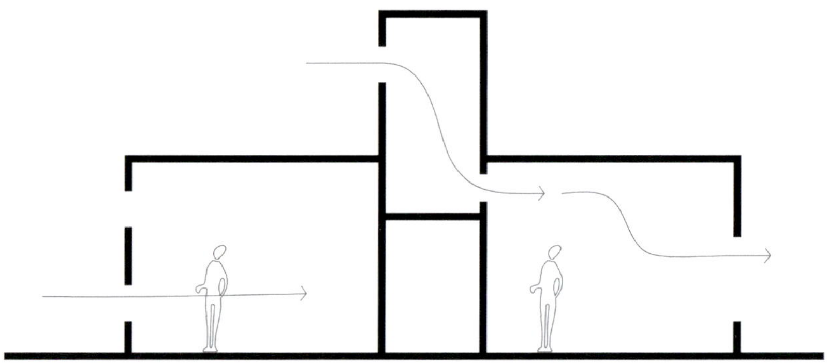

3 Above: Wind-cooled water reservoir, Yazd, Iran; Below: windcatchers are strategically placed to bring airflow indoors.

Airflow representation during the 1960s and 1970s — from physical properties to visual aids

From analogue to digital, airflow representation has changed little in seventy years. Streamlines of airflow and pressure fields remain the norm, regardless of scale. Numerical and graphical representations simplify and aid visualisations of turbulent or laminar flow. They are also used for schematic representations of wind patterns and speed at various scales. The landmark work from the 1950s and 1960s of Victor and Aladar Olgyay at Princeton University set the vocabulary of airflow representation for many generations to come.[4] Through a series of wind tunnel tests, their work extensively documented how airflow moves inside and outside buildings. The results helped explain why and how natural ventilation could be successfully implemented within small-scale buildings. The images that accompanied the technical explanation and design directives was essential to help readers understand the phenomenon. The streamlines generated by paths of kerosene smoke are more than illustrative: they show how to strategically position architectural elements that achieve specific outcomes in terms of natural ventilation.

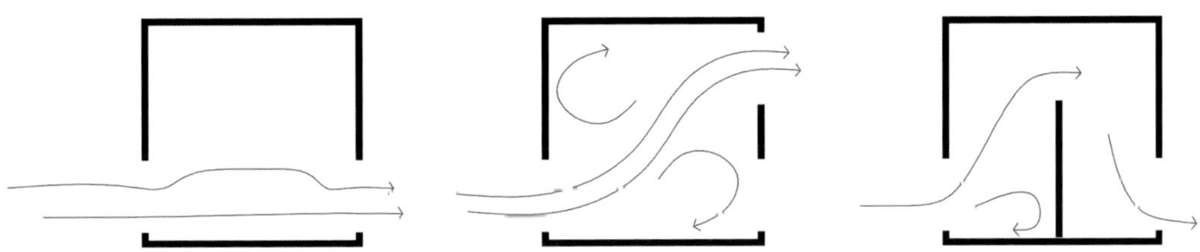

4 Flow patterns for different outlet locations.

In the later decades of the twentieth century, the Israeli-American building scientist Baruch Givoni enlightened audiences not only about how airflow behaves indoor and outdoors;[5] he also considered the magnitude of the resultant ventilation available indoors as a result of different combinations of inlets and outlets (Figure 4). When describing design factors affecting ventilation, Givoni mapped and communicated indoor airflow distribution and speed with simple, analogue 2D models including a multitude of combinations for inlet and outlet.[6]

In terms of practice, Givoni produced a road map for designing windows. This included their optimal locations and sizes to allow for ventilation to flow indoors, along with references about airflow distribution and speed. Further, he also provided guidance about the subdivision of the space and its subsequent impact on airflow distribution indoors.

This type of drawing is simple and effective, showing streamlines of airflow that seemingly move around architectural obstacles. Olgyay's and Givoni's work paved the way for how we represent airflow today. Their seminal work generated an architectural pattern book that could inform early-stage designs. What is remarkable about these works is that they translated the physical mechanisms of ventilation into a portfolio of visual aids that could be used by anyone, regardless of their technical knowledge. Information about airflow distribution and speed, which can be hard for the uninitiated to grasp, is powerfully communicated through simple, clear diagrams. This type of representation, along with the number of examples, becomes a catalogue of basic typologies that students and professionals can access many times. Further, the representation at the room level becomes a reference point for larger-scale extrapolations.

The computer takes hold

Computational Fluid Dynamics (CFD) tools started to be used to simulate airflow in the 1970s.[7] CFD methods can be deployed to solve equations that are relevant for fluids in motion and in interaction with solids. The simulation mesh used in CFD models contains multiple cells capable of going beyond basic calculations for the conservation of mass, momentum and energy. CFD is suitable for several applications within the scope of industrial ventilation. It has been used to simulate aerodynamics of specific architectural, air-conditioning and automotive components. CFD simulations also can include temperature and contaminants carried by the air, such as smoke. CFD tools are considered robust and have been applied with confidence to solve complex fluid flow problems. Comprehension of inviscid and viscous fluid equations is required for the development of models and interpretation of simulation results. The change from analogue to digital simulation of airflow has assisted in making experimentation during initial design stages more accessible to parts of industry. Initial studies of airflow in and outside of buildings once relied on physical models, which were then used in simulations in wind tunnels. These beautiful apparatuses are quite large and most often limited to educational and research facilities. While many of those organisations do perform robust consulting work for built-environment related purposes, it is unlikely that designers can easily access such facilities. Computer-aided simulation became more accessible to designers, and some large design and consulting firms have direct access to such tools in situ. Today the use of CFD simulation is still very much led by specialised consultants and findings may or may not be used to inform early design stages of a project.

Despite the significant advancements in computer simulation, the visual vocabulary used to represent airflow was not transformed by the birth of CFD: colourful streamlines and arrows for airflow distribution and speed along with pressure fields are still very much in use (Figures 5 and 6). Designers face two difficulties when it comes to designing for natural ventilation: one is technical and the other is of a sensorial nature. The movement of air relies on pressure differences to take place. The mechanics are ignited from temperature differences, called the stack effect, and air pressure differences, or airflow. Air changes direction and speed constantly and as such its performance is hard to predict. As a result, the amount of technical knowledge demanded to accurately predict how air will actually move inside and outside buildings is significant and not always part of a designer's education and skill set. Further, most people lack a developed sensorial relationship with airflow. Unlike light, which designers can manipulate well in order to imprint the desired atmosphere or 'feel' of a space, air has proven more difficult to control with the same level of mastery.

Perhaps this is because air cannot be seen. This lack of sensorial attachment means few designers know how to manipulate air as well as they know how to manipulate light, as there are fewer visual cues for airflow compared to light. As a result, the visual vocabulary and tacit knowledge one accumulates from ongoing exposure to light is absent when it comes to airflow.

Are there other ways of becoming more experimental when it comes to representing airflow that can also entice feelings? By observing and attempting new techniques of capturing such fluids in general, would it be possible to move from the vectors and pressure fields to new ways of representing airflow?

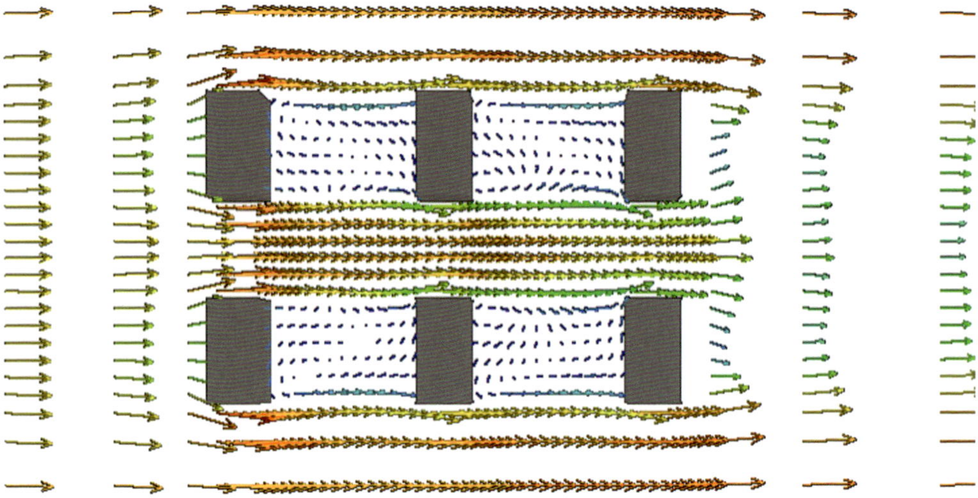

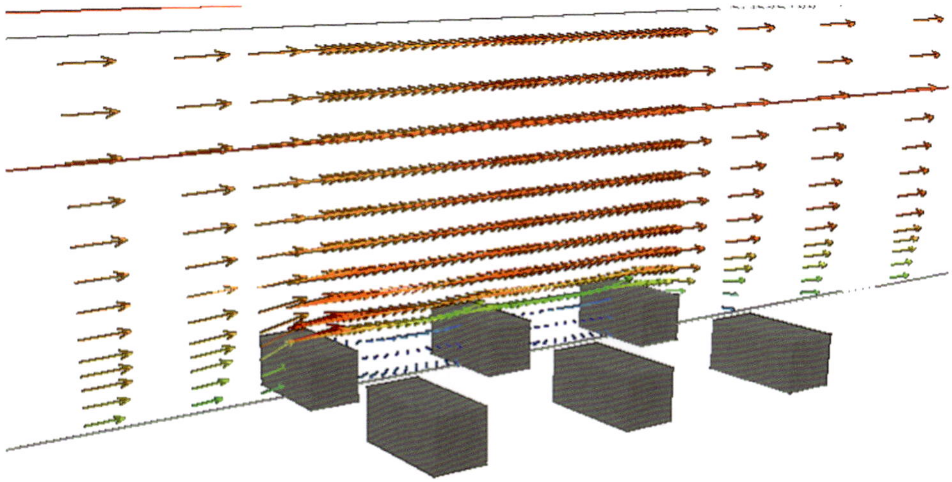

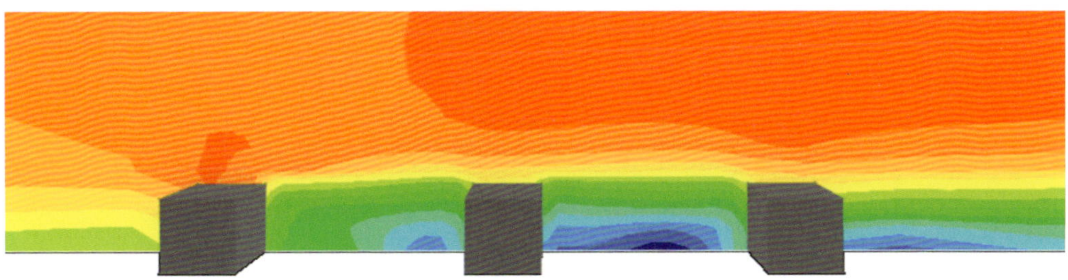

5 A CFD tool was used to simulate the impact of building orientation and overall arrangement on a site.

6 Airflow and pressure fields around buildings produced by a CFD simulation tool.

A rekindled interest in natural ventilation

There are successful examples of buildings that prioritise the use of natural ventilation in combination with other bioclimatic strategies. From *mashrabiyas* to *cobogos*, and then later carefully crafted corporate atria and windcatchers, designing for natural ventilation has resulted in a distinct and interesting architectural vocabulary. Yet the understanding of how to design to make the most of ventilation alone may not be enough in light of climate change. Designers need to be able to go beyond and include other variables that may be carried by airflow in order to make more resilient buildings, as a number of authors argue in this book. This is about designing for extreme weather events that are native and sometimes exotic to a location. It is both a necessity and opportunity to create buildings that must adapt constantly. It is not enough to design the built environment to cope with climate. It is about designing for organic, ongoing transformation—buildings that need to grow or shed skin from time to time, or urban spaces that need to become shelters from unpleasant hot breeze during a heat wave.

In this context, the way airflow is represented ought to move forward, too, but not focused on the aesthetic sense. The technical knowledge needed to understand, design for, with and later represent airflow is a key asset and a missing piece here. The basic technical understanding of how to design the built environment to make the most of airflow must be an integral part of the teaching and practice of architecture. The fundamentals of airflow behaviour around architectural objects is perfectly represented by analogue work. It is still relevant and just as sophisticated as Navier-Stokes equations underpinning CFD simulation. The porosity observed on the built environment itself has played a main role in the representation of airflow. It cannot be an afterthought captured by whimsical ribbons of airflow; it must be an integral part of an architectural statement and who knows, a moment.

1 *Thermal environmental conditions for human occupancy*, ASHRAE Standard 55-2013 (Atlanta American Society of Heating, Refrigerating and Air-Conditioning Engineers, 2013).
2 Ahmed-Shams Forruque Khan, Khan-Mohammed Masud Kamal Khan, Amanullah-Amanullah Maung Than Oo et al., 'Selection of suitable passive cooling strategy for a subtropical climate,' *International Journal of Mechanical and Materials Engineering*, 9:14 (2014): 1–11, https://doi.org/10.1186/s40712-014-0014-7.
3 Marieli Azoia Lukiantchuki and Rosana Maria Caram, 'Análise do conforto térmico na obra de João Filgueiras Lima, Lelé: hospitais Sarah de Salvador e do Rio de Janeiro,' *Paranoá: cadernos de arquitetura e* urbanismo, 12 (2014): 33–43, https://doi.org/10.18830/issn.1679-0944.n12.2014.12209.
4 Victor Olgyay, *Design with climate: bioclimatic approach to architectural regionalism* (Princeton: Princeton University Press, 1963). See also discussion on Olgyay in the introduction of this book.
5 Baruch Givoni, *Man, climate and architecture* (Amsterdam: Elsevier, 1969); Baruch Givoni, *Passive and low energy cooling of buildings* (New York: Van Nostrand Reinhold, 1994).
6 Givoni, *Man, climate and architecture*, 299–306.
7 Dean R. Chapman, 'Computational aerodynamics development and outlook,' *AIAA journal* 17:12 (1979): 1293–1313.

WET

Weathering the monsoon: affective relations

1 Photograph by Ong Chan Hao. The south cove waterway at Sentosa Cove turned pink after days of limited sunlight and copious rains encouraged an algae bloom. The water subsequently took on a murky red hue.

The contours of this self suggest a rich sense of connectedness, a kind of inevitable and mutually informing contact with surrounding terrain... A self that becomes part of a terrain rather than acting upon it. — *Tamsin Lorraine*[1]

In the first of these photographs, a woman in Punjabi dress is seated on a rattan chair within a suburban garden (Figure 2). An enormous headgear made of what looks like fruit is covering her head. In other photographs of the same series, more people appear as similar versions of 'fruit-becoming-head.' They are distinguishable only by these luscious fruits, which increasingly seem to adorn these individuals. The 'fruit heads' are photographed in their 'natural' environments—either relaxing in the garden, enjoying beer at the coffee shop (Figure 3), hauling up a catch on the beach or resting in their living room (Figure 4). These 'fruit heads' may be read as indigenous species found in the local markets—'we seem to be left on the outside unless we are prepared to "go native" and replace our own heads with something more fruitful.'[2] In each instance, there is something both appealing and worrying about the self behind each of these excessive tropical fruit headgears; a self being enveloped and reformed in a strange, unknown terrain. Yet through these visual images, nascent connections holding together notions of climate, fiction, myth, history, ritual, life and decay seem more tangible, if not increasingly real.

Simryn Gill's photographs from *A small town at the turn of the century* (1999–2000) are adopted as thought-images to contemplate the

2 Simryn Gill, *A small town at the turn of the century #5*, type C photograph, 1999–2000.

3 Simryn Gill, *A small town at the turn of the century #26*, type C photograph, 1999–2000.

4 Simryn Gill, *A small town at the turn of the century #28*, type C photograph, 1999–2000.

proposition of self and space borne *by* climate—in particular of the self and space being the 'weather fronts' of the monsoon.[3] To reposition the self in a dynamic and responsive relationship to climate, activists and feminists Astrida Neimanis and Rachel Loewen Walker argue for a 'transcorporeal' re-worlding of ourselves as 'weather bodies.' When our bodies intersect with the weather, 'rain might extend into our arthritic joints, sun might literally colour our skin, and the chill of the wind might echo through the hidden hallways of our eardrums.'[4] Gill's photographs allow us to think through a transcorporeal imagination that moves between a fruit and a head: transiting between tropical monsoonal nature and its cultivated interiors/exteriors, juxtaposing systems of knowledge that do not normally reside together. Thinking through the 'fruit-becoming-head,'[5] how do we incorporate the monsoon into our cities, our architecture and ourselves?

Monsoon fronts

The imperious monsoon results from a weather system of reversing winds—one wet, the other dry—moving between land and sea. With solar heating, contrasting terrestrial and oceanic temperatures as well as differential wind pressure occur, bringing on rain. The dry spell, however, is often marked by dust and, increasingly, pollutants in the atmosphere, resulting in a perennial and hazardous haze. While there are many monsoon systems located around the world, 'Monsoon Asia,'[6] covering East India, South China and much of Southeast Asia, remains the most consequential. Countries like Myanmar, Thailand, Singapore, Malaysia, Vietnam, Laos, Cambodia, Indonesia, Borneo, East Timor, the Philippines and western New Guinea feel its seasonal effects.[7] In fact, almost a quarter of the world's population[8] are subjected to this weather system of mild or severe drought and grand deluge.[9] As thunderstorms sweep through cities, suburbs and the countryside, rivers fill up and overflow; the smell of asphalt mingles with sweat; parched grass turns green, and dust becomes mud. A phenomenon that transforms landscapes and livelihoods, the word monsoon first appeared in English in the sixteenth century, likely derived from the Arabic word *mawsim* (meaning 'season').

> The monsoon is ground, water, and air; it is a relation of things in its very core. It is about atmospheric conditions, sea temperatures, dust particles... It is about water in the air, water in the ground, ground in the air. It is an extraordinary planetary wide system that no one really understands and yet is experienced

> very locally. It's what Timothy Morton calls a *hyperobject*—you can only know it in its local instantiations, it's about highly localised incidents and it phases in and out. The monsoon is an abstraction, except when you feel it on your head.[10]

The monsoon is relational. Architect-academic Lindsay Bremner beautifully sums up the entwined dimensionalities of the monsoon as a weather system endemic to the lived experiences, regions and spaces it influences. As a meteorological construction, it is a phenomenon driven by the mechanics of wind pressure and hot air. Yet the largest impact of the monsoon lies in its relationality—its planetary networks as well as its localised residues; particularly the way it envelops, the way the monsoon gets under one's skin. Its impact remains traceable in processes, spaces, cultures and physiologies. It is something in the background that is already enmeshed with that in the foreground. In this sense, just as it shapes us, the monsoon is co-produced by our actions in the world around us. For those of us who live in monsoonal regions and cities, the monsoon is not an abstract system. Its affects are influential and formative to who we are. Or as Bremner asks, what are the implications of shifting our knowledge of monsoons from an abstract concept to something that settles on the skin, that can be tasted, felt or sensed? In other words, can the monsoon be better understood through visual and sensorial attunements to its affects?

The monsoon is cultural. In Vietnam, the phrase *Sống chung với lũ*—'living with the floods'—is endemic to the Mekong Delta, fostering acceptance, adaptivity and diverse productive engagements in reaction to the inescapable annual monsoon floods.[11] The monsoon has shaped cities, influenced the migrations of people, recharged their lands and determined their fortunes. Rain is wished for, while its overabundance is guardedly accommodated. Myths, rituals and religions pursue the coming of rain as deities are worshipped across Asia to ensure a bountiful wet season, among them mass singing to appease the rain gods, the offering of gifts and flowers and the enactment of bodily penance are associated with the monsoon. The latter includes anthropological documentation of late nineteenth-century acts of hook-swinging, or *charak-puja*, a process of self-mutilation where a powerfully built young man would be lifted to 10–18 metres in the air, with hooks sewn into his back, or women dragging ploughs in the night across fields, stripped of their clothing, as invocation to the rain-gods.[12] Folk festivals like the *charak-puja*, link the coming of the wet season with prosperity, thus bestowing the monsoon a mythopoetic quality. In this way, the monsoon brings a measure of the extraordinary into everyday existence.

The monsoon is mythical. Throughout historical accounts of weather forecasting, speculative and mythical practices of inducing rain are embedded in a 'rich and complex cosmological system that included ancestors, ghosts and a variety of both helpful and dangerous spirits.'[13] These practices are taken as moral correctives to human activities and behaviours that would have resulted in the extremes of floods or droughts.[14] For example, the Kenyah Badeng rice farmers in Sarawak, East Malaysia rely on their observations of the natural, cultural and social phenomena and connect these patterns to a religious framework of deities, spirits and omen birds.[15] They believe that wrongful acts, such as trespassing in cemeteries, disrespecting the dead and mocking animals, contribute to violent thunderstorms and copious downpours.[16] To the same extent that spirituality has been woven into these speculative practices, ceremonial acts to worship and appease celestial beings also endure. In India, mass prayers for a good monsoon still draw thousands of devotees.[17] Overcoming cynicism and scepticism, ancient superstitions such as the marrying of frogs[18] continue to be performed to appease Indra, the Rain God.[19] Similarly in 2019, under the shadow of a regional haze and prolonged drought, thousands of Malaysian Muslims including the King and the Prime Minister gathered to pray in unison for rain (*solat istisqa*).[20]

The monsoon is physiological. The Kenyah Badeng predict weather through acute use of their senses. Weather patterns are intuited through bodies. The Badeng monsoon-bodies allow rice farmers to read cloud and wind patterns, sense humidity and temperature, and smell the changing winds.[21] Such tacit knowledge connects the body and its sensory capacities to the monsoon system. The Badeng people monitor personal symptoms such as fatigue, habitual changes and physical conditions as precursors to impending weather changes:[22] 'Turning inwards, changes in the internal states of human bodies may also indicate coming changes in the weather, with warm but rainy days expected when people become irritable, lethargic and suffer insomnia.'[23] In Chennai, leading up to the rainy season, people pray, fast and change their diets in anticipation of the monsoon's arrival. Responding with agility to 'weather, water and air,' altered eating habits 'prepare their bodies, [while] infrastructures are adapted, [and] city resources ... spent ...[on] the rains....'[24] Such bodily preparations are necessary to acclimatise and fortify oneself against the health perils brought about by rain including a prevalence of waterborne disease and illness, and humidity-induced skin issues.

The monsoon is matter; the monsoon is milieu. If these responsive monsoon-bodies reside primarily on the city periphery, how can the urban dweller recuperate their natural sensibilities to measure and understand the monsoon? The relationship between the built environment and the monsoon is tenuous, sometimes antagonistic. In the tropical monsoon city, architecture must respond equally to the scorching heat and the persistent rain. Office towers are still regressive in accommodating the monsoon, while bungalows and resorts have aestheticised the climatic need for deep-pitched roofs and broad verandahs.

Being alienating and aestheticising, there is a phenomenon particular to buildings in the monsoonal tropics. The architectures of monsoon cities offer instances of architecture-as-matter, or transcorporeal architecture—rain-slivered plywood, insect gossamers on metal frames and sun-burnt brick. The monsoon can make architecture rugged and well-worn, or it can make architecture vulnerable and brittle. In both cases, architecture becomes region-specific: there is a need to consider details, materials, labour and skill that prevail in such milieux or localities. Such architecture acknowledges its making as inevitably entangled with 'the social and material practices ... and [that] the forces at work in the realisation of [architecture's] objects ...range from the conceptual, to the practical and technical, to the institutional.'[25] Architecture that derives from—and resides in—amorphous matter evolves from within economies, events, processes and histories that continue to weather the monsoon. In shifting its emphasis towards actions and materiality, the architecture of monsoon cities may be rethought as 'a formless phenomenon.'[26]

The concept of formlessness coincides with Gilles Deleuze and Felix Guattari's *milieu*, simply and complexly translated to being in the 'middle,' or as architectural historian Andrew Ballantyne elucidates, constituting an inseparable part of an 'environment.'[27] Deleuze and Guattari give the example of the tick as an organism that survives on the precondition that its environment (or *milieu*), which is a part of the tick's body, is sufficiently protected. The radical significance of the Deleuzian figuration of architecture-as-*milieux* is how the boundary as an idea fundamental to architectural thinking, and especially pervasive in urban design practice, becomes multiply populated and subsequently ambiguous. If '*milieux*—environments—are formless,'[28] this does not mean spaces lack shape but rather that form is only one aspect in a constellation of forces that defines a space. An architectural *milieu* is constructed through social and political dimensions and exists as a self-organising network encompassing 'geographic, ethnic, linguistic, moral, economic, technological particularities.'[29] In a monsoonal milieu, like the fasting bodies of Chennai or the intuiting bodies of the Badeng farmers, architecture must learn to adapt and to speculate. It needs to return to engaging directly with ground, water and air.

Monsoonal milieu

Urban water systems are invisible until they malfunction. In June 2010, after two days of continuous rains, a freak flash flood swept through Orchard Road, Singapore's premier shopping precinct. Orchard Road had always been prone to flooding, exacerbated by its basin-like profile into which water from surrounding higher terrain flowed.[30] The June 2010 downpours measured a high volume of rainfall—101 millimetres, or the equivalent of 60 % of accumulated rainfall in the entire month, occurring within two hours.[31] The knee-to-waist-high deluge led to SGD 10 million in estimated damages.[32] Birkin bags, boxes of new iPhones, vials of expensive perfume, plastic fashion mannequins and branded merchandise were carried aloft from shop interiors by the surge of water streaming down in furious torrents, filling the ground floors and open semi-basements along Orchard Road. Photographs showed shopping centres marooned in moats of muddy water, their exterior pavements and semi-basements completely submerged.[33]

The flood lasted six hours. After the rain stopped, it took another three hours for the fetid water to be pumped away. During this time, the shop interiors went into accelerated decay—wooden floors became warped by damp, laminates peeled and curled, waterlogged carpets turned mouldy. An inquiry levelled blame at a maintenance fault in a choked underground drain culvert beneath Orchard Road. The culvert measured a massive cross section, large enough to accommodate a single-decker bus.[34] The size of the obstruction, caused by organic and inorganic waste including tree branches, leaf litter, paper cups, plastic bottles and aluminium cans, is hard to fathom. A waterlogged image of Singapore remains antithetical to the city's orderly reputation.

During the flood, common architectural features such as automatic sliding doors, staircases and escalators transformed into gushing waterways; basements and atria became temporary urban pools, albeit filled with putrid liquids. Amidst such confusion, a temporarily ludic atmosphere prevailed—passers-by helped themselves to the floating goods which drifted free from the boundaries of their shop owners, out into public space. Public space itself became temporarily undefined as property lines, street fronts and pavements were obscured in rank, muddy waters:

> Like puddles, mud often signifies a type of failed engineering, but it also takes on a larger metaphorical dimension in architecture. As an aspect of primitive architecture, mud was once associated with a lack of cultivation—a type of degenerate architecture. As a viscous substance, it operates against modern concepts of circulation; it slows the city down, like slush.[35]

Mud, an after-effect of a monsoonal deluge, is what architectural historian David Gissen calls 'subnatural matter,' a hybrid, denigrated form of nature made by and through our practices, industries and built forms in our urban environments. Gissen writes that urban water in undesirable states—stagnant pools, muddy puddles, slow trickles, gushing leaks, urban flooding—are forms of displaced subnatural matter, representative of imminent disorder.[36] Dirty water signals a malfunctioning city, portraying ruination, destruction, disease, backwardness and vulnerability. Eighteenth-century architects Giovanni Battista Piranesi and Robert Adam both utilised forms of denigrated water to depict the downfall of civilisation: Piranesi depicted the ruination of the Roman town of Albano, where stagnant contaminated pools of water were found inside underground drainage works; Adam portrayed aqueducts and once-grand fountains of the Roman palatial city of Split repurposed as bath pans for farm animals, where pure drinking water became mud-filled washing water.[37] In time, cross-sectional drawings of underground water and sewerage infrastructure became synonymous with the image of the progressive city, serving as evidence of the efficient system which functioned to protect urban dwellers. Yet, as a departure from these celebrated underground urban networks whose orderly states were directly linked to the health of the city's operational interiors, Gissen points out that from the mid-twentieth century onwards, a more tenuous image of the modern street emerged of the 'undrainable city' where 'waters inundating the modern city rained from above and surged from below.'[38]

Burst water mains, urban flash floods and overflowing drains further emphasised 'the fragile nature of modern architecture as it interacted with the environment over time.'[39] The city's 'natural' reaction to the torrential monsoonal downpour is one of resistance. Is there another way to think about deluge that salvages imminent urban disaster? Writing about the 1955 Paris flood, Roland Barthes describes the displacing power of the urban flood, 'thereby refreshing the perception of the world by introducing into it unaccustomed and yet explicable points of view,' radically altering the perception of normative urban boundaries, practices and possibilities.[40] Notwithstanding urban floods being precursors of climate change, Barthes' narrative of the Parisian flood illustrates a climatic event that defines a momentary re-enchantment with the city. Such a narrative forces a new way of seeing, feeling and behaving which takes seriously the value of observation, personal responsibility, spontaneity and intuition, reinvigorating the importance of feeling one's way through the city:

> ... the rising waters not only selected and displaced certain objects, they upset the very coenesthesia of the landscape, ... that angular stability which so well prepares the shapes of property, all that was erased, extended from angle to plane; no more roads or riverbanks, no more directions; a level surface going nowhere, thereby suspending human becoming, detaching it from any right decision, from a utility of sites.[41]

In a similar register, cultural anthropologist Stephanie Kane suggests in her ficto-critical account of the Orchard Road flood that an ancient river once flowed under this highly altered and engineered terrain.[42] Kane traces the alluvial conditions of Orchard Road's 'marine-sediment' rich geology, piecing this fragment together with the historical premise of once-thriving orchards in an originally hilly terrain.[43] Kane's 'ghost river' exposes the susceptibility of Orchard Road's now dry, insulated, impervious surfaces to flooding risks. She writes that 'flash floods can assume the force and form of the lost river and challenge the existential premise that the geological deep is fixed in our past.'[44] Kane's reading of Orchard Road carries both the past and the future in its imagination. It provokes questions about how the city might act to reclaim its historical geology while also embracing its monsoonal milieu. Against fertile orchards laden with tropical fruit, overlooking a river flowing in a valley fed by monsoon rains, Kane's speculation juxtaposes several spatio-temporal milieux: monsoon rains, a ghost river, historical fruit orchards and the present consumerist landscape. This vision comes from a position of accommodating and living with the monsoon. It is a particularly challenging stance in an urban environment where enclosures and interiors turn inwards, and where architecture's function is to keep the weather elements firmly outside and apart from our spaces within.

In the afternoon light

This essay closes with another work by the artist Simryn Gill, whose head-becoming-fruit photographs opened the chapter. *My Own Private Angkor* (2007–2009) is an elegiac tribute to the ravaging effects of the tropical monsoon on architecture (Figure 5).[45] Shot in Gill's natal seaside town of Port Dickson, located near the Strait of Malacca in Malaysia, the photographs are documents of a boom and bust cycle involving a housing estate which never fully materialised. In *My Own Private Angkor #35*, a piece of glass leans precariously against two neoclassical columns. The columns are bathed in velvety, late-afternoon light; the sunlight bends and distorts the angle of the leaning glass. The tiled floor is strewn with crinkled leaves, adding to its perceived filth. In the background are slender trees, with their branches dangling down as well as growing upwards and diagonally. In time, this garden-turned-jungle will engulf the columns; perhaps they will shatter the glass. The glass is burnished with a milky patina inked in by damp air, rain and heat. *My Own Private Angkor* simulates portraits of time and weather fronted by a half-built environment; itself slowly becoming ruin, becoming jungle, eventually dematerialising much like the light which passes languidly through the glass.

Not unlike *A small town at the turn of the century*, these photographs are thought-images, but maybe here, they go a step further. They provide evidence of what a monsoonal milieu could become, or could otherwise be. There is beauty and poetry but also regret and despair. The monsoon can be devastating; it can take lives, and cause irreversible damage and decay. Deeply affected by climate change, the seasonal rains are now more and more erratic in timing and volume, while hazy dry weather is increasingly prevalent. Yet it is easy to forget these transient changes. Gill's photographs offer clues for remembering. They are attuned[46] to decipher the monsoon affectively, unravelling this weather system into its elemental forms of rain, light, heat and wind. The photographs also capture a monsoonal milieu: a place and a time with specific meanings, stories and ambitions, and where its subject, architecture—here, represented in pieces of milky glass or neoclassical columns in semi-ruin—is always held in precarious balance.

5 Simryn Gill, *My own private Angkor #35*, silver gelatin print, 2007–2009.

Monsoon Journal: Singapore
Photographs by Ong Chan Hao

6/7 Left: Another afternoon of unexpected heavy rainfall. Caught unaware, pedestrians without umbrellas avoid being splashed by passing cars; a woman removes her shoes when the water reaches her ankles.

8/9 Right: The convenience store sells the much-needed umbrella, often purchased in the heat of a storm. Umbrellas are involuntarily amassed at home after many such thunderstorms. Some choose not to spend the money, finding instead a route with the least exposure to rain.

Monsoon Journal: Singapore
Photographs by Ong Chan Hao

10/11 Left: Some storms are fleeting. They stop quickly. A bus stop is a popular place to take cover but provides limited protection.

12/13 Right: To dry off his feet, a commuter puts up his legs on the seat in front of him.

14 Next page:
A secret garden thrives in the concrete gaps of a monsoon drain.

1 Tamsin Lorraine, 'Becoming-imperceptible as a mode of self-presentation,' in *Resistance, flight, creation: feminist enactments of French philosophy*, ed. Dorothea Olkowski (Ithaca: Cornell University Press, 2000), 181.
2 Wayne Tunnicliffe, 'Self selection,' in *Simryn Gill: selected work* (Sydney: Art Gallery of New South Wales, 2002), 5.
3 Astrida Neimanis and Rachel Loewen Walker, 'Weathering: climate change and the thick "time" of transcorporeality,' *Hypatia*, 29, no. 3 (2014): 559, https://doi.org/ 10.1111/hypa.12064.
4 Neimanis and Walker, 'Weathering,' 560.
5 Gilles Deleuze and Felix Guattari, *A thousand plateaus: capitalism and schizophrenia*, trans. Brian Massumi (London: The Athlone Press, 1988), 323. 'A becoming is neither one nor two, nor the relation of the two; it is the in-between, the border or the line of flight....'
6 Katherine Gibson et al., 'Community economies in Monsoon Asia: keywords and key reflections,' *Asia Pacific Viewpoint*, 59, no. 1 (April 2018): 3–16, https://doi.org/10.1111/apv.12186.
7 Yen Yi Loo, Lawal Billa and Ajit Singh, 'Effect of climate change on seasonal monsoon in Asia and its impact on the variability of monsoon rainfall in Southeast Asia,' *Geoscience Frontiers*, 6, no. 6 (November 2015): 819, https://doi.org/ 10.1016/j.gsf.2014.02.009.
8 'The South Asian monsoon, past, present and future,' *The Economist* (27 June 2019), https://www.economist.com/essay/2019/06/27/the-south-asian-monsoon-past-present-and-future.
9 Gibson et al., 'Community economies in monsoon Asia,' 4.
10 Lindsay Bremner, 'On monsoon assemblages,' *Migrant Journal*, 3 (2017): 93.
11 Gibson et al., 'Community economies in monsoon Asia,' 6.
12 J.H. Powell, '"Hook-swinging" in India. A description of the ceremony, and an enquiry into its origin and significance,' *Folklore*, 25, no. 2 (1914): 147–197; James George Frazer (c. 1890), *The golden bough: a study in comparative religion* (Edinburgh: Canongate Books, 2010).
13 Gotzone Garay-Barayazarra and Rajindra K. Puri, 'Smelling the monsoon: senses and traditional weather forecasting knowledge among the Kenyah Badeng farmers of Sarawak, Malaysia,' *Indian Journal of Traditional Knowledge*, 10, no. 1 (2011): 21.
14 Ibid., 23.
15 Ibid.
16 Ibid.
17 *Times of India*, 'Ajmer Urs: farmers pray for good monsoon' (5 April 2016), https://timesofindia.indiatimes.com/city/jaipur/Ajmer-Urs-Farmers-pray-for-good-monsoon/articleshow/51690945.cms.
18 Faima Bakar, 'Frogs who married "to bring rain" to Indian village gets divorced because of too much downpour,' *Metro UK* (15 September 2019), https://metro.co.uk/2019/09/15/frogs-who-married-to-bring-rain-to-indian-village-get-divorced-because-of-too-much-downpour-10745884/.
19 *The Star Malaysia*, 'Farms pray to Rain God' (26 September 2013), https://www.thestar.com.my/news/nation/2013/09/26/farmers-pray-to-rain-god.
20 *Malaysiakini*, 'Jakim calls on all mosques hold prayers for rain' (9 September 2019), https://www.malaysiakini.com/news/491244.
21 Garay-Barayazarra and Puri, 'Smelling the monsoon,' 21.
22 Ibid., 25.
23 Ibid., 21.
24 David Gissen, *Subnature: architecture's other environments* (New York: Princeton Architectural Press, 2009), 100–117.
25 Katie Lloyd Thomas, 'Introduction: architecture and material practice,' in *Material matters: architecture and material practice*, ed. Katie Lloyd Thomas (London: Routledge, 2007), 2.
26 Jonathan Hill, *Immaterial architecture* (London: Routledge, 2006), 3.
27 Andrew Ballantyne, *Deleuze and Guattari for architects* (London: Routledge, 2007), 85.
28 Ibid., 86.
29 Deleuze and Guatarri, *A thousand plateaus*, 433.
30 Vivian Balakrishnan, 'Increasing rainfall intensity on Singapore—flood prevention will need major infrastructural upgrades' (9 January 2012), http://vivian.balakrishnan.sg/2012/01/09/increasing-rainfall-intensity-on-singapore-flood-prevention-will-need-major-infrastructural-upgrades/.
31 Wee Keat Leong, 'Clogged canal caused flash floods, says PUB,' *Today Online* (18 June 2010); Grace Chua and Victoria Vaughan, 'Blocked Drain Blamed for Orchard Rd Flood,' *The Straits Times* (18 June 2010), https://wildsingaporenews.blogspot.com/2010/06/blocked-drain-blamed-for-orchard-road.html.
32 For estimated costs of the Orchard Road flood damages see Hui Theng Koh, 'No more handbags, it's sandbags,' *The New Paper* (22 July 2010), AsiaOne edition, https://www.asiaone.com/News/The%2BNew%2BPaper/Story/A1Story20100722-228306.html.
33 Kin Mun Lee, 'Someone call the minister of freak incidents! Orchard Road flooding!' Mr Brown (16 June 2010), https://www.mrbrown.com/blog/2010/06/someone-call-the-minister-of-freak-incidents-orchard-road-flooding.html.

34 Chua and Vaughan, 'Blocked drain blamed for Orchard Rd flood,' *Straits Times* (18 June 2010); this newspaper report includes a diagram showing the cross-sectional dimensions of the culvert as 2.7m × 2.7m, large enough for a single-decker bus.
35 Gissen, *Subnature*, 118.
36 Ibid., 100–117.
37 Ibid., 100–102.
38 Ibid., 104.
39 Ibid.
40 Roland Barthes, 'Paris not flooded,' in *Mythologies*, trans. Richard Howard and Annette Lavers (New York: Hill and Wang, 2012), 62.
41 Barthes, 'Paris not flooded,' 62–63.
42 Stephanie C. Kane, 'Engineering an island city-state: a 3D ethnographic comparison of the Singapore River and Orchard Road,' in *Rivers of the Anthropocene*, ed. Jason M. Kelly et al. (Oakland: University of California Press, 2018), 137.
43 Ibid., 147.
44 Ibid.
45 Anders Kreuger, "O, outside, show me your innermost!": Simryn Gill's My own private Angkor,' *Afterall — a journal of art, context and enquiry*, 33 (2013): 88–97.
46 Kathleen Stewart, 'Atmospheric attunements,' *Environment and Planning D: Society and Space*, 29, no. 3 (2011): 445–453. This essay was prepared with the support of the MOE Tier 1 Grant WBS R-295-000-156-115. The author thanks Sherilyn Yeo for her assistance, and greatly appreciates Ong Chan Hao's cinematic shots.

Clouding architecture

1 Finbarr Fallon, Photograph of A Simple Headquarters (design by author), 2020, Singapore.

'They are the celestial clouds, the patron goddesses of the layabout. From them come our intelligence, our dialectic and our reason.' — *Aristophanes, c. 420 BCE*[1]

As cities become denser, visual access to an endless expanse of clouds and sky becomes a rare occasion. In urbanised Singapore, the sky view is always obstructed by tall building skylines and access to open-sky terraces.[2] Recently, I have considered myself fortunate to be sitting atop my equatorial roof terrace, where I have been staring skywards. COVID-19 may have kept me house-bound, but it has created moments for pause and reflection as I consciously appreciate my breath and the air around me. Through my ascending gaze, the clouds in the constantly changing, moving and shape-shifting sky glide past in a variety of shapes, colours and figures. Looking up, my daughter points to a bunny rabbit, a dog or a T-rex in the sky. Alternating between ecstatic shrieks of laughter and wide-eyed wonder, she witnesses these ephemeral white forms dissolve and reconstitute into new shapes only moments later. Quickly changing colour from white to grey to greenish black marked by a monsoon thunderhead, the sky signals us to retreat back indoors, just as the clouds crack open with sheets of rain, flashes of lightning and claps of thunder. Such quotidian moments of dramatic monsoon skyscapes evoke realisations that this band of volatile cloud activity[3] over the Equator compensates for the lack of perceptible seasons—offering a dynamic context for architecture and lives therein.

These transient masses of water vapour, however distant from land, continue to wield strong physical connections to climate and culture and in turn frame architecture. In *Clouds and sky ceilings: landscape symbolism and the architectural imagination,*[4] John Roberts discusses the aesthetic roles of clouds and sky in the works of Erik Gunnar Asplund (Skandia Cinema and Stockholm Public Library), Alvar Aalto (Viipuri and Seinäjoki libraries) and Jørn Utzon (Bagsvaerd Church). Each project explores the sky ceiling as a programmatic and aesthetic choice ingrained into architectural narratives, combining landscape and history. They demonstrate the representation and symbolism of the sky and clouds as being intrinsic to the architectural imagination—particularly, sky views that have continued to emphasise the natural within man-made environments. Therefore, it can be argued that the sky and clouds are architectural elements just like a roof, window or door that position architecture into its own climatic landscape:[5] be it fictional, ideal or real.

Portraying clouds

However, in drawings of the architectural imagination, clouds are highly underrepresented, despite their ubiquity in our daily experience of climates—influencing how we conceive architecture and understand the climates we inhabit. They are not merely neutral, abstract bodies, but possess given scientific genres and species subsets based on their shape and altitude. First categorised by Luke Howard in 1802, all clouds are combinations of four cloud categories: Cirro, Cumulo, Strato and Nimbo.[6] Despite their geological variety and transience, representational clouds in drawings, paintings, photography and simulations have adhered to a single type — the puffy soft Cumulus Humilis. These are low-level clouds, with detached, dense morphologies—'resembling a cauliflower' with distinct edges,[7] reflecting light in a modelled manner. The sunlit parts of these clouds remain mostly brilliant, in an intense white colour; in contrast, their horizontal layers are relatively dark against a sky-blue background, which allows our imagination to anthropomorphise them into storyboard characters, making them the most recognisable clouds in the sky. As cumulus clouds develop on clear-sky days with rare precipitation, they are known as 'fair-weather clouds' which signify a rain-free, sunlit day. For architects, the predilection for the cumulus cloud implies a preoccupation for a clear blue-sky climate—an 'ideal, transparent backdrop' for their building and a preference for heliocentric atmosphere that amplifies a contrast of light and shadow.

Deployed universally despite climate, latitude or place, the cumulus cloud signifies the construction of a climatic ideal, fuelling the bias for

clear skies. Such bias creates more imageries of architecture and its surroundings existing in climatic utopias, particularly ones that disregard unpredictable, dynamic weather events—especially now as we witness alarming intensities of climate change worldwide. Such predilections for fair-weather cloud scenes amongst architects can be traced back to the French Renaissance period. In the depiction by Philibert de l'Orme, the idea of a builder emerges from a dark cave to become an architect in ideal weather conditions replete with cumulus in the background, establishing the context for the proper climatic conditions in which the architect practises. Several centuries later, architects and inhabitants continue to consume remnants of this imagery as a touchstone for aesthetic and performative choices in buildings, most of which are dangerously outdated given more accurate instruments for visualisations in the present day.

The reality of the equatorial region, for example, results in rare sightings of the cumulus cloud. Singaporean skies (located at 1° latitude above the equator) are replete with mid- and low-level strati:[8] for example, blankets of opaque, translucent greys and whites, offering only an occasional peek at blue skies. Yet, if you search online for images on the 'tropical architecture of Singapore' and 'modern architecture,' the results include photographs of beach-front villas set in verdant landscapes with deep blue crisp skies and a speckling of white puffy Cumulus Humilis—an indicator that the blue sky has become a universalised ideal. Rendered generic by internets algorithm, an architect's sky is defined broadly as an International Style sky,[9] free from pollution, clouds or water vapour. Only sunlight can penetrate the clear and cleaned-up air. It is an atmosphere of transparency that reinforces a parallel aesthetic in architecture itself. We find evidence for the same in a series of published works from Singapore that reinforce this image of a transparent climate through photographs of inset architectural projects. In *Singapore houses* (2012)[10] by Robert Powell and architectural photographer Albert Lim, tropical architecture gains legitimacy in the deployment of the 'universal' sky, through the use of the terms 'tropicality' and contextual practice. Darren Soh,[11] in many of his commercial architectural photographs, and Patrick Bingham-Hall for Singapore-based practice WOHA, showcase architecture set under a vibrant cerulean sky, rarely found in the cityscape.

By unconsciously privileging a blue sky and the cumulus cloud over grey skies, visual representations have become complicit in reinforcing a certain type of temperate, climatic prejudice. It places a singular cloud condition and its resultant weather as an ideal over all others—enforcing this model as the only acceptable backdrop for architecture. From Rome to New York, Seoul and Melbourne, architecture is surrounded by blue skies and puffy cumulus clouds—idolising an architectural aesthetic of tall, sharp-edged skyscrapers that non-temperate urbanscapes are forced to emulate, denying their climatic otherness.[12] Cloud-filled, hazy, rain-filled atmospheres—or climatic others—are burdened by expectations that they should be manipulated into a temperate vision of crispness, clarity and blue backgrounds: an idealised state that has long been valued in architectural thought and making. In fact, I argue that a very different set of architectural values and aesthetics are embedded in these other climatic variants—overcast, blurry, contaminated, soft, flexible, mutating and hazy clouds. These alternate forms provide climatic specificity that grounds architecture in situ and de-universalise the temperate hegemony prevalent in architectural discourses.

The heavenly foundations of temperate clouds

> [T]he background against which the architectural perspectives of Pompei [sic] are painted are always of a transparent blue, as are the cloudless skies of the mythological landscapes in the Vatican,which some art critics nevertheless persist in regarding as one the first examples of a 'pictorial' treatment of space... According to Riegl, cloudy skies were never to be found in ancient art, and it was not until the Middle Ages that painting paid them any attention.[13]

Tracing how clouds appear in architectural representations, the relationship between atmosphere, climate and architecture become perceptible. During the Renaissance (fourteenth to seventeenth century AD), clouds began as conspicuous motifs in the visual arts adorning the walls and ceilings of churches and palatial chambers. For instance, *The last judgement* by Michelangelo in the Sistine Chapel in Vatican City serves as a dramatic backdrop to the altar. It showcases a dramatic skyscape wherein heavenly figures are found flying, levitating, dancing and standing on clouds. Largely unclothed, full of muscular flesh, the rotund bodies painted in whites and pinks are choreographed with clouds modelled in the same vein. Traced in white bulbous outlines against a lapis lazuli[14] blue sky, the clouds here seem to depict stepping stones in a heavenly ascension above a dystopian mortal life. Through his sectional striations, Michelangelo creates a lamination between above and below, human and angel, earth and heaven glued together by air and the inhabitants of clouds. The cumulus cloud provides the underside of heaven, the foundation to which we look up to, while we search for shapes, figures and meaning from our position on earth. In *Fall of the giants* (1531–1533) by Perino del Vaga, we likewise view a stratification between the heavenly, white-hued figures above and the defeated underworld below by a band of stratocumulus cloud with dark grey undersides. Although the clouds occupy a thick line across the painting, this line embodies a soft, flexible material of interpenetration and the possibility of salvation. Implicit in these sectional narratives is that up-and-skyward with bright illumination is considered a good place, while downward and into the earth where dark, shade and heat loom is closer to the sins of hell. Crossing from a terrestrial existence to the skies, humans and their souls are required to traverse through air, passing through the lamination of the cumulus to find the angels above (Figure 2).

The amorphous nature of clouds—both their geometry and meaning—make them versatile devices of religious symbolism in the visual arts. As much as they serve to stratify the sky in the aforementioned paintings, they are also employed as representations of heavenly portals. For instance, in *Triumph of the virtues* (1502) by Andrea Mantegna, three figures Justice, Temperance and Fortitude punctuate the sky through a ring of clouds. This cloud form represents a soft, blurred portal between sky and earth, a conduit to heaven allowing saintly virtues to ameliorate the mayhem on earth: an umbilical cord suggesting that heaven on the other side of our earth-bound existence is fundamentally connected through the cumulus portal (Figure 3). *Fall of the giants* (1532) by Giulio Romano showcases a circular arrangement of cumulonimbus and gods on the ceiling in the Chamber of the Giants in the Palazzo del Te in Mantua, Italy (Figure 4). The outward ring of puffy clouds merges into an assemblage of gods, followed by a secondary ring of clouds pierced by an orifice of architectural columns with a dome; some of these figures stare back down to us while our gaze ascends. The rotunda allows us to peer into the architectural heaven above and to those who inhabit it, mirroring our own gaze albeit from a lofted sectional position. Their 'heavenly' perspective downwards shares the vantage point that architects assume—a privileged 'up on high' view when drawing plans or axonometric projections.

Cloudless ideals

However, the omnipresence, shapelessness and translucency of clouds—in contrast to the objects and figures on canvas, meant that their criticality in a visual composition would become less defined over time. In his landmark experiment on mathematical perspective (1415), Filippo Brunelleschi painted a picture of the Baptistery in Florence on a silver mirror, tracing its reflection in real time; the sky and clouds were left unpainted. The choice to render the two-dimensional drawing with

2 Perino del Vaga, *The fall of the giants (Jupiter in the clouds overhead striking the Giants with lightning)*, 1531–1533, Palazzo dei Principe, Genoa.

3 Andrea Mantegna, *The triumph of the virtues*, 1502, Musée du Louvre, Paris.

4 Giulio Romano, *The fall of the giants*, 1532, Sala dei Giganti, Palazzo del Te, Mantua.

5 Above: Luciano Laurana, *The ideal city*, *Urbino* panel, 1480–1490, Galleria Nazionale delle Marche, Urbino. Below: Fra Carnevale, *The ideal city*, *Baltimore* panel, 1480–1484, Walters Art Museum, Baltimore, Maryland.

the sky as a neutral mirror, absent from pictorial space, suggests that the sky did neither form a part of his idea nor support his mechanical construction of the perspective drawing.[15] In either case, Brunelleschi's experiment remains one of the first Western precedents where the cloud and sky became separated from the architectural object. In Botticelli's *Punishment of the sons of Aaron* (1480–1482), the viewers gaze not into the heavens, but instead their sightline is positioned across the horizon. The urban tripartite scene in the foreground is contextualised by a waterscape and a hill beyond, with a flock of stratocumulus on either side of the triumphal arch. Botticelli structures the painting as a series of layers in semi-perspectival projection where the sky and clouds serve an attempt at describing visual reality, not heavenly ascension. In *The ideal city*, *Urbino* panel, people are noticeably absent and so, too, are the clouds. A symmetrical composition displays the prominence of architecture and a gradient of blues that define the sky. The city represents a sanitised ideal, a city removed from human contamination, a city of geometry and control, a city where the heavens and the clouds are no longer foundational to the structure of the scene. In *The ideal city, Baltimore* panel, the traces of a few figures in the forecourt reappear, diminished in relationship to the architecture, while a neutral-hued sky features wispy cirrocumulus clouds. This aesthetic of these two panels suggests a shift in the representation of landscapes, where people and clouds become contaminants, intrusions and expendable objects—where the architectural vision for the city's construction holds prominence over human bodies and the presence of climate (Figure 5).

Hazy clouds down here

While temperate manifestations of cloud figures focus on objects and pictorial representations, there are other painterly approaches that produce clouds in other variations. In a multitude of examples in Chinese paintings, we find clouds as negatives, absences, hazy in-betweens and emptiness intermingled with the landscape, architecture and atmosphere. In Wang Hui's (1632–1717) *Kangxi Emperor's southern inspection tour, Scroll three: Ji'nan to Mount Tai*, a series of mountains, waterbodies, vegetation, people and architecture are deployed throughout the scroll. Clouds, mist and fog percolate throughout the work, operating not as a figural representation of clouds, but as a form of absence. White spaces of the scroll bleed through the painting, linking mountain peak to mountain peak. At other moments, the hazy, effervescent quality of the clouds drains into rivers and passageways, transforming one terrain into another (Figure 6). Such vaporous representations envisage the air and atmosphere as being integral to the landscape. This unified, contiguous vision suggests that clouds can operate as an atmospheric connection that conjoins us with each other and with the physical world we inhabit.

In Guo Xi's (1020–1090) *Early spring* (1072), trees, roots, landform and air intermingle in shape and visual technique. The river folds into roots, transforms into rocks and then into trees, only to shift back into the horizon on another mountain. Traversing the scroll from bottom to top, in a snake-like figure, the ink inscriptions slither and move oscillating between the spaces of clouds, mist and air. The clouds shift in their visual associations, serving as foreground and background as the beholder's eyes move across the scroll (Figure 7). These compelling visual techniques that manifest the presence of clouds and their climate are unified with the specificities of their associated landscapes. Unlike the clouds in the Urbino panel, these clouds cannot be removed from the composition. They remain fundamental to the scroll's visual techniques, serving as both foreground and background simultaneously.

6 Wang Hui, *The Kangxi Emperor's southern inspection tour, scroll three: Ji'nan to Mount Tai*, 1698.

7 Guo Xi, *Early spring*, 11th century, National Palace Museum, Taipei.

樹纔發葉溪
開凍樓閣仙
居最上層不
藉柳桃間點
綴春山早見
氣如蒸
己卯春月
御題

Drawing out clouds

The erasure of clouds (and the sky) from architectural representations can be traced back to the geometric methods of inscribing single lines to compose a plan.[16] The architectural plan requires positioning the eye above buildings in a god-like position (as from the ceiling in the Chamber of the Giants), so far removed that convergent lines are eliminated. In comparison, axonometric drawings from the eye of the architect privilege the roof and two elevations. In both representations, the space between the eye and the drawing is emptied, coloured by an assumed atmosphere free from cloud, breeze, dust or storm. Such a space of transparency, free from any contamination, renders climate and the presence of atmospheric elements external to the architectural representational repertoire. This visual strategy cements the ideal setting for an architecture focused on form, structure and shape, comparable to Brunelleschi rendering the sky outside of the perspectival space.[17] While this atmosphere is empty of any physical obstructions, a series of moving photons of sunlit illumination traverse this void, tracing from above. The illumination of the drawing—a typical white background with black lines—assumes a heliocentric privilege, permitting the movement of light between the unobstructed sun, the drawing and the architect's eye. The architect's medium thus became narrowed to sunlight and the mechanical drawing from Alberti onwards—censuring, erasing and concealing clouds, atmosphere and climate from representation.

With photography, absolute removal of climate in architectural drawings began to be replaced by a sanitised representation of climate. The drawings showcased an idealised, pictorialised, temperate construction universalised across time and place—enforcing and idolising the contamination-free sky. This was not only an ideal photographic technique for representing architecture, but also for constructing the architectural photograph as a climate-free drawing in the twentieth century, reducing clouds to an inkling of fair weather. We can observe the presence of two to three strategically placed cloud forms that puncture the monotony of the skyscapes, while also conveying the aspirations of the architectural artefact. In Frank Lloyd Wright's *Golden Beacon apartment tower for Charles Glore* (1956), three white wisps of cirrostratus traverse a blue background (Figure 8) while his Mile-High Illinois diagram showcases clouds that interrupt the view of the tower. While Wright's high-altitude clouds largely appear in his tower projects in an attempt to pierce the sky, ovoid singular clouds can be found in Le Corbusier's section of the Unité d'habitation published in *La maison des hommes* (1942) where two grey, oblong cumulus clouds hover in the background.

8 Frank Lloyd Wright, Golden Beacon apartment tower for Charles Glore, 1956.

9 Yona Friedman, Ville Spatiale over the Seine, 1959.

Paul Rudolph deploys a similarly figured cloud in his *Milam Residence* (1959–1961) perspective, where black shadows inscribed on the underside of the brise soleil suggest a bright, sunlit day. Oblong cumulus clouds, a single palm tree and a dune-like landscape set the stage for a 'desirable' beach front experience embedded in the drawing's rhetoric. This is an idealised image of sunlit skies, puffy clouds and subtropical fantasies, not the hurricane-impacted landscape of northern Florida where the house sits. In the tropics, Geoffrey Bawa draws cumulus clouds, rolling waves and incoming catamaran—signs of a paradise for the holiday traveller in the elevation of Club Méditerranée (1972).

While Wright, Le Corbusier, Rudolph, Bawa and others deploy conventional clouds in their representations, Yona Friedman employs the cloud as an urban metaphor in his Ville Spatiale (1959). He transforms Michelangelo's cloud—a foundational structure for heaven—turning it into a utopian ideal with an array of box-like volumes floating above the city (Figure 9).[18] Friedman's clouds suggest, as Mark Wigley points out,[19] a network of architecture, spaces and volumes of continual adaptability: where urbanism operates as in the cloud-filled sky. Physically, these cartesian clouds also hint at the digital clouds that construct our online world today.

Virtual clouds

In the twenty-first century, the 'cloud' continues to serve as the foundational underside, not between heaven and earth as in Renaissance paintings but our bridge between the material and the digital worlds. Clouds of virtual space dominate our online presence through a networked architecture—a growing entity of pooled data, whose edges are networked and rendered invisible. Moving from Michelangelo and the drawings of Le Corbusier to the digital information stored in the cloud and constructed of clouds of data, the point cloud[20] takes on a new metaphorical figure in architectural discourse.[21] Here, clouds represent surface topology, topography or geometry rather than an ecology of climate. A point cloud prioritises surfaces of objects, as energy reflecting off material surfaces; this digital figure, with increasing data-point density, creates meshes or closed, non-permeable outlines. In so doing, the point cloud fails to consider not only the metaphorical origins of original stratiform and nebulosus veils, but also the shifting, moving and material-rich presence of air, cloud and climate itself. The point cloud reinforces the surface of objects rather than the qualities of air in which they are positioned, reaffirming an eminently geometric obsession rather than a climatic one.

Virtual tools borrow principles that relegate clouds to compositional elements in a scene, similar to factoring their impact into the creation of architecture. Sky dome in Autodesk 3ds Max defaults to a blue, cloudless San Francisco sky as its backdrop. This convention suggests a culturally embedded predilection. Simulation software, from Ecotect to Diva, privileges the sun path over all other forms of climate features, implying an architecture where humidity and cloud cover does not exist. In Singapore, as in the case of most tropical cities, the presence of cloud cover in the atmosphere and intense humidity levels in the air create conditions where 50% of solar radiation annually received on a building is caused by diffusion. Favouring the path of the sun instinctively directs architects to work with only half of any these climatic possibilities, a significant impediment to environmental design despite an assumed digitally enabled prowess.

Contemporary clouds—moving the heavens to earth

10 Fujiko Nakaya, Experiments in art and technology, Fog Sculpture #47773 of the Pepsi Pavilion, 1970, Expo '70, Osaka.

11 Transsolar and Tetsuo Kondo, Cloudscapes, ZKM, 2015, Karlsruhe, photograph by Wolfgang Kessling.

If *The last judgement* (1536–1541) constructed a heavenly world above, a pictorial space that my daughter enjoys, architects have fantasised about bringing architecture into the clouds through vertical expressions that defy gravity or, more contemporarily, pulling clouds from the sky down to earth that evaporate architecture dissolving it into a cloud.[22]

The Blur Building (and its earlier precedent in the Pepsi Pavilion at Expo '70 in Osaka, Japan, by Fujiko Nakaya) by Diller and Scofidio is a recent example where a fabricated cumulus cloud serves as a media pavilion for Swiss Expo 2002.[23] A volume of mist held together by a tensegrity steel scaffolding manifests as a lake-hugging cloud, enabled by 13,000 nozzles that vaporise the lake water below. Here, the architecture begins to unsettle several of the aforementioned historical constructions wherein their designer cloud—firstly, moves from heavenly skies to terrestrial earth; secondly, reduces architecture to a series of micro

12 Kevin Scott, Photograph of A Simple Terrace House (design by author) with party wall elevation in the background after a monsoon rain, 2014–2017, Singapore.

details and experience; thirdly, camouflages the architecture of pumps, pipes and nozzles to create the cloud and finally, becomes an entity pierced by human bodies—rather than souls (raincoats included) (Figure 10).

Transsolar Energietechnik climate engineers in Germany approach the cloud as a scientific phenomenon with spatial implications, as they develop specific climatic conditions enabling clouds to form within spaces.

> *'Making a cloud is climate engineering at its best. It is about working with the physics of the environment and challenging a project's constraints to do more with less.'*
> *– Wolfgang Kessling, Transsolar Energietechnik*

For Transsolar, clouds are formed by the stratification of atmospheric conditions—temperature from below and humidity from above (while in the Blur Building the cloud was produced by vaporising and projecting water). *The unidentified scented object* (2019) displays a cloud contained in a simple rectangular glass vitrine that separates two atmospheres sectionally, as in Perino del Vaga's *Fall of the giants*.[24] The lower cool, conditioned and fragrance-free atmosphere is separated by a permeable cumulus band from an upper, signature-fragrant atmosphere accessible by a central spiral staircase. In *Cloudscapes* (2015) they produce a cumulus at eye level where the viewer is in horizontal alignment with a cloud—an improbable view where as mortals we no longer experience the underside of the cloud or from above as imagined gods (Figure 11).

Dutch artist Berndnaut Smilde similarly creates terrestrial-based clouds within architecture as momentary apparitions, temporary constructions that emerge and dissipate within seconds. In the work *Nimbus* (2015–present) it is only the photograph that captures the cloud as a trace of its presence and its physicality. While the Blur Building and the Cloudscapes of Transsolar imply the ability to design climate, Smilde's constructions suggest the impossibility of controlling and disciplining heavenly bodies from above. For Smilde, the representation—the photographic drawing—takes on more presence and materiality than the cloud itself.

Equatorial clouds

Clouds and their climatic presence in architecture have been rendered through one variant manifest in one ideal climate and its associated 'fair-weather' transparent air. Tropical fantasies do not visualise the monsoon storm or billowing thunderhead; rather it is the reflective swimming pool mimicking the azure sea beyond with subtle puffs of the cumulus cloud (that hardly appear there). The temperate climate has gripped the architectural imagination regardless of place, climate or latitude.

The temperate climate depicted in Albert Lim's or Darren Soh's images is rarely part of the daily climate in Singapore. Singapore has a wet, cloudy, hot and humid atmosphere full of amazing drama and moving cloud formations above. The tones of billowing clouds change, grow and collide minute by minute. Light and shadows are rendered diffuse because of the very pregnancy of the air. Greys become black, colour bounces, and contrasting perimeters and crispness get camouflaged by washed-out edges. Bleaching whiteness pervades, where the silhouette of the sun hides behind the vapour, lost in its own reflected daylight. The equatorial cloud is not merely a visual canvas from above, but acts as a solar reflector, reducing solar gain[25] on the surface of the earth by 50%. On the equator, specifically in Singapore with 88% cloud cover[26] there is a persistent canopy of shade and reduced air temperatures, producing a more hospitable exterior. The clouds above the equator work in unison with our terrestrial bodies.

In my own architectural practice, I have tried to shed these cumulus prejudices and sought out photographic representations in cloudy, overcast, rainy conditions representative of the realistic equatorial conditions in which I work. In A Simple Terrace House, photographer Kevin Scott was brought in to capture the dynamism of inhabitants and architecture in and after the rain. Puddles, umbrellas and overcoats collaborate with the architecture and climate in that frame against a flat, bleached-out overcast sky. The light quality produced by this diffusion is what I am after in my buildings, made dramatic not by the sun or clouds, but by the filtering of architecture itself through screens, perforations and filters across the architectural envelope (Figure 12).

In A Simple Headquarters (2018–2020), working with photographer Finbarr Fallon, we wanted to achieve evidence of being on the equator: awaiting the hanging underside of a large cumulonimbus cloud to unleash its physicality in a monsoon downpour. The dramatics of the grey and black sky and the amplified depth of the cityscape embroider the building's visual context bearing similarities to the apocalyptic

13 John Martin, *Seventh plague of Egypt*, 1823, Museum of Fine Arts Boston, Massachusetts.

Sublime[27] as seen in John Martin's *Seventh plague of Egypt* (1823). Here, Martin focuses on an all-encompassing and turbulent composition of clouds overpowering the towering monuments of Thebes,[28] celebrating the powerful forces of nature over the well-formed and aesthetically pleasing elements that appear to be in flux with the constantly evolving skyscape (Figure 13). Photography here beyond its representation of climate concentrates not solely on the architectural edifice but enables a closer calibration between my design work and the atmospheric context in which I practise. Other values including haziness, the blurry and the washed-out visual fields are prospective opportunities at the crossroads of equatorial aesthetics, culture, architectural technique and climate science (Figure 1).

Clouds are not simply a representational idiosyncratic concern of architects but remain fundamental to how we think about air, atmosphere and the climate around us. By upholding the cumulus cloud, we are complicit in the reinforcement of a given set of values around transparency, clarity and crisp edges; we have obfuscated the possibility of another architecture culture—one that is hazy, blurry, bleached out, full of water vapour and rain, denouncing the diversity of atmospheres around the earth. The more attuned we are to these subtle but important foundations in architecture, the more diverse our architecture will become. In an age of climate change, it is imperative that the clouds, as important climate signifiers (and modifiers), are always in the picture, present and centred as an inhabitant of the built environment. No longer can climate be relegated as an external participant to architecture, or as a repository for the excesses of an internally controlled climate. Architects can become the custodians of clouds in all their varieties, championing the dynamics of climate in architecture. When gazing upwards into the heavens, look at the presence of the dynamic cloud formation in the overcast, grey underbelly just before the storm's rain and wind—this, too, is our climate to be cherished and celebrated. The more we centre climate and all its variety in our photography, in our diagrams, drawings and as inhabitants in our own domain, the more care and consideration for climate will begin to inform the creation of meaningful, sensorial architecture.

1 As quoted in the Introduction to Richard Hamblyn, *Clouds: nature and culture* (London: Reaktion Books, 2017).
2 UN-Habitat, *Housing practice series*, Singapore (2020): 80% of Singapore's residential population lives in the predominant public housing with little to no access to sky terraces: https://unhabitat.org/sites/default/files/2020/08/singapore_-_housing_practise_series.pdf.
3 Intertropical Convergence Zone (ITCZ) is a region circling the earth near the equator where trade winds from both the North and South Hemisphere blow towards and ascend as a broken line of thunderstorms.
4 John Roberts, 'Clouds and sky ceilings: landscape symbolism and the architectural imagination,' *Proceedings of the 27th International Society of Architectural Historians, Australia and New Zealand Conference*, Newcastle (2009), https://ogma.newcastle.edu.au/vital/access/%20/services/Download/uon:9739/ATTACHMENT01.
5 The term 'climatic landscape' refers to the scientific and phenomenological aspects of climate (temperature, humidity, sky, wind, solar irradiation, rainfall, etc.) that shape and are shaped by humans and architecture.
6 Richard Hamblyn, *The invention of clouds: how an amateur meteorologist forged the language of the skies* (London: Picador, 2001).
7 For a general visual description of the Cumulus Humilis see https://www.metoffice.gov.uk/weather/learn-about/weather/types-of-weather/clouds/low-level-clouds/cumulus.
8 Fu Yingzi, 'Photographing the Singapore house: the construction of a tropical fantasy,' dissertation, unpublished, National University of Singapore, 2013.
9 *Modern architecture: international exhibition*, New York, 10 February to 23 March 1932, Museum of Modern Art, https://www.moma.org/calendar/exhibitions/2044.
10 Robert Powell, *Singapore houses* (Singapore: Tuttle Publishing, 2012).
11 His non-commercial work is often more experimental, depicting the cityscape of Singapore during lightning storms, rain and overcast conditions. It is presumed that Soh's commercial work requires the blue sky, cumulus signification to gain currency with clients and publishers.
12 Rome (41.90°N), New York City (40.71°N), Seoul (37.56°N) and Melbourne (37.81°S) all share similar latitudes. Adding Sydney, Los Angeles, Cape Town and Tokyo as well as Chicago, San Francisco and Shanghai, we find a collection of temperate cities and their associated architecture located in a narrow band of climatic hegemony. From 30° to 40° either north or south, this geographic band measures only 1,126 km wide and represents only 11% of the earth's latitudinal zones.
13 Hubert Damisch, *A theory of cloud: toward a history of painting, trans. Janet Lloyd* (Redwood City: Stanford University Press, 2002; original French edition 1972), 126.
14 Lapis lazuli is a deep-blue metamorphic rock, with references in the Old Testament, mined in Asia Minor and exported to Europe for its expensive blue pigment, used by Renaissance and Baroque artists.
15 Damisch, *A theory of cloud*, 123.
16 Robin Evans, 'Architectural projection,' in *Architecture and its image: four centuries of architectural representation: works from the collection of the Canadian Centre for Architecture*, ed. Eve Blau et al. (Montreal: Canadian Centre for Architecture, 1989), 20.
17 Samuel Y. Edgerton, *The mirror, the window, and the telescope: how Renaissance linear perspective changed our vision of the universe* (Ithaca: Cornell University Press, 2009).
18 Sou Fujimoto's cloud for the Serpentine Gallery pavilion continues Friedman's network metaphor through the production of a lattice-like cumulus cloud composed of 40 mm pointed hollow sections. Located in Hyde Park, London, and designed for the 2013 exhibition, Fujimoto's metaphoric construction of painted steel and embedded circular discs allows visitors to circulate around and within.
19 Mark Wigley, 'The fiction of architecture,' in *Out of site: fictional architectural spaces ed. Anne Ellgood, Rhonda Lane Howard and Mark Wigley* (New Museum of Contemporary Art, 2002), 37–50.
20 A point cloud is defined as a set of data points in space. Point clouds are generally produced by 3D scanners or photogrammetry software, which measure many points on the external surfaces of objects around them.
21 Natalie P. Koerner, 'Beyond millions of plans: a geometry of clouds,' in *The artful plan: architectural drawing reconfigured*, eds. Martin Søberg and Anna Hougaard (Basel: Birkhäuser, 2020), 166–181.
22 From the Tower of Babel, the Burj Khalifa, to Star Wars depictions of Cloud City above Planet Bespin, architects have fantasised about structures with vertical muscularity and gravity-defying proportions that lift slices of the earth into the clouds. While the typology of the tower typically is imagined with technological advances in steel, concrete and glass, the construction of a cloud at ground level works with attributes of temperature, humidity, wind, particulates and vapour.
23 Spray nozzles used originally on the Pepsi Pavilion were designed by cloud physicist Tom Mee from Pasadena, California.
24 See Transsolar Energietechnik GmbH OSNI.1 Unidentified scented object, Cartier, Paris, 2017, https://transsolar.com/projects/osni-1-le-nuage-parfume.
25 NASA, 'Clouds and the energy cycle' (Greenbelt: Goddard Space Flight Centre, 1999), http://nenes.eas.gatech.edu/Cloud/NASAClouds.pdf.
26 Fu Yingzi, 'Photographing the Singapore house,' 31. Using data from the Meteorological Service Singapore, Yingzi estimates that Singapore skies have cloud cover around 88% of the year. Only 12% of the time is the sky clear, and about 54% of the time the sky is cloudy to the extent that one cannot see direct sunshine. And within that, 50% of the time, it rains.
27 Edmund Burke, *A philosophical enquiry into the origin of our ideas of the sublime and beautiful* (London, 1761 [1757]).
28 *The seventh plague of Egypt*, one of Martin's grandest paintings, depicts the Biblical narration from Exodus 9:23—'And Moses stretched forward his rod toward heaven, and the Lord sent thunder and hail, and fire rained down onto the earth.'

90% chance of rain: downpour as event

NATHAN ETHERINGTON

1 Le Corbusier, Preparatory sketch of a rainwater spout for the Chapel at Ronchamp, 1951.

Rainfall arrives in many guises. It can be destructive or mundane, a cause for celebration or terror. As a climatic certainty, precipitation cannot be ignored by architects, but as a source of design expression its status is contentious. Unlike sun or wind, the downpour tends to be excluded from architectural representations in the twentieth century: after all, how does one draw a condition that is incalculable in terms of direction, intensity and duration? How, for example, could a designer represent crucial distinctions between a week of steady rain and a thirty-minute flash flooding event?

A common way of experiencing urban rainfall is through a series of increasingly certain probabilities (for example, 90% chance of precipitation on Friday) that culminate in an event represented on a screen by electronically generated blobs of colour, updated as close to real time as possible (Figure 2). Cycles of urban life rely on short-term probabilities in order to avoid disruption to daily activities; here, the weather tomorrow is critical for one's schedule rather than rain predicted for next week. For activities that rely on longer cycles, it can be more important to know the probability of rain over the next six to twelve months. For agricultural production this is certainly true and for those in charge of water supply where the catchment and storage of rainfall is the primary source of potable water; the same holds true for bushfire planning, which needs to calculate the build-up of fuel loads in the absence of rain. For architects and urban planners, such a timeframe can extend to decades and sometimes centuries. The likelihood of a 1-in-20 or 1-in-100-year rainfall event determines the minimum sizing for a building's gutters and

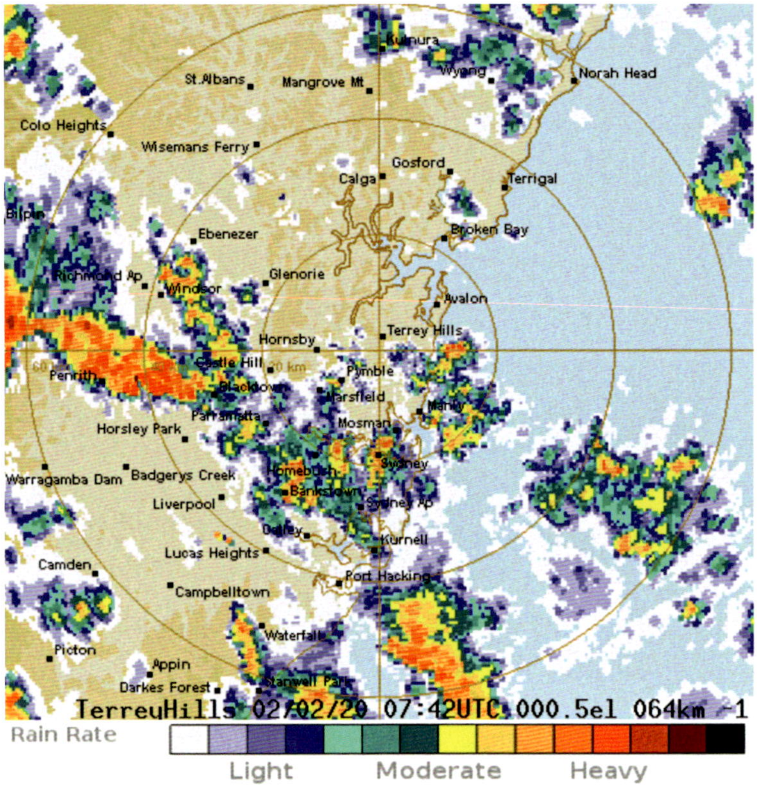

2 Screenshot of radar loop of rain rate at Terrey Hills, Sydney, 2 February 2020, Australian Bureau of Meteorology.

downpipes. A 1-in-100 or even 1000-year event becomes the motivating factor behind flood control and coastal protection systems.

Differences between short- and long-term probabilities also exemplify the separation of weather from climate; the event of the downpour itself is experienced as weather against long-term shifts in the probability of rainfall. The fact that these events are occurring more frequently today as a result of a changing global climate has resulted in a marked shift in attitude by designers towards the event of rainfall. Here, the former notion of control of the downpour by buildings has become supplanted by concepts of resilience.

From 'everywhere' to 'somewhere'

Anuradha Mathur and Dilip da Cunha, whose work spans architecture, landscape and planning, speak of rain as water that is based 'everywhere' rather than 'somewhere,' such as rivers or lakes, where water is 'framed, held in place and distinguished from land.'[1] Mathur and da Cunha take an unusually discerning attitude to water and rain, but it is curious that architects more broadly have not sought to scrutinise this distinction further. Unlike sun or wind, architecture has a direct and material impact on the transition of rainfall from being 'everywhere' to 'somewhere.' Buildings collect, shed and disperse rainfall, and as buildings accumulate into urban agglomerations so, too, does their impact on patterns of water runoff, with increasingly tangible effects. The downpour event has, however, had seemingly little impact on visual representations and the architectural imagination. An obvious reason for this is that rainfall, unlike sun or wind, is excluded from the internal rooms of a building at all costs. Due to its unpredictability, the downpour plays no reliable part in the control of the internal environment of a building. It is therefore resistant both materially and scientifically to architectural diagrams. A second explanation is that the dual event of rain—the storm itself and the change in state from 'everywhere' to 'somewhere'—is difficult to capture in an architecturally meaningful drawing. It is seemingly more atmospheric than climatic, better suited to sublime paintings and cinema than to the functionalist rhetoric accompanying twentieth-century investigations into climate control.

However, the phenomenon of the downpour has not gone entirely unnoticed by architects. This chapter will outline an interest in ephemeral events and their relationship to architectural systems, where precipitation is gradually accommodated, celebrated and integrated into architecture. This development can be traced to a parallel shift from the passive reception of rainfall through the design of spouts, gutters, downpipes and even rainwater tanks, to an active use of rainfall in the form of temporary pavilions and installations. In the twenty-first century, the occurrence of a number of destructive climate events prompted a further movement, this time away from the aesthetics of the event towards a more complex synthesis of design expression and strategic planning. Visual representations of rain have assumed a number of guises within this evolving attitude to precipitation. From sketches, diagrams and digital collages, the image of the downpour, as elusive as the event itself, has tended to be captured as effect: an overflow of flooding water, an architectural detail of rainwater equipment or a diagram of concentrations of cooling spray, each of these examples alludes to architecture's complex attempts to anticipate, control or integrate rainfall.

This chapter will consider a number of projects, primarily through drawings and other modes of architectural representation that demonstrate this evolution. I will argue that the shift in thinking is accompanied by shifts in scale, from the architectural detail and the individual raindrop to the scale of the watershed, the city and the region. This scalar shift parallels a conceptual shift from weather to climate, whereby the downpour becomes subsumed within a complex set of long-term urban challenges. This shift, however, does not necessarily follow a neat, linear progression: scalar leaps are often made within an architect's design process as analogies to climate, landscape and engineering, often manifest across scales. The projects examined in this chapter are presented chronologically but are not intended to comprise a comprehensive narrative of architecture's relationship to rain. Rather they are examined as exemplars of architectural confrontations with the downpour.

'Reconciliation of architecture and water'

Le Corbusier's ambition to reconcile architecture and water is one of the earliest, and certainly most explicit, attempts to develop a formal response to rainfall. While a number of his late buildings, particularly at Chandigarh, express this relationship, it is the chapel at Ronchamp that is most intriguing. The spout at the rear of the building represents a well-known detail. Carefully sculpted in concrete, the bifurcated spout releases water into a cistern below (Figure 3). However, its formal role in the building as a whole is a curious one. The need to collect and store water was a requirement of the brief,[2] but Le Corbusier could have chosen to conceal this process behind the parapet and retain a focus on the larger arrangement of forms. The decision to transfer collected rainwater to a cistern via a spout was certainly not an afterthought.

3 Notre-Dame du Haut by Le Corbusier, Ronchamp, France, photograph of 2005 by author.

Danièle Pauly has noted an origin of the spout and cistern's design in a sketch of a dam by Le Corbusier drawn in 1945, several years prior to the Ronchamp design.[3] What she does not mention is that the 1945 sketch represents Le Corbusier's own speculative design for the Chastang Dam (Figure 4). The drawing appears adjacent to an earlier dam sketch in the *Oeuvre complète* with the caption 'I had tried, in 1939, a first reconciliation of architecture and water (M. Coyne's dam). This year (1945) once more (the Chastang Dam).'[4] The origins and purpose of these sketches are unclear. Jean Petit claims that in 1951, 'Le Corbusier, at the request of engineer André Coyne, carried out several studies for the Chastang dam.'[5] That the earlier sketches may also have been requested by Coyne present an intriguing possibility for understanding Le Corbusier's attempt to synthesise architectural form with engineering necessity.
The 1939 sketch mentioned by Le Corbusier was created for the Aigle Dam, which was constructed between 1941 and 1946 on the Dordogne River in central France, appearing very close to the completed structure. The 1945 sketch of the Chastang Dam is remarkably different from the dam on the Dordogne (located only ten kilometres downstream from the Aigle Dam), ultimately completed in 1952. However, the dramatically elevated spillways were in fact constructed.

B2 18
182
FONDATION LE CORBUSIER
PARIS
1
2
F
LC

What then does Le Corbusier mean by the 'reconciliation of architecture and water'?[6] In 1946, the same year as the *Oeuvre complète*, Le Corbusier also published the two dam sketches in *Propos d'urbanisme*. The accompanying text provides a small but significant distinction:

> In 1939, I attempted to achieve a new form in the architecture of fluids (on the lines of the barrage of M. Coyne). In 1945 I tried again (the barrage of Chastang). But I had the impression that I preached into the desert: to jettison the ballast of habit so completely and so light-heartedly shows a certain lack of good manners perhaps … and engineers, oh miracle! Are the least daring of men.[7]

Le Corbusier is, in fact, attempting a double manoeuvre. First, to draw on the poetic energy of the hydroelectric dam to bring architecture into the realm of hydraulic engineering, where he sees a poetic synthesis between water and built form. He then endeavours to use the architect's grasp of form to refine and invigorate this relationship, usurping the engineer's pragmatism. By appropriating the engineer's control of water, the architect gives life to the relationship of design and nature. In both sketches, the energetic overflow of water in the spillway dramatises the release of water that symbolises a further reconciliation; architecture's role here is the making-visible of the event of flooding rainfall. When this concept is rescaled as a rainwater spout and cistern in the design of Ronchamp, Le Corbusier aspires once again to synthesise architectural expression and engineering through the capture of rainwater (Figure 1). A closer examination of the spout and cistern reveals further dynamism in the building: the water collected on the roof is received by a cylindrical sculptural well and conveyed to the underground cistern. As the cistern fills up, excess water overflows into the decorative pond on top, in what may be seen as a tribute to the poetry of the dam spillway.

Creek beds and gutters

While Le Corbusier attempted to synthesise engineering and architecture through the expression of the rainwater spout, Australian architect Glenn Murcutt pursues a similar reconciliation between building and landscape. Murcutt's highly synthetic design process intertwines modernist planning principles with commonly used local materials and a sensitivity to climatic conditions. This approach is manifested in buildings that tend to be uncomplicated in plan while dynamic in section, relying on the articulation of individual components as the basis for architectural expression. Although Murcutt does not literally draw rain

4 Le Corbusier, Sketch of the Aigle Dam, 1939 (above); Sketch of the Chastang Dam, 1945 (below).

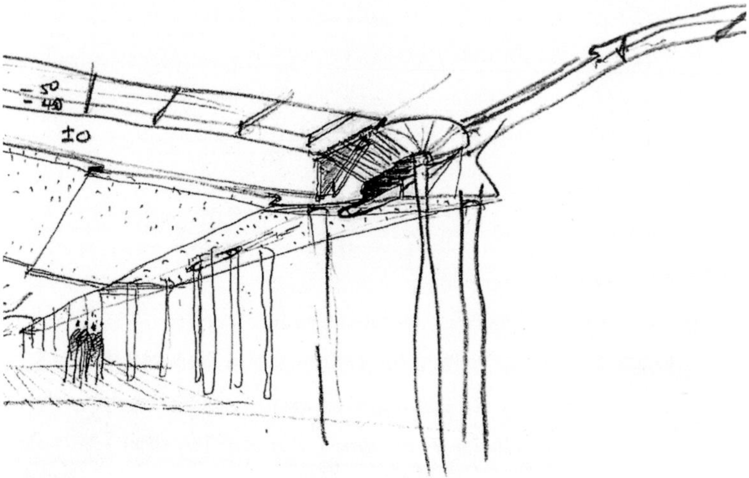

(unlike sun and wind, which appear in many drawings), his design sketches and buildings represent an analogical relationship between the downpour and the Australian landscape. This is nowhere better demonstrated than in the design of the gutters and downpipes of his regional buildings—critical elements that, like a dry creek bed, appear to hold the building in a state of perpetual anticipation of flooding rain.

In Murcutt's works of the 1980s and 1990s, the design of these elements follows a strict pattern: an apparently oversized gutter feeds a large conical rainwater head which conveys water to a circular downpipe pulled away from the main volume of the building stopping just short of the ground (Figure 5). Murcutt explains the reasoning behind the scaling of gutters as a poetic and functional correlation to the natural landscape:

> These are the sorts of details I am interested in. In the dry creek bed where there is no water at all but every now and then 75 millimetres per hour of rain will fall, the dry creek becomes a powerful body of water. The same applies to a gutter which needs to be sized to cope with the volume of water it receives.[8]

This analogy correlates with a tendency to use wide, shallow gutters, much too big for an occasional shower but more than adequate for a 1-in-50-year rainfall event.

5 Glenn Murcutt, Detail of architectural drawing of Visitors Information Centre and Park Headquarters, Kakadu, in association with Troppo Architects, 1992.

6 Glenn Murcutt, Kempsey Museum, photograph by Max Dupain, 1983.

The expression of the movement of water is further accentuated in the design of downpipes which are round in profile and almost always detached from the façade and the ground. In the detailing of the downpipes for the Kempsey Museum (Figure 6), Murcutt goes a step further, giving them a decorative helical form, which 'reflects the movement of water internally in the pipe. In other words, the water does flow down inside the pipe not exactly in that fashion, but it is a suggestion of the movement of the water.'[9] The use of the circular downpipe holds further justification as an auditory mechanism; it produces a pleasant trickling sound rather the 'crashing noise' of a square downpipe. Murcutt's attention to the sensorial dimensions of rainfall preempts experiments in the atmospheric qualities of rain that will be considered in the next section.

Murcutt is quite deliberate in his isolation of the downpipes. He speaks of them as precious objects that are 'not part of the structure, they are not attempting to be columns.' The whole system of water conveyance is ultimately, for Murcutt, an homage to architecture's connection to climate:

> One has to recognise the great importance of water runoff, where the water goes, the water-table. So one might celebrate that.[10]

In a country that experiences frequent and often extreme periods of drought, the value of water, its collection and storage has become a common trope in Australian architecture. Murcutt's celebration has morphed into occasionally extreme levels of preciousness, with copper and brass rainwater goods vying for attention on the façades of buildings.

Murcutt's concern with the atmospheric qualities of rain becomes amplified in projects at the turn of the millennium, as architects became increasingly fascinated by events as generators of architectural form. Advances in digital design and interactive computing are employed in numerous installations and pavilions in which formal fluidity and tectonic ambiguity have flourished. Water has transformed into the subject and material of experimental projects defined by their ephemerality and temporality.

From 'somewhere' to 'everywhere': architecture as event

> Why still speak of the real and the virtual, the material and the immaterial? Here, the categories are not in opposition or in some metaphysical disagreement, but more in an electroliquid aggregation, enforcing each other, as in a two-part adhesive; constantly exposing its metastability to induce animation.[11]

Lars Spuybroek's NOX H2O Expo (Freshwater) pavilion (1994) exemplifies this convergence. The project embodies an 'event' in every way. The form of the building results from an iterative process through which internal factors (programme and movement) and external factors (topography and weather patterns) act to 'deform' the geometry of the pavilion. The waterlike fluidity of the exterior is carried through to the internal articulation where the passage through the pavilion takes on metaphorical fluidity:

> Since the sections are continuous and floor blends into wall and wall into ceiling, the building forces the visitor to rely on his or her own motor system to balance...The visitor must act like water to pass through the building.[12]

As people enter the building, the metaphor is literalised in the presence of water throughout:

> The building's first part, which features a three-dimensional door, is constantly flooded with water. Visitors arrive at the 'glacier-tunnel', which is completely frozen with melted water spilling onto the floor. Further into the building are 'springs' spraying mist and water, a 'rain bowl' with stroboscopically illuminated rain and the 'well', which contains 120,000 litres of water...[13]

7 NOX, Sketch of H2O Expo, 1994, The Frac Centre-Val de Loire, France.

An early concept sketch by NOX illustrates this literal and metaphorical fluidity of water events arrayed across an internal landscape (Figure 7). The conceptual continuity of external and internal landscapes is clearly represented in this diagram, overlaid by a secondary landscape of events.

H2O Expo presents an absolute theatre-of-water event that is real and analogous. The building form and visitors 'flow,' and water is encountered in various states, each event (such as flooding, melting raining, misting) amplified by an interactive sound and light show (Figure 8). The event of the downpour is disaggregated into components each of which is experienced in isolation in a building which, in turn, isolates the visitor from the outside world—the water event is contained entirely 'somewhere' under mechanical control. The anti-didactic nature of the building—it appears only to want to dazzle, not to inform—reinforces the totalising paradigm of event architecture. The choreography of water here is contained, controlled yet entertaining, the lovechild of a water park and a nightclub.[14]

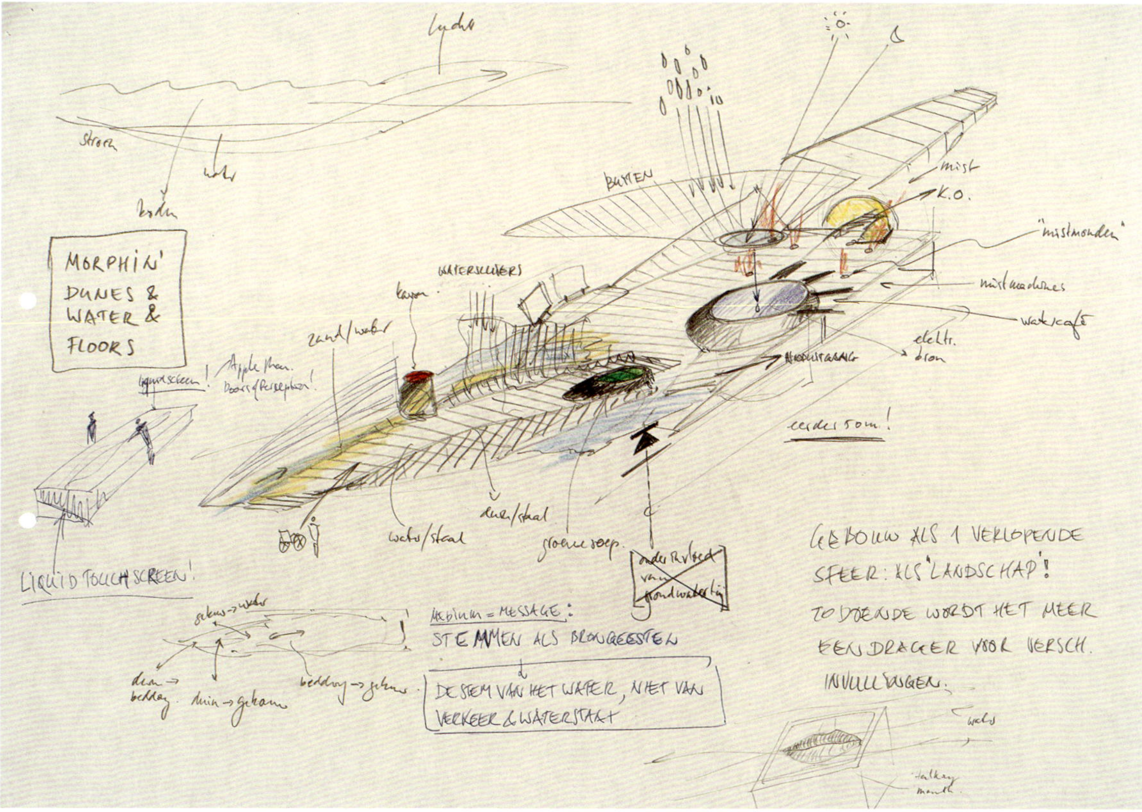

H2O Expo finds its antithesis in the Jade Eco Park by Philippe Rahm, a large park that takes a 'meteorological' approach to the design of a landscape.[15] Rather than construct a series of theatrical encounters with water in various states, Rahm's project opens up the internalised control of water to the real climatic and meteorological conditions of Taichung in Taiwan. Completed in 2018, seven years after winning the design competition, the design of the park is structured around the creation of strategically located, semi-artificial (or simulated) microclimates.[16] Through a detailed climatic analysis of the park, Rahm identifies a spectrum of microclimatic interventions that provide localised cooling, dehumidification or depolluting depending on park programme, adjacent context or prevailing climatic conditions. Building upon experiments and experience with highly controlled exhibition work, Rahm sets out to calibrate rather than control the physiological experience of the park.

Central to the design and execution of the park, and indeed to Rahm's projects, is a particular form of representation that takes a

scientific approach to diagramming architecture. It has been noted that Rahm eschewed conventional architectural drawings in his competition entry, presenting the project as a spectrum of hot and cold temperatures (Figure 9).[17] Within this framework, the representation of rain is conveyed in the form of an evaporative cooling diagram. Among the 'climate devices' scattered throughout the park are 'cirrus clouds,' structures that release mist providing local cooling (Figure 10). This release of 'rain' from artificial clouds is represented as a gradient of cooling capacity, a graphic equivalent to the physiological mechanisms of the other devices in the park (regardless of the specific technologies involved). The original diagram of the park is thus actualised through the climate devices which produce a dynamic gradient of microclimatic effects now at the whim of real climatic conditions.

It is impossible not to draw comparisons between Rahm's cirrus clouds and Diller and Scofidio's Blur Building for the 2002 Swiss Expo.[18] Though both are technically 'clouds,' the modes of representation employed by the two firms present clear conceptual and theoretical distinctions. Diller and Scofidio's attempt to dematerialise architecture is conveyed by the collaged image of a fluffy white cloud floating over Lake Neuchâtel. The engineered skeleton is obscured in both the presentation drawings and the cloud 'event' of the realised pavilion. Conversely, Rahm's highly diagrammatic drawings convey a tight synthesis between the engineering

8 Lars Spuybroek, H2O Expo, 2004.

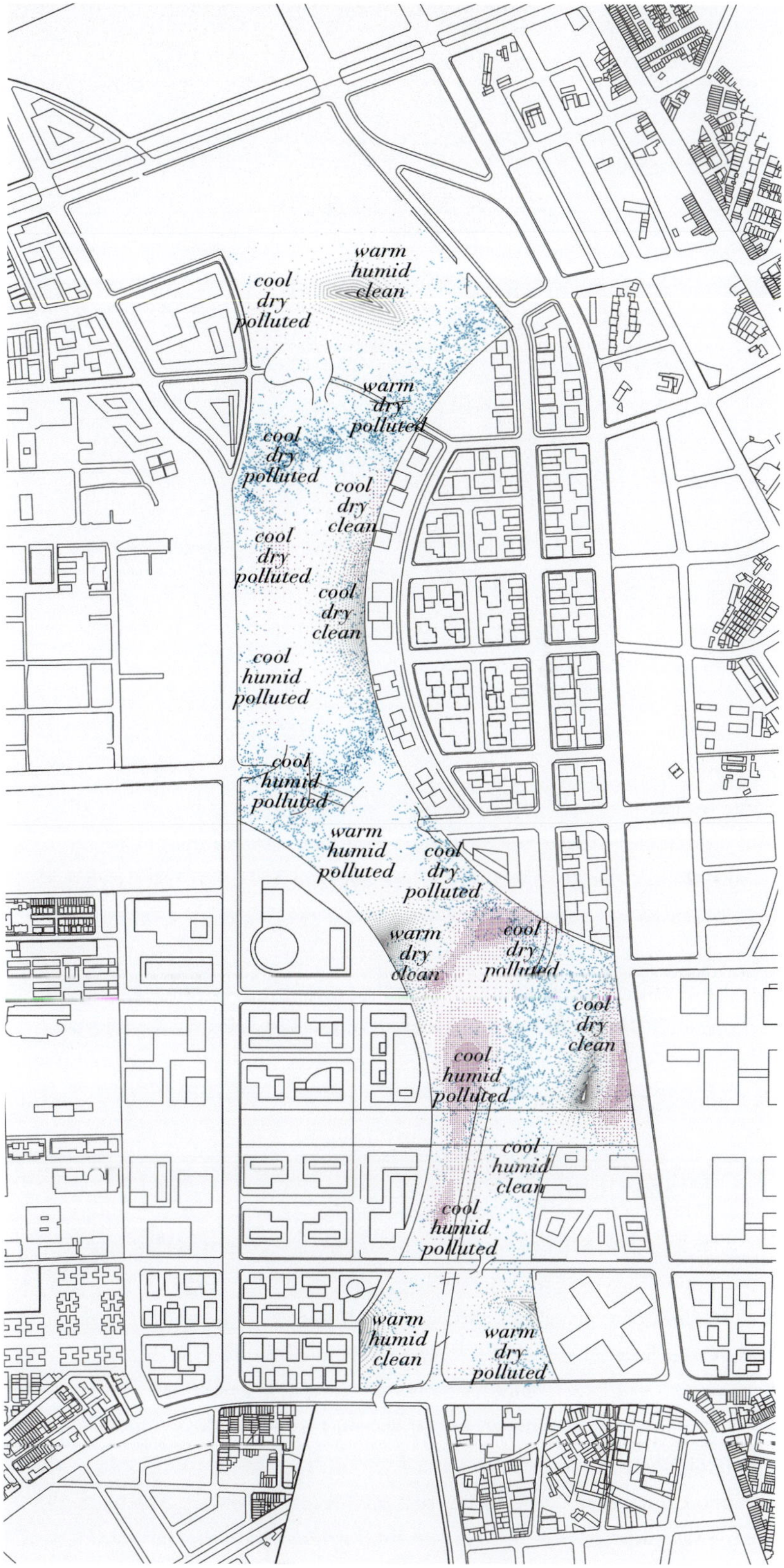

9 Philippe Rahm architectes, Mosbach Paysagistes, Ricky Liu & Associates, Jade Eco Park site plan annotated with Microclimates, 2013.

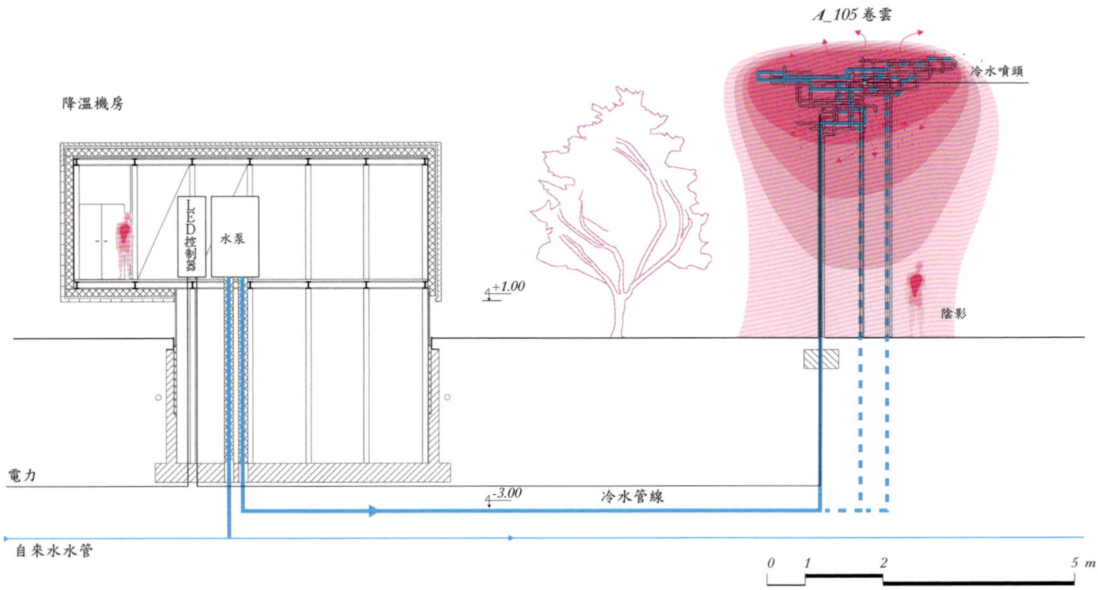

10 Philippe Rahm architectes, Mosbach Paysagistes, Ricky Liu & Associates, Cirrus cloud diagram, 2013.

and architectural expressions of the climate devices, a climate event that sits, paradoxically, between retention and relinquishment of climate control. Rahm is explicit in this distinction, asserting that 'I try to avoid references to images, and try to work more readily from a scientific and technical point of view… The purpose of our devices isn't as much to represent the image of a cloud as it is to provide a variety of thermal sensations.'[19] This tension between design and engineering (as well as modes of control and submission) characterises another recent trajectory in design, that of urban resilience.

Water out of place

In this new millennium, a series of catastrophic weather events combined with a growing sense of urgency around climate change has set a new course for architecture's relationship to rainfall, characterised by interdisciplinary collaboration and pragmatism, rather than form and expression. This new trajectory appears to run counter to the architectonic concerns of Le Corbusier and Murcutt and the atmospheric experiments of NOX. In formal terms this may be true, but strategically what occurred was rather a rescaling of architectural thinking. For example, Murcutt's analogous relationship to landscape became concretised in a new set of relationships between architecture, landscape and risk management. The oversizing of stormwater equipment now extends to urban infrastructure. The interactive, technological ideas that constituted the motivating factor in the event pavilions can now be seen implemented at the scale of the landscape.[20]

At the architectural scale, risk of inundation has been managed through regulatory processes and building codes. The increasingly urgent problems of flash flooding and storm surges at the urban scale has necessitated collaborative approaches to risk. At the heart of these approaches was an expansion and multiplication of scales of design, now extending from macro regional or even continental scales to micro architectural details. A further result of this shift was to de-emphasise the aesthetics of the event in favour of solving imminent problems rather than disciplinary concerns. This trend has escalated in the face of climate-driven urban catastrophes set against the backdrop of increasingly urgent global environmental movement.

Hurricane Katrina in 2005 marked a key event driving this new pragmatism. As William Taylor and Michael Levine have argued, the 'Katrina effect' laid bare a litany of failures in the design, planning and governance of cities worldwide, not simply in New Orleans.[21] Subsequent disasters such as the flooding of the Brisbane River in 2011, Hurricane Sandy in 2012 and Typhoon Haiyan's destructive impact on the Philippines demonstrated that Katrina was not an isolated case; cities such as New York were equally vulnerable to worsening climate events. A key term to emerge from these events was urban resilience. What appeared to be the greatest failure in the face of these storm-generated disasters was the ability for cities to absorb the impact of flooding rain and contain the possibility of extensive damage. The problem lay with water being 'out of place' or uncontained. During a flood, water that should be kept 'somewhere' appropriate—contained in a river, behind levees, stored in a dam—is suddenly everywhere. As Taylor and Levine point out, the cause of these events is not just the weather event itself, but in fact, lies within a history of planning decisions. Urban resilience possesses a much larger scope than merely disaster relief and control; it impacts design, engineering and policy across scales. Importantly, concepts of resilience acknowledge that the effects of climate and other shocks are not absorbed equally by all city dwellers—low-income neighbourhoods and vulnerable people tend to be at far greater risk from these events, and strategies for urban resilience must account for these issues.[22]

For designers, the move from containment or control of water to resilience is a paradigm shift. Murcutt's creek analogy and Rahm's microclimates are supplanted by an imperative for cross-disciplinary collaboration: the hydrology of watersheds, the engineering of embankments, the absorptive capabilities of landscape surfaces and the site coverage of buildings all become strategic elements on a scalar continuum. This continuum has a correlative in the reconceptualisation of urban boundaries. A city located in a flood plain is re-established as part of a set of regional mechanisms aimed at resilience that renders so-called city limits arbitrary.

The emergence of resilience in urban planning theory has a long history, but broader awareness among design practitioners, and architects in particular, has lagged. A notable shift occurred, however, in the period between the post-disaster responses to Hurricanes Katrina and Sandy. Where the focus after Katrina was on rebuilding and in particular the idea of 'building back better,' in the wake of Sandy the design disciplines showed a trend towards larger-scale storm protection schemes with broader collaboration with other fields of expertise. Some of this can be explained by the specifics of each case: the devastation wreaked by Katrina came in the form of breached levees that focused destruction in particular on low-income neighbourhoods creating a necessity for reconstruction. Sandy, by contrast, manifested as an external force through a coastal storm surge, leading to a debate that incorporated wider issues of climate change and sea level rise. I would argue, however, that progressing interests in landscape design and ecology have influenced the nature of the responses between 2005 and 2012.

11 Stoss, Aerial view in clear weather of East Boston and Charlestown coastal resilience solutions, 2017, Boston, Massachusetts.

12 Stoss, Aerial view in rain of East Boston and Charlestown coastal resilience solutions, 2017, Boston, Massachusetts.

The Rebuild by Design competition organised after Sandy in 2014 gave graphic expression to the challenges facing urban development in a changing climate. The dynamism of resilient cities and landscapes creates a representational challenge for architects. Collaboration between disciplines, acting at the scale of the landscape, has the immediate effect of sidelining architectural instincts for form-making and expression. In the place of formal concerns—either expression or dissolution—is the representation of dynamic processes: not the analogous response by way of Murcutt's details or NOX's design process, but active climatic and ecological changes. Rather than representations of architecture, we see a strong emergence of the representation of conditions and the incorporation of multiple forms of representation including maps, diagrams and charts, alongside more conventional architectural drawings and perspectives.

In addition to evolving representational techniques within multidisciplinary design teams, there is the difficulty of communicating complex ideas and strategies to policy-makers and local communities which, as noted, are often low-income or vulnerable. In discussing the Blue Dunes project, an entry for Rebuild by Design, Claire Weisz

and Mark Yoes argue that the development of representational practices constitutes an important part of the design process:

> These techniques [of representation] form a body of research and iterative investigation through which designers and planners seek to create tools to gather feedback on alternate designs or outcomes. The challenge is to source data as much as it is to project it.[23]

From this perspective, drawing plays a dual role as a key element in design research and a more traditional communicative device between specialist and 'client'; however, the process is again rescaled to address a new spectrum of physical scales as well as broad swathe of actors.

An example of this communicative necessity can be illustrated by a recent coastal resilience project by Stoss Landscape Urbanism for Boston's Charlestown waterfront. The design for a recreational space that doubles as protection against storm and sea surges is captured in aerial perspectives of the landscape. Unusually, however, the views are paired, showing landscape conditions under clear skies and heavy downpour (Figures 11 & 12). This representational pairing gives a striking and immediately comprehensible indication of design strategy intended to accommodate water both in and out of place. The shift to a resilience mindset here sees a further development on the movement of water from everywhere to somewhere. It now recognises that patterns of urbanisation can be designed to adapt to an oscillation of water moving from somewhere to everywhere and back again, a view of water that does not see rainfall as needing to be naturally contained but in flux.

The occurrence of a downpour may only be anticipated as a probability, but it is increasingly certain that extreme rainfall events will become more frequent and destructive. The regulatory nature of architectural practice means that architects will be forced to adapt to these conditions as governments face up to reality. The projects considered here demonstrate, however, that an expressive, experimental or collaborative approach to rain and its consequences can provide a pathway for architectural practice that is progressive rather than reactive. The uneven social effects of rainfall events should be reason enough for architects to incorporate a responsible attitude towards the movement of water from being everywhere to being somewhere. There remains an untapped potential for drawing to embrace the downpour as a means of bringing architecture into a closer relationship with temporal events.

1 Anuradha Mathur and Dilip da Cunha, eds., *Design in the terrain of water* (Philadelphia: Applied Research Design Publishing with the University of Pennsylvania School of Design, 2014), xi.
2 Danièle Pauly, *Le Corbusier: the chapel at Ronchamp* (Basel: Birkhäuser, 2008), 52.
3 Pauly, *Le Corbusier: the chapel at Ronchamp*, 72–75.
4 Le Corbusier, *Œuvre complète*, Vol. IV, *1938–1946* (Basel: Birkhäuser, 1995[1946]), 152.
5 Jean Petit, *Le Corbusier lui-même* (Genève: Éditions Rousseau, 1970), 110. Quotation translated from French by the author. Petit's chronology appears flawed as the Chastang Dam was completed in 1952, prompting the question as to why an engineer would request input from an architect for a project nearing completion.
6 Le Corbusier, *Œuvre complète*, Vol. IV, 152.
7 Le Corbusier, *Concerning town planning* (Propos d'urbanisme), trans. Clive Entwistle (London: The Architectural Press, 1947), 43.
8 Philip Drew and Glenn Murcutt, *Touch this earth lightly: Glenn Murcutt in his own words* (Potts Point, N.S.W.: Duffy & Snellgrove, 1999), 112.
9 Ibid., 112-113.
10 Ibid., 113-114.
11 Lars Spuybroek, 'Motor geometry,' in *The digital turn in architecture 1992–2012*, ed. Mario Carpo (Chichester: Wiley, 2013), 116.
12 Lars Spuybroek, *NOX: machining architecture* (London: Thames & Hudson, 2004), 18.
13 Ibid., 18.
14 In the wake of H2O Expo, a number of other architects and designers have sought to experiment with precipitation within the context of exhibitions and installations, notably Random International's *Rain room* (2012) and Carlo Ratti's *Cloud cast* (2015).
15 Philippe Rahm architectes, *Form follows climate. About a meteorological park in Taiwan* (Rionero in Vulture: Oil Forest League, 2017).
16 Philippe Rahm in conversation with Sascha Roesler, 'Thermal sensations: the case of the Jade Eco Park in Taichung (Taiwan),' in *The urban microclimate as artifact: towards an architectural theory of thermal diversity*, eds. Sascha Roesler and Madlen Kobi (Basel: Birkhäuser, 2018), 112.
17 Gene K. King, 'The tao of Rahm,' *The architectural review*, 241, no. 1442 (1 June 2017): 31; Rahm, 'Thermal sensations,' 112.
18 Sascha Roesler broached this comparison in his interview with Rahm, 'Thermal sensations,' 104.
19 Rahm, 'Thermal sensations,' 118.
20 See the projects in Bradley Cantrell and Justine Holzman, eds., *Responsive landscapes: strategies for responsive technologies in landscape architecture* (New York: Routledge, 2016).
21 William M. Taylor and Michael P. Levine, 'Catastrophe and the "Katrina effect",' in *The Katrina effect: on the nature of catastrophe*, eds. William M. Taylor, Oenone Rooksby, Joely-Kym Sobott and Michael P. Levine (London: Bloomsbury, 2015), 1–24.
22 See Lawrence J. Vale, 'The politics of resilient cities: whose resilience and whose city?,' *Building research & information: resilience in the built environment*, 42, no. 2 (4 March 2014), 191–201; William M. Taylor, 'Architecture after Katrina: lessons from the past or designs for someone else's future?' in *The Katrina effect*, 255–285.
23 Claire Weisz and Mark Yoes, 'Engaging design: complexity and contradiction by design,' in *Blue dunes: climate change by design*, eds. Jesse M. Keenan and Claire Weisz (New York: Columbia Books on Architecture and the City, 2016), 57.

COOL

Casting shadows and seeking shade

1 Jan Pietersz. Saenredam after Cornelis Cornelisz. van Haarlem, *Plato's cave*, engraving on laid paper, 1604, Ailsa Mellon Bruce Fund, National Gallery of Art, Washington, D.C.

In the beginning, as the book of Genesis tells us, God created the heavens and the earth. Earth 'was formless and empty,' immersed in darkness, until there was light.[1] Light was hereby deemed to be good, and thus separated from the darkness, which by implication was something to be read as negative. From this beginning, as it is presented by the Hebrew sources, light and dark were seen as dualistic. Light was something to be defined as much by its presence as by its absence or its opposite. Light and dark, day and night, would become entangled with other binary concepts such as knowledge and ignorance, good and evil, and even masculine and feminine. In between these conditions of lightness and darkness, was *shade*—being a state of comparative darkness, often transient, that was made possible by the interruption of light. While facilitated by the presence of and contrast with light, it was more commonly associated with darkness.

Shade has been oft-overlooked in the history of art, literature and philosophy—overshadowed if you will—by accounts and interpretations of light and darkness, and their meanings and its representations.[2] It has received more attention in histories of architecture and the built environment, due largely to climatic design and interest in shade-bearing elements, such as the verandah or brise soleil. However, the role of shade as both a negative and positive condition warrants further investigation, particularly as it pertains to its representation in architecture and the built environment.

Shade—as it has been represented in Western art and architecture—traditionally fell into two distinct categories of interpretation.

At various times and places, it was both feared and sought, and this dualism will inform the structure of our discussion. The first part of the chapter, 'Throwing shade, casting shadows,' considers the historic interpretation of ideas of shade and shadow in art and architecture. Beginning with a discussion of its integration in early histories of art, it considers the problem of shade through a number of negative conditions, including those that emerged as a result of the evolution of the high-rise in the first half of the twentieth century, as well as strategies for dealing with the ongoing issues of shade and shadow in the built environment. Returning to the nineteenth century, but this time to the southern hemisphere, the second half of the chapter 'Seeking shade in the Global South' examines the opposite condition, when shade is sought, especially in the context of offering relief from environmental conditions. It traces how the phenomenon of *Pteridomania* (or fern mania), captured a European desire to seek shade and fulfilled a nostalgia for the cooler spaces of 'home' when confronted with warmer climates of the southern hemisphere. It pays particular attention to the 'temperate' retreat the shade house or fernery offered occupants of the tropical and subtropical garden in Australia, its use by women and children, and its intersection with contemporary anxieties surrounding race and climate. As such, the two parts of the chapter reflect on different geographies, to consider how climatic conditions in various parts of the world influenced the reception of shade. The discussion will thus also highlight how the eventual 'adoration of shade' became apparent in the Western canon as it expanded to include work and places from beyond Europe and its own particular climate, paralleling the expansion of European exploration, colonisation and empire.

The emergence of shadow

Ideas of shade and shadow have a long history in Western culture. In *Republic*, written in the fourth century BCE, the inhabitants of Plato's allegorical cave knew the world only though its shadows (Figure 1). In Classical mythology, the Shades were spectral inhabitants of the underworld, who subsequently featured as characters in the works of Homer and Dante Alighieri. In the late nineteenth century, inspired by Dante, Auguste Rodin's *Les trois ombres (The three shades)* would feature prominently atop his *La porte de L'enfer (Gates of hell) of* c. 1890. More generally, shade and shadow took on important symbolic roles in literature and art, becoming emblematic of death, and the shadow of death, as well as qualities and states such as ignorance and melancholy. The latter was illustrated, for example, in Albrecht Dürer's sixteenth-century

2 J. J. Grandville, Four men whose distorted shadows are cast on the wall: an apothecary casting the shadow of a clyster, a censor casting the shadow of a devil, a hereditary peer casting the shadow of a pig, and a Jesuit casting the shadow of a turkey, lithograph, 1830.

engraving *Melencolia I,* which depicted the allegorical figure of Melancholy partially immersed in the shadows to further emphasise her melancholic and depressive state.

In contrast, an 1830 caricature by J. J. Grandville depicted the projected shadows of four Frenchmen—a Jesuit, a peer, a censor and an apothecary—as representing their concealed characters: a goose, pig, demon and a bottle, respectively (Figure 2).[3] Shadows were here projected as silhouettes, directly onto the architectural background, acting like ghostly doppelgangers, standing tall with the figures themselves. The shadow was used as a device that revealed a sinister truth. In each of these examples, characteristics of shade and shadow were invoked in ways that were in distinct opposition to the symbolism of light, which was commonly seen as emblematic of not only God and life, but knowledge and enlightenment. The shadow was a negative presence, summoning ghostly presences, or revealing emotional gloom or dubious characters.

Art historian Thomas DaCosta Kaufmann suggested that shadow first became a prominent concern among Renaissance artists, with the recognition that shadows and shading were important components for achieving a convincing representation of the three-dimensional world.[4] The first known discussion of the projection of shadows, Kaufman notes,

3 Michelangelo Merisi da Caravaggio, *The calling of Saint Matthew*, 1599–1600, Contarelli Chapel, San Luigi dei Francesi, Rome.

was in the context of geometry and astronomy, observing that these sources were later incorporated into artistic treatises like the *Commentarii* by Lorenzo Ghiberti. In astronomy, shadows were used to calculate time, as well as seasonal and celestial events such as solstices and eclipses.[5] Kaufmann argues that the first original studies of shadow projection in relation to art were in the work of Leonardo da Vinci, followed by Albrecht Dürer.[6]

Beyond the symbolism commonly attributed to it in art and literature, shade played an important role in the techniques of drawing and painting, through a variety of meanings. The word 'shade' was itself associated with colour (hue); as a verb, 'to shade' was to hatch or to tint. The contrast between light and dark was to become an important tool in Baroque painting, as evidenced through the use of *chiaroscuro* in the work of Caravaggio, for example, that united the technique of shading with its symbolism. In Caravaggio's *Calling of Saint Matthew* (1599-1600), the use of chiaroscuro on the figures was heightened by the dramatic use of shade and heavenly light in the architectural interior (Figure 3). Light and shadow were manipulated in the pictorial frame, to add emphasis to the human figures, while in the lower half of the pictorial space, the architectural background was immersed in shadow.

4 Honoré Daumier, A country house near Paris: --Well, my dear... it's a good thing we had the idea to plant a house. Without it, we wouldn't have had shade all summer! from *The pleasures of a country holiday*, lithograph on newsprint, 24 May 1858, *Le Charivari,* Elisha Whittelsey Collection, Metropolitan Museum of Art, New York City, NewYork.

The dramatic contrasts between light and dark facilitated Caravaggio's stark naturalism that both endeared and shocked audiences for centuries to come. In his seminal study of shadows in Western art from 1995, E. H. Gombrich identified three 'species' of shadow, where shadow is one of the following: light interrupted, colour that is gradually diminished to give a sense of form, or a painterly tool used to give an understanding of pictorial space, in particular depth.[7]

In architecture, shade took on very different connotations. Excessive shade was commonly held in suspicion, particularly on the grounds of healthfulness. In particular, miasmas and other contagions were feared to lurk in damp and dark places. Summarising historic attitudes towards darkness and health, Alain Corbin wrote:

> Baudelocque noted that dark places made flesh soft, puffy and flaccid; inadequate light slowed circulation, brought on the young girl's terrible chlorosis; Jean Starobinski has stressed its effect on the imagination. Darkness made nocturnal animals sad and perfidious; uncertain light was a threat to health, zeal for work and sexual morality. A young husband's first duty, stated Michelet, was to give his child and its young mother 'the joy of good light.'[8]

Thus, in such circumstances, the negative associations with shade were not always just symbolic. In contrast, light was generally associated with ideas of healthfulness, especially by the early twentieth century, when heliotherapy became a common treatment for conditions such as tuberculosis.[9] Excess of light and glare were, however, equally to be avoided. By the mid-nineteenth century domestic treatises such as those written by Catherine Beecher, cautioned against the excessive use of white in the interior of homes, for fear of the harmful effects of glare.[10] In 1858, the discomfort of glare outside of the house was mocked by Honoré Daumier (1808–1879) in his print series *Les plaisirs de la villégiature* (*The pleasures of a country holiday*).[11] On the other side of the world, the discomforts of light—of glare—and the benefits of shade depicted by Daumier (Figure 4) leave the realm of mockery to become a lived reality and genuine concern, as demonstrated in the second part of this essay.

5 Vanderbilt Avenue, from E. 46th Street, Manhattan. New York Public Library digital collections, Miriam and Ira D. Wallach division of art, prints and photographs: photography collection, The New York Public Library, New York City, New York.

Throwing shade, casting shadows

The refuge of the shade, as satirised by Daumier, was not always to be relished, particularly in urban settings. During the early years of the twentieth century, there was growing concern for the impact of overshadowing in large cities, in particular New York City, where the rapid influx of densely packed skyscrapers was having a noticeable impact. In 1907 the architect Ernest Flagg, who designed the 10-storey Singer Building, once the tallest building in the world, bemoaned:

> The time is upon us when high buildings are becoming a nuisance and a peril, and we are only just beginning to take fright. We are now looking about for remedies, which had much better have been applied a dozen years ago. We now see before us the prospect of streets little better than deep canyons. With the clearest atmosphere of any great city in the world our rooms and offices are becoming so dark that we must use artificial light all day long.[12]

The conditions to which Flagg alluded were to yield the phenomenon that would be known as the canyon street or urban canyon (Figure 5). At their worst, these would result in urban microclimates that resulted in wind tunnels and dust storms, such as that captured in John Sloan's famous painting *Dust Storm, Fifth Avenue* of 1906, as well as buildings and streets cast in perpetual shade.

In New York the tipping point was seen to come in 1915 with the construction of the Equitable Building that occupied an entire city block in Manhattan's Financial District, where the deviation from the cartesian

ONE - WAY
NO PARKING
LIMIT
PUBLIC

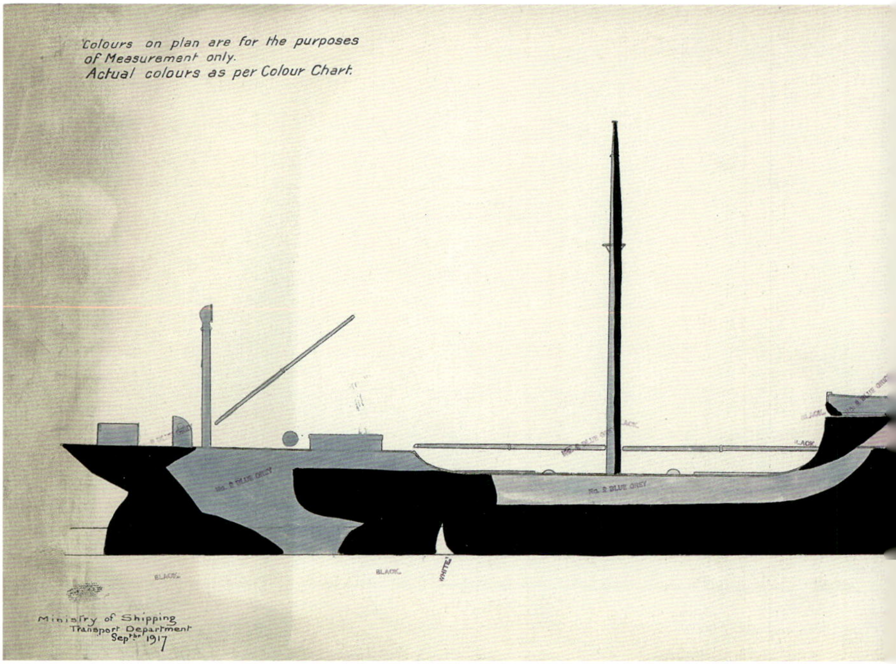

urban grid that characterised the majority of Manhattan exacerbated the ill effects caused by its mass. At certain times of year, the building famously yielded a shadow more than seven and a half times larger than its own 0.4 hectare footprint. Although the role of this building actually played in these changes has been disputed, the resulting outcry was widely credited with prompting a reconsideration of the planning of the city and the introduction of zoning regulations in 1916.[13] These laws governed the implementation of setbacks to allow for light and air to reach the streets, that would characterise the forms of many of the city's skyscrapers. In his 1929 book, *Metropolis of Tomorrow,* Hugh Ferriss reported that within a decade of the conception of these laws in New York, they had been adopted by more than 300 municipalities.[14]

In 1920 the Welsh architect, planner and critic A. Trystan Edwards also addressed growing anxiety about the accessibility of sunlight on streets. Of particular concern was the healthfulness of the sunlit street.[15] Edwards endeavoured to compile the basic information necessary to make informed decisions about legislating for adequate sunlight. While not addressed overtly in these terms, it seems Edward's preoccupation with the accessibility of daylight echoed ideas he would later articulate in his 1924 book *Good and Bad Manners in Architecture* that argued for greater civility and consideration for the urban context when designing and constructing buildings.

6 British Camouflage, type 3, Design C, Starboard. Camouflage design drawings for U.S. Navy commissioned ships, National Archives, College Park, MD.

During the World Wars the problem of shade and shading was to generate an entirely new set of concerns. Considerable work during WWI went into disguising the forms of ships, using the technique of dazzle camouflage (Figure 6). In recognition of the Renaissance understanding of shadows and shading to convincingly depict three-dimensional forms and space, at this time, camoufleurs used painted abstraction to distort the perception of space, in order to disguise military infrastructure. As has been noted by various scholars, during WWI camouflage was the domain of the artist, with paint being the principal tool, whereas during WWII it increasingly became the concern of the architect. While much of the activity of the camoufleur was dedicated to decoys and disguising built forms and military infrastructure, as part of these activities, considerable research went into disguising shadows, or countershading, to ensure that forms were not easily discernible from the air.[16] The shadows cast by buildings were seen as signs of habitation and industry. This was potentially an alarming vulnerability for cities during a war that, as Jean-Louis Cohen observed, was for the first time fought from the air.[17] The threat posed by architectural shadows was evident in the 'Shadow reveals!' poster designed by artist and camoufleur Frank Hinder for the Department of Home Security. Countershading thus became an important tool for the camoufleur, and the study of shadows became a new area for investigation for the military and architects alike.

Returning to the problem of urban shadows in peacetime, despite efforts to minimise the conditions that prompted the introduction of New York's 1916 zoning regulation, in the century that followed, the issue would resurface periodically in zoning amendments around the world. In 1982, for example, New York introduced sunlight provisions that specified '75 percent of the sky surrounding any new building remain open.'[18] Thus these rules were effectively legislating for access to the sun, sky and air, as much as restricting the occupation of the ground. Two years later, in 1984, San Francisco introduced sunlight ordinances to protect open spaces. The planning code triggered the need for special approval for new buildings that exceeded 12 m in height and were likely to generate shadows on properties owned by the Recreation and Parks Department.[19] In 1987, concerned over the impact of a proposed development in Columbus Circle, 800 New Yorkers staged a synchronised line of umbrella openings as a dramatic protest against the winter shadows cast in Central Park by the development.[20] Three decades later, on the opposite side of the world, the Melbourne Planning Scheme of 2017 included a 'Sunlight in Public Spaces', provision that echoed the San Francisco ordinance, to ensure: 'overshadowing from new buildings or works does not result in significant loss of sunlight and diminish the enjoyment of public spaces for pedestrians,' and also, '[t]o protect, and where possible increase the level of sunlight to public spaces during the times of the year when the intensity of use is at its highest.'[21]

In 2016, ongoing concern with the impact of urban shade caused by architecture motivated the *New York Times* to document 'the struggle for light and air' in New York City, by mapping the shadows produced by every building in the city.[22] Published on the winter solstice, the interactive online maps demonstrated how the city's architecture impacted on the urban fabric, including parks and public spaces, as well as other residential and commercial spaces. In 2019, Anika Burgess would celebrate the poetry of shadows problematised in these studies, suggesting they created a second city that 'unfurls throughout the day and is gone by night: a city of shadows.'[23] Such poetics aside, the problem of urban shadows highlighted the city's ongoing conflict between private enterprise and public good, an issue that had also been addressed a decade earlier in a 2005 piece published in the *Washington Post*. Here Emily Badger wrote:

> For cities, shadows present both a technical challenge … and an ethereal one. They change the feel of space and the value of property in ways that are hard to define. They're a stark reminder that the new growth needed in healthy cities

> can come at the expense of people already living there ... [S]hadows even turn light into another medium of inequality — a resource that can be bought by the wealthy, eclipsed from the poor.[24]

In recent years, the problem of urban shadows has also impacted on other aspects of the city, such as the effect of shadows on solar panels in the city.[25] It also includes the perceived associations between shaded environments and shady activities, such as those identified by Sam Bloch in his 2019 essay 'Shade,' which focused on the lack of shade in Los Angeles. Bloch noted:

> police urge residents in high-crime neighborhoods to cut down trees that hide drug dealing and prostitution. Shade trees are designed out of parks to discourage loitering and turf wars, and designed off streets where traffic engineers demand wide lanes and high visibility.[26]

Interestingly, Bloch's discussion on the sun-loving city of Los Angeles concentrates predominantly of the lack of shade in the city, establishing it as much as a social issue as a climatic one. Bloch's essay inverted Badger's earlier concerns about the inequality of shadows, by noting how the inequitable distribution of shade across the city of Los Angeles paralleled socioeconomic boundaries. He argues this was at times a result of the city's neo-liberalist urges.[27] During the 1980s, for example, the city outsourced construction of bus shelters to advertising companies resulting in the placement of these structures being driven by marketing analytics rather than urban planning principles.[28] The inequitable distribution of shade that resulted from this, Bloch argues, is evident throughout the city of Los Angeles, especially when contrasting the leafy affluent suburbs with the poorer areas of the city. Bloch notes, that in Los Angeles, 'shade is often understood as a luxury amenity.'[29]

Despite the adverse associations with shade in urban environments (especially that caused by architectural components in the city) evidenced in much of the discussion so far, there is currently a growing recognition and advocacy for increasing the amount of shade in cities. Notably, this is predominantly being addressed through the introduction of gardens and landscapes, rather than architectural elements, at pedestrian level, through the implementation of urban forests and planting programmes. Such interventions are being implemented as one of number of measures to mitigate the urban heat island effect of cities, as well as providing for biodiversity in cities.[30] These recent discussions serve as fitting

reminders for the very different approach to the issue of shade that emerged in different climates, that resulted in what might be regarded as a parallel history of shade. Where shade was at times to be feared, it was also, in other places, something to be revered.

7 Eugene von Guérard, *Ferntree Gully in the Dandenong Ranges*, oil on canvas, 1857, National Gallery of Australia, Canberra.

Seeking shade in the Global South

Crossing to the southern hemisphere, the benefits of shade continue to be seen. In the mid-nineteenth century, in the Australian colony of Victoria, shade, as captured in the image and idea of the ferntree gully, represented both a desired sanctuary or retreat for European settlers the midsummer heat and a feature that was deemed to be distinctive of the Australian climate. In 1857, the Austrian painter Eugene von Guérard exhibited *Ferntree Gully in the Dandenong Ranges* at the Victorian Society of Fine Arts in the southern city of Melbourne (Figure 7).[31] Painted in the studio but based on sketches produced by the artist in the field, the painting depicts one of the many ferntree gullies found in the temperate rainforests of the coastal hinterland of southeast Australia. The appeal of the image, as art historian Ruth Pullin has suggested, lay in its association

8 N. J. Caire, The ladies' Fern Bower Bloomfield, c. 1886, from *Gippsland Scenery*. State Library of Victoria, Melbourne, Australia.

with 'simple mid-summer sensations of cool temperatures.'[32] The image depicts a dried riverbed framed by tree ferns and flowers that provides a sanctuary for two lyre birds. The foreground foliage, despite the absence of any visible water, is dense and green, suggesting an oasis in an otherwise hot, dry and dusty landscape, and one that is depicted in the background of the picture. Primordial tree ferns clump together to form what naturalist Alfred Howitt, a contemporary of von Guérard's, described as 'a perfect roof so shady that the temperature becomes instantly cooler the moment you enter the gully,' creating 'strange effects of light and shade.'[33] Artistically executed and scientifically precise, the image was also interpreted by contemporary commentators as a worthy example of the 'grand style in landscape painting' as described by the German naturalist Alexander von Humboldt (1769–1859). In *Images in opposition: Australian landscape painting 1801–1890*, environmental historian Tim Bonyhady explained that von Humboldt argued that each climatic zone of the world had a distinctive aspect and that it was the artist's responsibility to represent these.[34] He also identified the ferntree gully as 'one of the most characteristic features in Australian scenery,' an idea that was later embraced by Melbourne's art and scientific community in the early to mid-nineteenth century.[35] Quickly becoming the 'people's choice' of the exhibition, a campaign was established by the local press to raise funds for the purchase of the image as the foundation piece to a new national art collection or as a gift to the Queen.[36]

The ferntree gully as a representation of shade remained a popular subject in the art of settler communities in Australia into the late nineteenth and early twentieth centuries. These scenes had, however, now become populated by people; recreational tourists and amateur naturalists from nearby coastal cities who could now access the hinterland ranges via train.[37] The familiar landscapes of tree ferns were now littered with amenities—paths, bridges, benches, stairs—which aided access for the tourist, often formally dressed (and often feminine), shown relaxing in the cool, temperate and often heavily shaded glades (Figure 8).[38] The fern enthusiast could extend their visit by staying in one of the many guest houses such as the Hermitage on the Blackspur in the Yarra Ranges owned by the photographer John William Lindt. Described by Lindt in a promotional postcard as the 'perfect pleasure resort,' the Hermitage, it was claimed, fulfilled the poet's call for a 'lodge in some vast wilderness' that offered a 'boundless contiguity of shade.' In the postcard itself, two women stand on a road, their figures casting long shadows. These in turn are echoed by strips of shade thrown by giant mountain ash which create the canopy, shelter and shade for the tree ferns clustered below.[39]

A roof so shady

The experience of the ferntree gully was also, around this time, transported from the hinterland ranges to the coastal cities of the Australian colonies including Melbourne in Victoria, Sydney in New South Wales and Brisbane in Queensland, where large plant collections were curated in botanical and acclimatisation gardens.[40] Seeking to recreate the protected microclimate of the ferntree gully in coastal conditions, ferneries were erected to house these collections (Figure 9). These were often large, decorative structures constructed of timber laths (occasionally cast iron)[41] and partially enclosed on all sides, including the roof, by carefully spaced laths that controlled the quantity of light, wind and water that penetrated the interior of the fernery (Figure 10). The arrangement of laths resulted in geometrical patterns and forms that gave visual interest to otherwise simple structures; the addition of bargeboards and finials allowed the addition of stylistic affectations. The spaces created were filled with ferns and other shade-loving plants planted directly into the ground (or raised garden beds) placed around paths, fountains and seating carefully arranged for the recreational visitor.

9 The Fernery, Creswick Lake and Gardens, Victoria, c. 1890–1901, State Library of Victoria, State Library of Victoria, Melbourne.

The light, depending on the time of day, was striated, and like later camouflage, created unusual effects of sun and shade, light and dark, allowing the structure to dissolve and merge with the surround-ing vegetation.

The association of the ferntree gully with distinctive Australian scenery and climates also resulted in the inclusion of ferneries in the promotion of the Australian colonies at national and international exhibitions. In 1862, von Guérard's *Ferntree Gully,* was exhibited at the 1862 *International exhibition* in London, where it was identified by local commentators as an example of the natural beauty and the unique scenery of the Australian colony of Victoria.[42] Living displays were also shown at the Melbourne international exhibition (1880), the Franco-British exhibition of 1908 and the Adelaide jubilee international exhibition of 1887–1888. In 1897, Queensland constructed an International Exhibition around the acclimatisation gardens in Bowen Hills. Here, a large fernery

(also referred to as a bush house) was created to connect the annexes to the main exhibition building. Designed by the curator of the acclimatisation gardens, William Soutter, the space was stocked with 'more than 3000 staghorn, bird's nest and elkhorn ferns collected from the Blackall Range, ... 9550 potted plants and "many thousands" of "other plants"'[43] and described by local commentators as 'nature made perfect'; a 'dream of greenery, an enchanted bower of ferns, palms, and orchids.'[44]

10 The Fernery, Botanic Gardens, Ballarat, postcard, printed, c. 1908, State Library of Victoria, Melbourne.

The fernery at the Queensland exhibition was unusual. First, the display was based on native subtropical plants taken from the Blackall Ranges. While few tree ferns were to be seen, these were Queensland's local equivalents; cool (if not temperate) climate rainforest plants located on the coastal hinterland of southeast Queensland. Second, the Fernery was labelled a 'bush house' by the curator of the acclimatisation gardens, while the more traditional use of the term 'fernery' was adopted by reporters writing for the local papers.[45] While this may have been a reference to the use of native plants, it could also be interpreted as a reference to the regional solution developed for 'ferneries' when built in the subtropics and tropics of Queensland: how to increase shade levels at the height of summer, when the sun was at its most intense, and then reduce it again with the change in light that comes with the cooler seasons of autumn and winter. The solution, as landscape historian Jeannie Sim has argued, and borrowed from India was the addition of tea tree

(Melaleuca) leaves or bush to the roof of the structure,[46] and the growth of climbing vines on the exterior of the shade house in the summer months. While it is unclear if this strategy was used at the International Exhibition, which took place in the cooler months of May to October, it was a practice that was common in the private gardens of Queensland where the bush house, at the height of summer, protected plants and people from the extremes of the summer sun.[47]

Unusual effects of light and shade

The appeal of the bush (or shade) house for the Queensland gardener appears to have been the greater need within the state to protect cool climate and even temperate rainforest plants from the extremes of local subtropical and tropical climates. In 1930, writing for the *Sunday Mail*, one commentator observed that the bush house was a useful and attractive addition to any garden 'whether it be topped by laths or brushwood.' Noting that Queensland was, for the larger part of the year, troubled by 'too much sun,' he also suggested that 'foliage and flowering plants which grow out in the open show to better advantage when they are not affected by the excessive heat of summer.' With less effort and little attention, he argued, the same plants could 'grow to greater beauty and perfection in a well-appointed though cheaply constructed bush house.' While ferns were rarely the sole focus of Queensland's bush houses, it was acknowledged that they were the 'principal attraction.' Suggesting that ferns were difficult to grow and needed 'constant attention,' it was also recommended that the 'most suitable ferns' were 'those found in the temperate parts of Australia.'[48]

Intended to be both a practical and ornamental structure, it was also recommended the bush house be planned to look like an extension of the family home. This, it was suggested, could be achieved by building the structure adjacent to or as an extension of the back verandah. This had the advantage of offering the occupants direct views of the cultivated plants (Figures 11 and 12).[49] The bush house, it was also suggested, should be built on the north, east or west side of the house. The south side, however, and recalling Daumier's earlier satire, should be avoided as the larger house would throw too much shade in the winter, resulting in a bush house that was cold and damp. While the ground plan was not fixed and could be anything that appealed to the homeowner, raised garden beds bordered with natural rocks were recommended. Social activities were also taken into consideration, with the central area of the space set aside for tables and chairs and identified as 'convenient and pleasant for afternoon teas.'[50]

When constructing a bush house, commentators suggested that walls facing the prevailing winds (west, north and south) be closed. The key focus of the bush house, however, appears to have been on the intensity of light produced the unusual effects of light and shade that recalled the ferntree gully, and which, in the man-made environs of the bush house, could be tweaked and modified throughout the season via the spacing of the laths, the addition of brush or the growth of vines on the exterior of the structure. Whether roofed with laths or brushwood, it was recommended to have one half of the roof closer than the other, so plants such as ferns and palms, which reserved shady conditions, could be grown alongside flowering and foliage plants which needed additional light.[51] As Soutter explained in 1914, 'should the shading be too thin a few extra twigs may be added on the thin places.' On no occasion, however, was the shade to be made too dense as this would cause the plants to become 'drawn and too soft to stand the cold of winter.'[52]

It was widely agreed that the shade generated from the bush house, and the view of the plants it offered (ideally from the verandah), would create a 'restful and refreshing space' that gave, especially on hot

11 New fernery at 'The Hollow,' Mackay, Central Queensland, 1877, State Library of Queensland, Brisbane.

12 View of the fernery from the verandah, 1875, State Library of Queensland, Brisbane.

days, 'real pleasure and comfort' that could be enjoyed by all 'no matter whether they are lovers of the beautiful or less fortunate individuals'[53] (Figure 13). A. M. Cowan, a resident of the goldmining town of Kalgoorlie, suggested that the bush house should be adopted in the western regions of Australia as it would improve the comfort and quality of life in the arid and hot goldfields and make it more bearable. Encouraging all residents of the regional city to build a bush house 'opening off one of your verandahs,' and filled with plants from the 'cooler states of Australia,' Cowan argued that the 'shade created' would result in 'supreme satisfaction' and elevate the 'enjoyment of life.'[54]

Darkened houses

While the bush house was appreciated as a cool retreat or room that ran off the back of the house, its appeal can also be linked to the light or shade it created. In 1905, the American doctor Charles Edward Woodruff argued that an overlooked danger for the European settler in the tropics/subtropics was the intensity of tropical light or glare.

13 Edith Townsend in bush house at Canamble, c.1912, Sunshine Coast Libraries, Queensland.

Identified as a cause for a variety of medical complaints including neurasthenia, migraines and malaise, especially in women and children, Woodruff suggested that every attempt should be made to avoid such outcomes. 'Darkened houses,' he argued, were particularly important. These, he observed, should be surrounded by wide verandahs 'whose roofs came well down' and whose lower edge be 'about four feet above the floor line.' Screens built to that level, could also be introduced. Recalling Catherine Beecher's nineteenth century association of glare and the colour white, Woodruff also suggested that 'white houses' be avoided in the tropical city as they produced additional 'glare for their neighbours' and had been known to cause 'serious eye disease.'[55]

In Queensland, the darkened house had long been a reality. Often protected on three sides by verandahs, these were covered with deep and low roofs. Screens or blinds were added for additional protection. Ensuring that no direct sun could penetrate the interior of the house, a cause assisted by covered or small windows, the verandah offered a

14 Pot plants in an enclosed verandah at Umbercollie Station, Goondiwindi district, c. 1900. State Library of Queensland, Brisbane.

cool intermediary space on the edge of the home where, like the shade house, diffused light created a space that was suitable for gardening, retreat and social activities. If elevated to suitable heights, areas under the house could be put to similar uses.

While the bush house was often joined to or located in close proximity of the house, the verandah (and under the house) also offered screened and protected spaces for the display and appreciation of ornamental and shade-loving plants. 'Verandah gardening,' as Sim has previously argued, has long been an 'essential feature of horticulture in the tropics.' However, unlike the bush house or fernery, where plants were cultivated in the ground or in raised flower beds, verandah gardening was reliant on freestanding pots, decoratively arranged on stepped frames or in baskets hanging from the rafters. Showcasing 'the gardener's bush-house skills,' the bush house also provided a continuous supply of potted plants in peak condition. When their vigour on the verandah waned, however, plants were returned to the bush house 'to rest' or be repotted.[56]

It is suggested that the bush house was conceived in a similar way for its human occupants: a temperate space where the tropical heat and glare are tempered by shade that not only protects cool climate, rainforest plants, but also white women and children who need to avoid the full intensity of the subtropical and tropical outdoors. It is significant that in the photographic record, the bush house features as a backdrop for portraits of women and children, who formally dressed—and often in white—either pose outside or sit within the shaded confines of the bush

house. The shady spaces of the bush house and verandah are also represented as a domestic spaces where women can comfortably tend a garden, alongside their other domestic duties, without entering the outdoors 'proper' and exposing themselves fully to the intensity of the subtropical or tropical sun (Figure 14).

In 1925, Dr Raphael Cilento, Director of the Australian Institute of Tropical Medicine, argued that settler communities could thrive in Australia's tropical and subtropical environments. However, while the process of acclimatisation was seen to be successful for men, Cilento and his colleagues identified the white woman and child as 'weak links' and requiring additional support.[57] While the darkened house made suitable to its climatic context was singled out by Cilento and others as fulfilling this ameliorative function,[58] the bush house, it is suggested, can be understood in similar terms: shaded and cool outdoor living spaces that could not only be safely occupied and enjoyed by white women and children but where they could also regain a 'vigour' that was lost while acclimatising to their new climatic contexts. Like the 'foliage and flowering

plants' which 'show to better advantage when they are not affected by the excessive heat of summer,' the white woman and child would successfully 'grow to greater beauty and perfection' if time was spent productively in a 'well-appointed and carefully planned bush house' or one of its equivalents.[59] Shade, it is suggested, facilitated the domestication of the subtropics and tropics in Australia, first in the ferntree gullies of eastern Australia and later in the houses and gardens of southern and northern Queensland.

North meets south

15 Peter Heathwood, Speare House, 1959, Indooroopilly, David Knell and Associates, The John Oxley Library, State Library of Queensland, Brisbane.

The shade offered by the bush house and the cultures it supported remained an important trope for subsequent generations of Queensland architects. In postwar Brisbane, Peter Heathwood created a 'fernery' as part of the Speare House (1958)—a narrow space set between Thurlow blinds and the glazed walls of the house (Figure 15)—which was inspired by a childhood memory of the 'cool comfort' of the slatted lean-to that ran

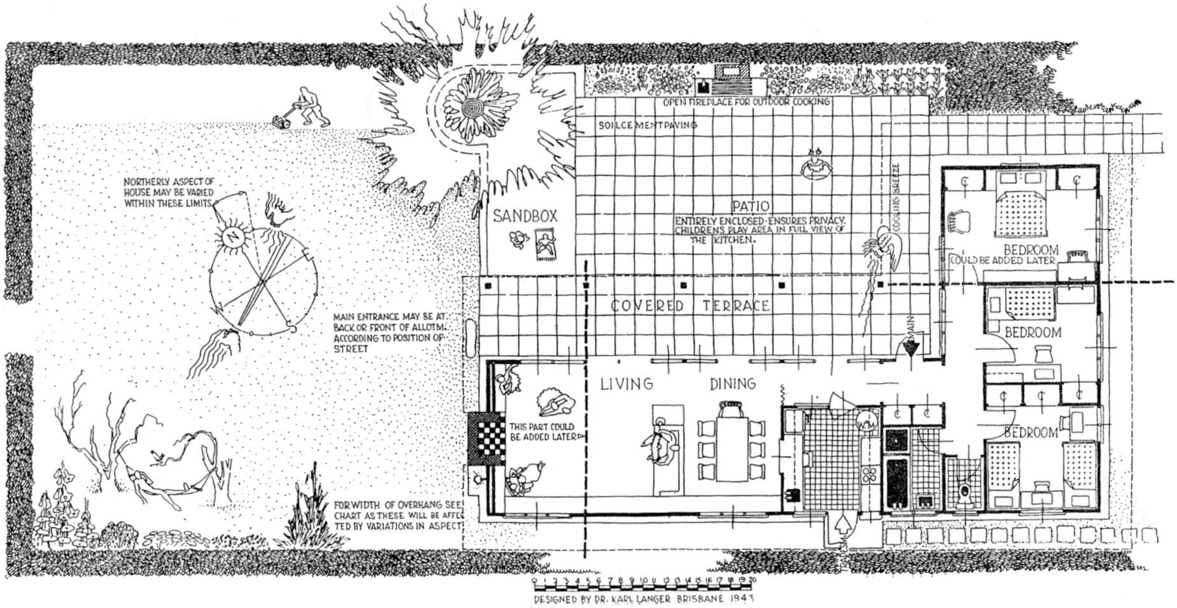

16 Karl Langer, Plan for sub-tropical house, 1943, Plate 5, *Sub-Tropical Housing*, published as an original paper of The University of Queensland, vol. 1, no. 7, 1944.

off the back verandah of his grandparent's home.[60] Rex Addison, on the other hand, adopted timber laths, evenly spaced, as part of the aesthetic for his own home (1974), recalling the decorative effect of the bush houses of old, a suggestion that is accentuated in a photographic representation of the house in the 1990 book on *Australian architects* (no. 5), where it is embedded in a bushland gully and surrounded by bracken fern.

A postwar architect who broke with tradition, however, was the recently arrived Austrian émigré Karl Langer. Dismissing the traditional Queensland house as a dark 'cave,' Langer proposed five modernised house plans as alternatives.[61] Rejecting the shade offered by the elevated home and screened verandah, Langer's proposals embraced the sub-tropical sun of southeast Queensland and the outdoor living he felt it promised (Figure 16). This is suggested in a plan he developed for the subtropical house where a histogram (consisting of a sun, the four compass points and anthropomorphised annotations of the prevailing breezes) dominates the garden space which is shared with a modular man mowing the grass, sweat dripping from his face, and another (or perhaps the same one once he had finished the lawn) having a nap in the hammock slung in a bare tree in the corner of the garden. Abundant garden beds, hedges functioning as living fences, and lush lawns collectively cool the microclimate surrounding the property, counter reflected glare and represent at the same time the botanical fecundity supported by a subtropical climate.[62] A child skipping on an open terrace, others playing in a sandbox and an unprotected barbecue or cooking fire further suggests a life that is largely lived outdoors and the climate that supports this. Except for a small area of covered terrace, achieved by overhanging eaves indicated on the plan by dotted lines, and a single tree with spreading foliage, Langer's plan gives little evidence of shade or its necessity.[63]

Drawn in 1943 and published in 1944, Langer's plan (one of five) is produced soon after his arrival in Brisbane while the appeal of the Brisbane sun and the lifestyles it suggested were still strong. This attraction, however, appears to fade for the European architect over the next decade and he develops subtle but significant strategies to reintroduce shade to the Queensland home and garden. In his own house and garden, built in 1950 in the Brisbane suburb of St Lucia, Langer tints the house pink to reduce glare, introduced a front, north-facing terrace for enjoying the winter sun, and cultivated a unique 'bush' garden behind the house (Figure 17).[64] Providing a cool, south-facing and shady refuge, a photo taken of Gertrude in the garden suggests the Langers were also drawing from another tradition: the nineteenth and early twentieth century association of the ferntree gully and its (Humboldtian) association with the Australian climate.

By 1955, a modernised bush house had been added to Langer's garden and house schemes, as demonstrated by his design for the Levy House (Southport, Gold Coast, 1955). His earlier preference for an exposed outdoor terrace and garden is now replaced by a semi-enclosed pavilion shaded by a roof of carefully spaced bamboo laths and enclosed on three sides by the house, a solid brick wall and a moon gate next to a built-in oven or barbecue. Featured in colour on the cover of the popular magazine *Home Beautiful*, Mrs Levy and son Thomas are shown relaxing in butterfly chairs by a Japanese-inspired pond. While the garden and pond are in full sun, Mrs Levy and Thomas occupy a part of the terrace, which they share with a collection of ferns and elkhorns, that is protected from the full sun by strips of shade.[65] In the architectural drawings produced for the home, Langer described this area of shaded outdoor living—one that ran directly of the living room—as the 'bush house.'[66]

17 Karl Langer, Gertrude Langer among the ferns, backyard of Langer residence: Native Bush Garden, c. 1950, Fryer Library, University of Queensland, Brisbane.

1 Genesis 1:2 (NIV).
2 Sources that have dealt with shade and shadows in art and architecture include: Victor Ieronim Stoichiță, *A short history of the shadow* (London: Reaktion Books, 1997); E. H. Gombrich, *Shadows: the depiction of cast shadows in western art* (London: National Gallery Publications, 1995); Stephen Kite, *Shadow-makers: a cultural history of shadows in architecture* (London; New York, NY: Bloomsbury Academic, 2017).
3 'Caricature,' Universal Museum of Art, http://legacy-uma.org/oeuvre/caricature-shadows-worn-j-j-grandville/.
4 Thomas DaCosta Kaufmann, 'The perspective of shadows: the history of the theory of shadow projection,' *Journal of the Warburg and Courtauld Institutes* 38 (1975): 258–287.
5 Ibid., 263.
6 Ibid., 258–287.
7 Harry Rand, 'Review of *Shadows: the depiction of cast shadows in western art*, by E. H. Gombrich,' *Leonardo*, 29, no. 4 (1996): 333. Rand states: 'Gombrich considers the shade created when something interrupts light flowing toward another plane, the gradual diminution of light upon an object's surface by which we adjudge the source and intensity of the illumination and an object's form, and a shadow that ties things to their spatial position by touching the object and another surface.'
8 Alain Corbin, *The foul and the fragrant: odor and the French social imagination* (Cambridge, Harvard University Press, 1986; original French edition 1982): 154.
9 See for example: Margaret Campbell, 'What tuberculosis did for modernism: the influence of a curative environment on modernist design and architecture,' *Medical history*, 49, no. 4 (2005): 464.
10 Bridget A. May, 'Advice on white: an anthology of nineteenth-century design critics' recommendations,' *Journal of American culture*, 16, no. 4 (Winter, 1993): 21.
11 Honoré Daumier, *The pleasures of a country holiday*, published in *Le Charivari*, (24 May 1858), Lithograph on newsprint. [62.650.455], The Elisha Whittelsey Collection, Metropolitan Museum of Art.
12 Ernest Flagg, 'Is New York becoming a city of canyons and ravines?' *New York Times* (29 December 1907): 39.
13 Sally A. Kitt Chappell argues that the planning reforms were already underway when this building was being completed, and that it became a convenient symbol of the problem, rather than the catalyst for change. Sally A. Kitt Chappell, 'A reconsideration of the equitable building in New York,' *Journal of the Society of Architectural Historians*, 49, no. 1 (March, 1990): 90–95.
14 Hugh Ferriss, *The metropolis of tomorrow* (New York: Ives Washburn, 1929), 72.
15 A. Trystan Edwards, 'Sunlight in streets,' *The Town Planning Review*, 8:2, no. 2 (April, 1920): 93–98.
16 For a discussion of countershading and research into this see for example, Ann Elias, *Camouflage Australia: art, nature, science and war* Sydney: Sydney University Press, 2011).
17 See Jean-Louis Cohen, *Architecture in uniform: designing and building for the Second World War* (New Haven: Yale University Press, 2011). Cohen includes a chapter on camouflage.
18 'Of sunlight, shadows and new midtown zoning rules,' *New York Times* (18 July 1982): 114.
19 San Francisco Planning Department, 'Shadow analysis: informational and supplemental application packet,' (17 August 2020), https://sfplanning.org/sites/default/files/forms/SHD_SupplementalApplication.pdf.
20 'Hundreds rally against towers at coliseum site,' *New York Times* (19 October 1987), https://www.nytimes.com/1987/10/19/nyregion/hundreds-rally-against-towers-at-coliseum-site.html. This protest was mentioned in Quoctrung Bui and Jeremy White, 'Mapping the shadows of New York City: every building, every block,' *New York Times* (21 December 2016).
21 Melbourne Planning Scheme, 22.07 'Sunlight to public places,' (31 August 2017): https://planning-schemes.delwp.vic.gov.au/schemes/melbourne/ordinance/22_lpp02_melb.pdf.
22 Quoctrung Bui and Jeremy White, 'Mapping the shadows of New York City,' *New York Times* (21 December 2016).
23 Anika Burgess, 'The Shifting City: Shadows of New York City,' *New York Times* (5 September 2019), https://www.nytimes.com/interactive/2019/09/06/multimedia/shadows-new-york-photos-skyline.html.
24 Emily Badger, 'In the shadows of booming cities, a tension between sunlight and prosperity,' *Washington Post* (5 May 2015), https://www.washingtonpost.com/news/wonk/wp/2015/05/04/in-the-shadows-of-booming-cities-a-tension-between-sunlight-and-prosperity/.
25 Ibid.
26 Sam Bloch, 'Shade,' *Places journal* (April 2019), https://doi.org/10.22269/190423. See also Tim Arango, '"Turn off the sunshine": Why Shade Is a Mark of Privilege in Los Angeles,' *New York Times* (1 December 2019).
27 Ibid.
28 Ibid.
29 Ibid.
30 Jason Barr, 'Skyscrapers and shadows: the value of sunshine in the city,' Building the Skyline (13 March 2019), https://buildingtheskyline.org/city-shadows/. In 2019, Jason Barr argued that the shade generated by tall buildings offered respite from for the Heat Island Effect, as well as hazardous reflections from neighbouring buildings, commonly labelled 'death rays.'
31 Tree ferns and ferntree gullies are found in the coastal hinterlands of eastern Australia from Victoria to Queensland. Treeferns are shade-loving plants and with few exceptions require low to medium sun to survive.
32 Ruth Pullin, *Eugene von Guérard: Nature revealed* (Melbourne: National Gallery of Victoria, 2011), 158. This would have been a concept appreciated by a Melbourne audience all too familiar with the city's hot summer months, and which is suggested by the landscape of eucalyptus and glare depicted in the background of von Guérard's painting.

33 A. W. Howitt to A. M. Howitt, 15 January 1858, A. W. Howitt Papers, State Library of Victoria, MS9356. Howitt visited the Dandenongs soon after von Guérard's painting was shown. Cited in Pullin, *Eugene von Guérard*, 158.
34 Alexander von Humboldt, Cosmos, vol. 2 (1849), 453; Tim Bonyhady, *Images in opposition: Australian landscape painting 1801–1890* (Melbourne: OUP, 1985), 66.
35 Ibid. See also Catherine De Lorenzo and Deborah van der Plaat, 'More than meets the eye: photographic records of Humboldtian imaginings,' *Mosaic*, 37:4 (December 2004), 237–253. The fern-tree gully remained representative of Australia's climate for international audiences well into the early twentieth century when images celebrating the intensity of Australian light and sun, such as the work of the Heidelberg School grew in popularity.
36 The image is now held by the National Gallery of Australia.
37 Julia Horne, *The pursuit of wonder: how Australia's landscape was explored, nature discovered and tourism unleashed* (Melbourne: Miegunyah Press, 2005).
38 Deborah van der Plaat and Catherine De Lorenzo, 'Sublimity and amenity at Lindt's hermitage,' *Studies in Australian garden history*, 2 (2006): 39–62.
39 See postcard by John William Lindt, *A Perfect Pleasure Resort. The Hermitage on the Black's Spur: Oh for a Lodge in some vast wilderness/ A Boundless Contiguity of Shade (Cowper)*, State Library of Victoria, Melbourne, Australia, H85.40/37. See also earlier discussion of this image in De Lorenzo and van der Plaat, 'More than Meets the Eye.'
40 Botanical gardens were also popular in larger regional towns.
41 See Fernery at the private residence and garden of Rippon Lee in Melbourne.
42 Eugene von Guérard *Ferntree Gully in the Dandenong Ranges*, 1857, https://artsearch.nga.gov.au/detail.cfm?IRN=36997.
43 Jeannie Sim, 'Tropicalia: Gardens with tropical attitude,' Queensland Review, November 2003, 1–24; quoting 'The Bushhouse,' *The Queenslander* (15 May 1897): 1066.
44 'The International Exhibition,' *The Queenslander* (19 June 1897): 1344.
45 'Queensland International Exhibition,' *Brisbane Courier* (22 December 1896): 6.
46 Sim has suggested the term 'bush-house' derived from early use of tea tree *(Melaleuca)* leaves for roofing; in India and elsewhere such structures were also known as canvas houses, lath houses (timber strips), chick houses (split bamboo) or betel houses. *The Oxford companion to Australian gardens*, edited by Richard Aitken & Michael Looker, South Melbourne, Vic.: Oxford University Press, published in association with the Australian Garden History Society, 2002.
47 Jean Sim, 'Climate and Garden Design in Queensland,' in Childs, I. and Hudson, B. (Eds.), Queensland Geographical Perspectives. Royal Geographical Society of Queensland, Australia 2006, pp. 189-215; and Ken Duxbury, 'Fabulous ferneries,' *Australian garden history*, 13:4 (January/February 2002): 21–23.
48 'In the bush-house,' *Sunday Mail*, November 1930: 21.
49 'In the garden,' *Queensland Times* (19 September 1925): 5.
50 Ibid.
51 'Bush houses,' *Sunday Mail* (2 November 1930): 21.
52 Coolibah, 'The bush house,' *The Queenslander* (10 January 1914): 34.
53 'In the garden,' *Queensland Times* (19 September 1925): 5.
54 A. M. Cowan, 'Bush house gardening,' *Kalgoorlie Miner* (18 July 1904): 2–3.
55 Charles Edward Woodruff, *The effects of tropical light on white men* (New Delhi: Isha Books, 1905, reprinted 2013), 328.
56 Sim, 'Climate and garden design in Queensland,' 14.
57 Raphael Cilento, *The white man in the tropics: with especial reference to Australia and its dependencies* (Melbourne: Department of Health Service Publication and H. J. Green, 1925).
58 W. A. Osborne, 'The physiological factors in the development of an Australian race,' *The medical journal of Australia* (18 September 1920): 261–267.
59 'Bush houses,' *Sunday Mail* (2 November 1930): 21.
60 Elizabeth Musgrave, 'The plywood exhibition space: an investigation of local idiom,' *Additions to architectural history, the 19th conference of the society of architectural historians, Australia and New Zealand, Brisbane 2002*, https://espace.library.uq.edu.au/view/UQ:9501.
61 These were first drawn in 1943 and published in 1944 as 'Subtropical housing,' an original paper published by the University of Queensland, 1:7 (1944), plates 1–5 and page 8.
62 Karl Langer, 'Town planning and the tropics,' Paper presented to the Australian Academy of Science. Symposium 'Man and animals in the tropics,' Brisbane, 24–25 May 1956; Karl Langer Collection, UQFL 158, Box 39, Fryer Library, The University of Queensland.
63 While Langer does give considered attention to the problem of subtropical glare and getting natural light into the interior of the house while avoiding full sun, the outdoor areas of his plans are represented in his plans as places of full sun and where little protection is needed.
64 Karl Langer, Langer residence, St Lucia (Brisbane), 1950; Karl Langer collection, UQFL 158, Box 44.
65 Keith Dunstan, 'House behind bamboo,' *The Australian home beautiful* (April 1955): 32–35.
66 See Karl Langer architectural plans, John Oxley Library, State Library of Queensland, R83, Roll 27/15, R83/27/15, Box 15734 O/S. I would like to thank Andrew Wilson for drawing this example to my attention. See Andrew Wilson, 'Bridging continents. Karl Langer's contributions to housing,' in Deborah van der Plaat and John Macarthur, eds., *Karl Langer: modern architect and migrant in the Australian tropics* (London: Bloomsbury, forthcoming).

From crystal to cryosphere: architecture for the future ice age

1 Frank E. Kleinschmidt, Building an eskimo [sic] igloo, Library of Congress, Prints and photographs division, Washington, D.C.

In his study of the relationship between fire and climate change, Stephen J. Pyne observes that 'some 90 per cent of the past 900,000 years have been icy,' and it should come as no surprise that 'most calculations reckon that the Earth is due—maybe overdue—to swing back to ice.'[1] Within the general discourse regarding climate change, however, the overriding theme is that the climate will become hotter: temperatures will rise, polar ice caps will melt, 1-in-100-year fires will run rampant and water will become scarce. Yet what these models fail to consider is that climate change—or, more accurately, climate volatility—includes both extremes, and, as a result, the future will also be marked by periods of exceptional cold. Historically, ice ages have been more decisive events of greater frequency and duration than heat waves, and it is only within the past two centuries that the planet has begun to grow steadily warmer.[2]

Within architecture, ice is often discussed as a seasonal or temporary inconvenience to be thwarted rather than harnessed, but the challenge for future architects will be how to confront new sets of cooler climatological norms. Whereas in the past, ice, snow and chill were all defining factors of earthly habitation, these conditions largely predated the recent record of human history and intervention; yet in the coming years, building with, against and in ice will become more and more necessary. There is already evidence of such trends with the recent boom in polar research stations, Nordic expansion and land grab battles for Arctic extraction sites, paralleled by increased interests in icy environs stretching from Antarctica, Canada, Russia, and even to Mars. This fascination is not new—Arctic zones have long attracted the attention of intrepid explorers and artists for promise of the unknown or final frontier, inspiring Renaissance maritime expeditions and the Romantic notion of an 'Arctic sublime.'[3]

These frigid landscapes bring a host of unexpected challenges in addition to cold temperatures, including issues related to static charge, violent winds, extreme isolation, impenetrable permafrost, snow loads, ice blocks, as well as rapid and unpredictable cycles of freeze and thaw. With limited local raw materials and shortened timeframes for construction, the difficulties of ice architecture also extend to more prosaic aspects of building, such as availability of resources and timely assembly. Taken together, these factors place pressure on the architect's ability to ensure thermal comfort and provide refuge in response to the harsh realities of polar microclimates, leading most designers to focus on keeping weather out and mobilising architecture as a protective shield against rather than in collaboration with ice and its surroundings. Furthermore, as extreme weather events become more prevalent, architects and engineers will need to account for the presence of and damage from atmospheric ice in all of its forms, among them, frost, hail, sleet and snow.

Unlike clouds, sunlight, wind or other natural phenomena addressed in this volume, ice constitutes a climatological factor and climatic environment. But despite its many manifestations, depicting ice has proven difficult. Ice challenges the human eye's visual apprehension due to its translucence and changing states, as bemoaned by nineteenth-century artists and explorers whose accounts of whiteouts and temporary 'blindness' suggested the very impossibility of representation.[4] Similarly, when ice does appear in architectural drawings, its presence is paradoxically suggested *in absentia:* pitched roofs and snow guards preemptively protect against unseen ice and snow, or the frozen elements are eagerly anticipated, as in Frank Lloyd Wright's description of Taliesin: 'I wanted a home where icicles by invitation might beautify the eaves. So there were no gutters.'[5] Yet there is another, rich history of ice architecture and architecture's engagement with ice as design inspiration, building material and site. Although overlooked for some time, it is perhaps in revisiting this multi-layered past that avenues for future development might be unearthed.

2 Robert Hooke, Observations of several kinds of frozen figures showing frozen urine (1), snowflakes (2) and ice flakes (4, 5, 6), 1665, from *Micrographia: or some physiological descriptions of minute bodies made by magnifying glasses with observations and inquiries thereupon*, Jo. Martyn and Ja. Allestry, printers to the Royal Society, London.

'Abundance of curiosity and neatness'[6]

In 1665, the natural philosopher Robert Hooke published *Micrographia*—a richly illustrated compendium detailing the 'abundance of curiosity and neatness' to be found in the natural world (Figure 2).[7] Within a lengthy study of water, Hooke dedicated particular attention to snow and ice, celebrating the complexity of their crystal formation and

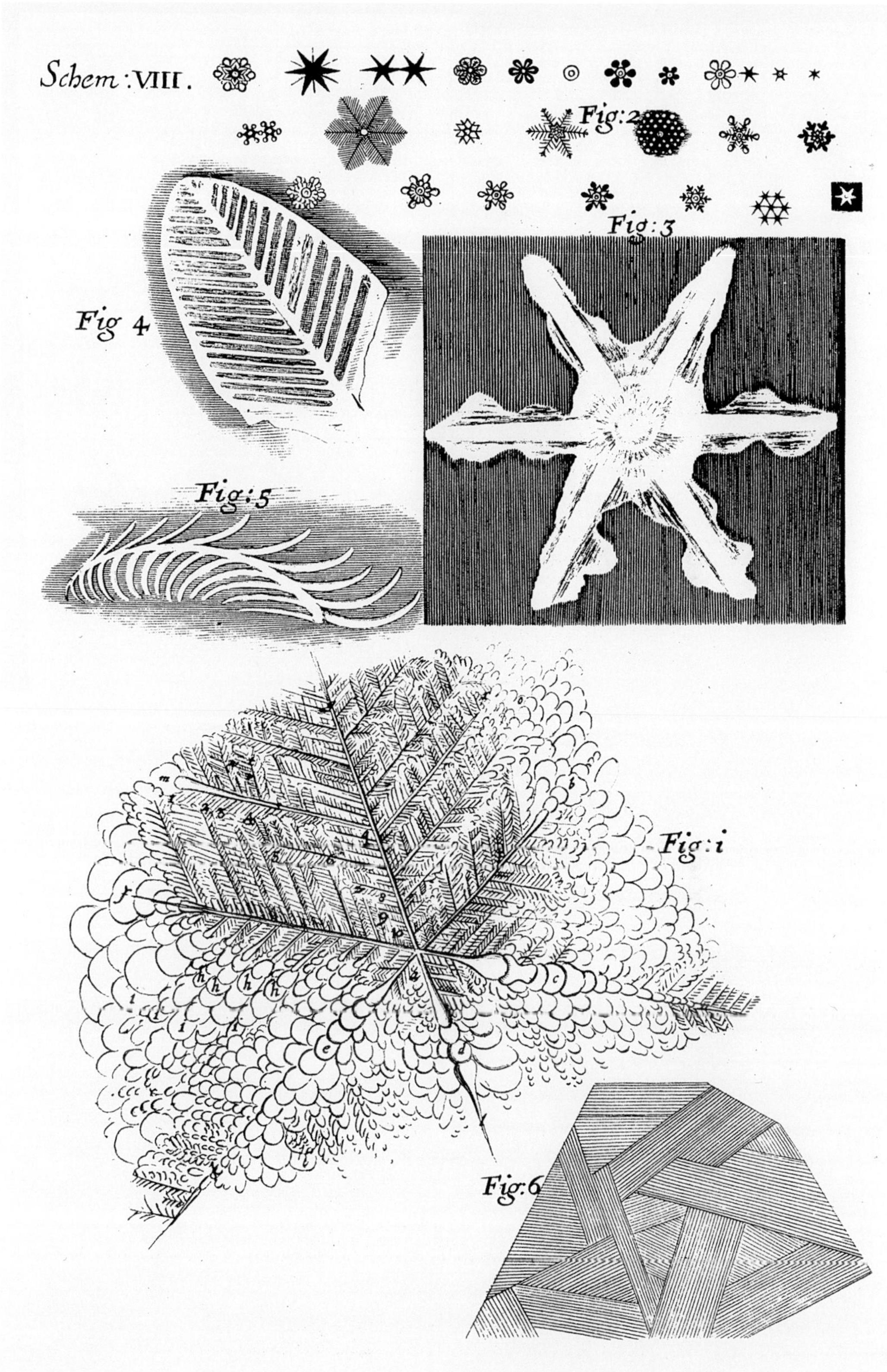
Schem: VIII.
Fig: 2
Fig: 3
Fig 4
Fig: 5
Fig: i
Fig: 6

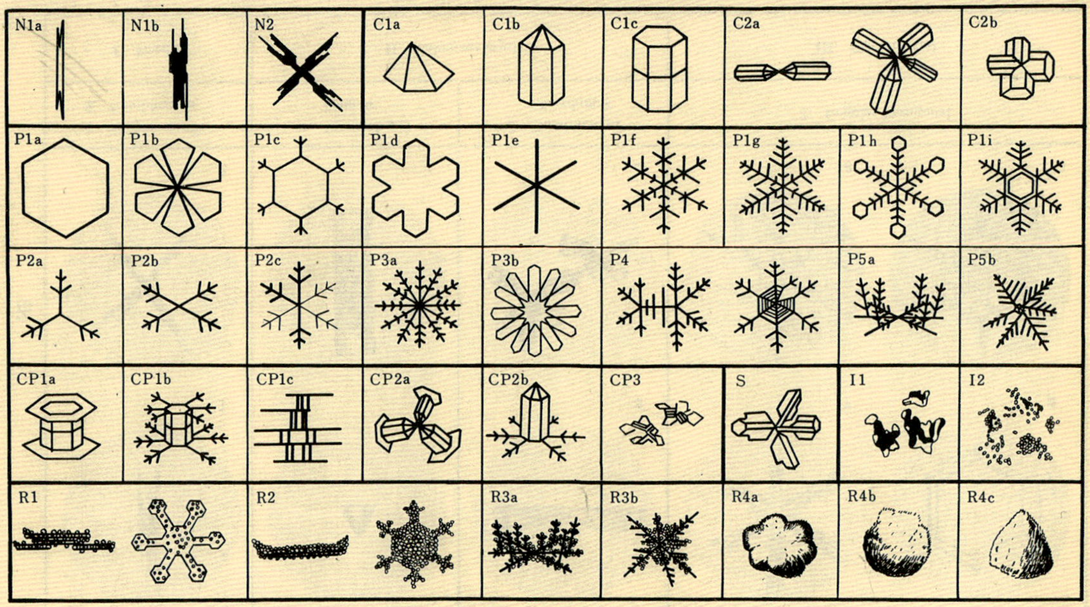

FIG. 197. General classification of snow crystals, sketches.

3 Ukichiro Nakaya, General classification of snow crystals, sketches, 1954, from *Snow crystals: natural and artificial.*

intricate symmetry: 'I have often with great pleasure, observ'd such an infinite variety of curiously figur'd *Snow*, that it would be as impossible to draw the Figure and shape of every one of them, as to imitate exactly the curious and Geometrical *Mechanisme* of Nature in any one.'[8] Undeterred by the supposed 'impossibility' of total classification, Hooke succeeded in outlining characteristic features of snow and ice formation, noting that snowflakes are composed of six identical branches of equal length placed at 60° angles to one another, whereas ice tends to grow in asymmetrical, linear patterns.

Some 350 years later, a complementary study was undertaken by the Japanese physicist and nascent founder of glaciology, Ukichiro Nakaya, who published the encyclopedic review *Snow crystals: natural and artificial* in 1954.[9] Like Hooke, Nakaya was seduced by the wide array of snow, ice crystal shape(s) and their arrangement. Yet, in contrast to Hooke's somewhat lyrical observations, Nakaya applied rigorous scientific analysis, subjecting water vapour to a set of controlled temperatures, atmospheric pressures and water saturation levels, yielding a comprehensive classificatory scheme that continues to be today's default reference on ice crystal formation for geophysicists (Figure 3).

These two studies nurture the oppositional poles of architectural practice, combining creative design with empirical science. Yet although ice and snow present real physical challenges for architects, when the two elements appear in architectural drawings, they most often serve as vehicles of design inspiration. Like Hooke and Nakaya, many architects have been blinded by the sheer visual presence of snow, while their fascination with the perceived order and purity of ice crystals have propelled architects working in varying disciplines and languages to attempt to translate the element's naturally occurring logic to their own practices, rendering ice and snow critical design references.

Among the most fervent proponents of crystal-inspired architecture were the early twentieth-century German Expressionists, whose faith in transcendentalism led them to propose socially utopian projects.[10] The clearest manifestation of this ideology can be found in Bruno Taut's *Alpine Architektur* (1919), a romantic treatise espousing the benefits of isolated, rural communities committed to innocence and purity in response to the horrors of World War I (Figure 4). Inspired by the writer Paul Scheerbart, who advocated for the practical and, particularly, symbolic appeal of glass, Taut argued that crystalline architectural forms could facilitate a spiritual regeneration of society, wherein glass or similar natural elements (i.e. ice) would encourage deeper self-reflection. Not only would the mountain air and beauty of alpine architecture be restorative, but the built edifice and its relationship to the landscape would also nourish self-growth and collective betterment. This utopian project was never realised in practice—but not because Taut thought building with ice or in the snow-covered Alps was unachievable. Rather, he noted: '[t]he execution would certainly be incredibly difficult and full of sacrifices, but not impossible. One so seldom demands the impossible of people.'[11]

The allure of ice's visual transparency and its associative symbolism persists today, having recently provided popular motifs for government-funded cultural facilities. This is particularly the case in former Hanseatic League municipalities where the community's relationship to water and thriving port economies constitutes civic identity. Following the success of Snøhetta's design for the Oslo Opera House (2008), other waterfront music halls and theatres have been completed in Poland and Germany, as seen in the Szczecin Philharmonic (2014) by Barozzi/Veiga studio and Herzog & de Meuron's Elbphilharmonie (2017) in Hamburg. In each of these examples, waves of frigid water, ice floes and snowdrifts are conjured through the crashing of angular planes, cool palettes and varied use of clear, cloudy and opaque glass. Substantiating the political watchword of the first decade of the twenty-first century, 'transparency' in all its forms is harnessed in these projects, inviting identification and reflection on behalf of its users.[12]

Der Kristallberg
Der Fels ist
oberhalb der
Vegetations-
zone behauen
und geglättet
zu vielfachen
kristallinischen
Formen.
Die hinteren
Schneekuppen
sind mit
Glasbögen-
architektur
bebaut
Vorne Kristall-
nadelpyra-
miden
Über dem Ab-
grund eine
Brückenver-
gitterung aus
Glas

Consider the igloo

Ice is not only a visual reference in architecture but also serves as a foundation for construction. Like the American log cabin or Gottfried Semper's proverbial tent, the archetypal 'ice house' can be traced back to the igloo (Figure 1). First constructed by the Indigenous Inuit and Dene peoples of Alaska, Canada, Greenland and Siberia, igloos were conceived to provide both stable, seasonal winter dwellings for communities as well as temporary shelters for individuals during hunting expeditions.[13] Igloos are formed from either windblown snow or improvised cut snow masonry arranged in a spiral formation to yield a conical hut. Structurally, the igloo's logic lies in its use of a catenoid section, harnessing ice and snow's compressive strength while mitigating pressure on structural tension by diverting gravity's vertical pull outward towards forces that secure the arch's curve.[14] In terms of thermal comfort, ice's high insulating properties afford a comfortable interior environment generated by human body heat alone. To thwart any loss of this precious warmth, igloos are often outfitted with small tunnel entrances, which also prevent wind and snow from entering the primary chamber.

The ingenuity of the igloo does not end with physics and thermodynamics: indeed, perhaps the igloo's greatest achievement is the exclusive use of naturally abundant and available materials. These materials bear no cost—financial or otherwise—since when the weather changes and snow melts, the igloo simply disappears; its life cycle has no net or negative impact upon the landscape and exists in harmony with local environmental conditions. The budgetary and ethical debates regarding building duration and demolition that plague so much of the built environment have no currency here. With its do-it-yourself design and as-found building components, the igloo marks a radical departure from hierarchical architecture as it is commonly understood, exemplifying the values heralded in Bernard Rudofsky's *Architecture without architects* (1964).[15]

With this summary in mind, the pejorative description of the igloo as a 'primitive' structure seems ill-suited, while its illustrative merits of building in ice suggest possibilities for far greater applications. As a naturally occurring, crystalline inorganic solid with an ordered structure, ice shares classificatory properties with minerals, and its high compressive strength and insulating qualities make it, given appropriate weather conditions, a practical building material. Throughout the history of human construction, ice has existed as a natural and economical solution but it has generally only been exploited for radical experimentation. Luxury ice hotels are now common sights in Finland, Iceland and Sweden, ushering in a wave of Arctic tourism. Prior to this 'cool' fad for the nouveau riche,

4 Bruno Taut, Snow, ice, glass, 1919, from *Alpine Architektur*.

5 Saint Paul Winter Carnival Ice Palace in Minnesota, Minnesota Historical Society, Minnesota.

6 Valery Ivanovich Jacobi, Ice house, 1878.

7 Space exploration architecture & clouds architecture office, Mars ice house, 2015.

showstopping ice palaces and seasonal expositions offered architects imaginative release to demonstrate human mastery over the natural world, such as the Harbin International Ice and Snow Festival in China (the largest, and most spectacular, of its kind) or the Winter Carnival in Saint Paul, Minnesota, an annual event that has taken place—complete with an Ice Palace—since 1886 (Figure 5).[16]

In another case, the Empress Anna Ivanovna commissioned an elaborate ice fantasy during the harsh winter of 1739–1740 (Figure 6). Designed by Pyotr Yeropkin, the ice palace was built to house a court wedding and celebrate a recent victory over the Ottomans. The absurdist extent to which this display of ice craftsmanship was taken was detailed by the Marquis Jacques Joachim Trotti de la Chétardie, a French ambassador invited to attend the festivities who recorded in his travelogue: 'there was an entry hall and a bedroom on the left, where stood a bed, curtains and a dressing table along with a pair of slippers and night caps—all made of ice; to the right, there was a drawing-room with an ice table, ice chairs, armoires, a wall clock and maps. The newlyweds were put to bed and left in the space until 8 o'clock in the morning. The ice blocks looked like well hewn stone both in size and in construction. The most amazing architectural element was the façade of the building, which incorporated eight ice cannons on mounts. These cannons, when fired, could sustain charges of three quarters of a pound of gun powder!'[17]

As these examples demonstrate, in most parts of the world, ice and snow embody ephemeral conditions, causing ice architecture to primarily operate in the realm of festival and fantasy. However, ice has recently come under consideration for structures of longer duration, with two proposals illustrating preliminary approaches. In the 2015 edition of the NASA Centennial Challenge Mars Habitat Competition, architects were invited to envision how 3D printing technologies might facilitate human life on Mars. Entrants Space Exploration Architecture and Clouds Architecture Office posited that the solution to this challenge lay in ice. However, one common problem of building in ice-covered environments is that of transporting additional or alternative building supplies to the site—a difficulty that is only magnified when working at planetary distances. Thus, rather than send building materials to Mars (as other schemes proposed), the team settled upon using and extracting what was readily available, drilling down into water below the Red Planet's surface.[18] This strategy mobilises the phase change of liquid into solid to its advantage, yielding a double-shelled ringed structure composed of transparent ETFE membranes enclosing 3D printed ice blocks, which is not dissimilar in profile to an igloo (Figure 7). Although the igloo tends to inspire nostalgia and the Mars Ice House seems more like science-fiction fantasy, these two designs rest upon the shared principles of ice's high compressive strength and insulation, providing refuge to intrepid explorers in frontier environments previously deemed inhospitable to human life.

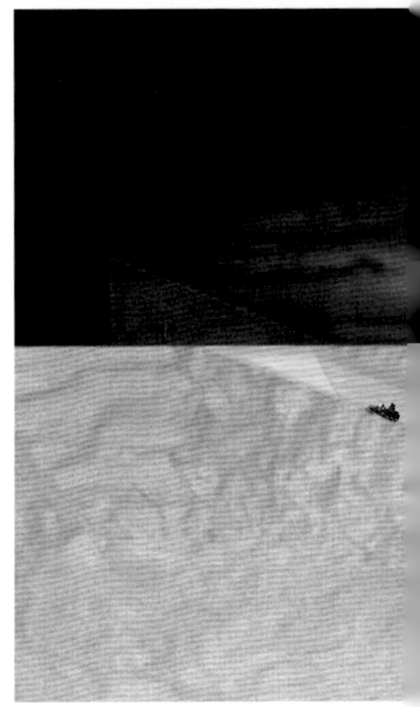

Although most examples thus far have considered building with ice as an additive process, working from the opposite end of the problem via extraction is an equally fruitful approach. Faced with accommodating increased Antarctic tourism (an approximate 80,000 tourists in 2010 alone) while minimising environmental impact, the Danish firm MAP Architects proposed excavating from, rather than erecting atop, polar terrain (Figure 8).[19] In an environment continually under siege by warming waters, melting glaciers and ice shelves cracking and separating, the decision to build on a mobile iceberg wisely anticipates the landscape changing rather than remaining stagnant; it reflects the cyclical nature of ice shifting between solid and liquid chemical states. However, unless the course of climate change is radically altered, this proposal also envisions its own demise, with the host iceberg and architectural intervention ultimately succumbing to a watery fate.[20]

8 MAP Architects, Antarctica iceberg living station, 2010.

Building in the cryosphere

Not surprisingly, ice architecture is most at home in its natural habitat: the cryosphere. This term is employed to link all frozen territories of the world, encompassing ice sheets, ice caps, ice fields, ice streams, frozen rivers and lakes, glaciers, permafrost, snow lines and snow fields.[21] Geopolitically speaking, this area includes Antarctica, the Arctic and territories in over one hundred countries. Although previously this region seemed to be an inaccessible, frozen wasteland, the discovery of rich mineral assets and material resources to be harvested or unearthed in Antarctic, Arctic and Alpine tundras have yielded increasing political and financial interest. In tandem, the effects of climate change have also encouraged northward migration of everything from trees to humans, a trend that will likely continue as sea levels rise.[22] Consequently, the cryosphere is viewed anew as a final frontier of utopian promise. This idealisation is in keeping with how the region has been romanticised for the past century, during which the poles were frequently idealised as safe havens in times of political instability and ecological crisis; these 'distant' realms were considered pure, seemingly endless pristine, sublime landscapes despite—or perhaps because of—their radical isolation. But as the world becomes more interconnected, further expansion into and subsequent architectural interventions within the cryosphere appear inevitable.

This move will present unique risks and challenges for architecture. Historically, cold climate and environment-specific design indications were limited, such as gabled roofs and snow stops as common features to combat excessive snow loads or hazardous falling ice. But apart from these modest gestures, the majority of architects building in the cryosphere have transplanted designs for temperate climes with little to no adaptations.[23] Not surprisingly, the results were often disastrous. Revisiting the first documented structures in Antarctica which, unlike the Arctic, was devoid of human habitation prior to the nineteenth century, one finds simple constructions resembling Scandinavian wooden cottages fashioned from plank walls and outfitted with gabled roofs, or British-style timber frame houses affixed to the unforgiving landscape by ropes approximating the look and organisation of a military campsite. In these examples, clichéd Nordic and Alpine architecture is transplanted from the mild winter environments of northern Europe; the forms recall the German notion of *Heimat* or homeliness, incorporating pitched roofs that are reminiscent of Tyrolean chalets, while the overall construction distinctly sits atop the landscape rather than being incorporated into it.[24]

For many early Antarctic explorers, the decision not to utilise the surrounding landscape and benefit from the energy-efficient insulation of

9 Ralph Erskine, An ecological Arctic town, 1970.

packed snow proved fatal. As a result, mastering ice and protecting against frigid temperatures came under the purview of engineers rather than architects, which, in turn, led to a utilitarian approach devoid of any romantic visual references to *Heimat*. The work of Atelier des Bâtisseurs (ATBAT) and other engineering firms involved in planning for the International Geophysical Year in Greenland in 1957 illustrates this shift in Arctic and Antarctic design. Contracted by the French government, ATBAT rigorously tested and built an Arctic habitat intended for occupancy by six researchers from the French Polar Expedition for one year. Working with Jean Prouvé, ATBAT devised a structure directly implanted into its snowy environs. With a hollowed-out entry tunnel and domed profile peeking out above, the structure is both a technological update and homage to the native igloo. The project also seems to draw inspiration from an earlier proposal by Charlotte Perriand and Pierre Jeanneret, whose 'barrel shelter' represented a prototype for minimalist high-altitude living. Yet unlike its aluminium predecessor, the ATBAT model is composed of lightweight plastic panels brought to the site, relying upon future snow buildup to partially bury and insulate the hut from strong winds and bitter cold. Both structures demonstrate that in order to successfully build in the cryosphere, designers need to embrace rather than work against the difficult conditions and dearth of local materials.

The self-anointed champion of such a climatically conditioned approach to polar building was Ralph Erskine. In his proposals for a 'sub-Arctic habitat' in the 1960s, Erskine argued for 'house and towns [that] open like flowers to the sun of spring and summer but, also like flowers, turn their backs on the shadows and the cold northern winds,' burrowing into the landscape and nestling within its protective coves and ridges.[25] In two proposals for 'An ecological Arctic town' and 'Resolute Bay' in Canada, Erskine provided visual corollary for these poetic ideas (Figure 9). Yet despite his call to honour local landscapes and incorporate preexisting culture and customs, Erskine's plans blatantly overlooked the rich traditions of Indigenous construction in sub-Arctic Europe and North America and relied upon importing foreign materials to the site. By neglecting these practices, Erskine ushered in a period of polar projection defined by tabula rasa technological fantasy rather than rooted, regionalist consideration, the latter of which he paradoxically believed himself to be a foremost proponent.

Frei Otto's and Kenzo Tange's proposal for an 'Arctic city' envisions a city of 40,000 people to be housed under a massive, transparent dome, evidencing unshakable faith in technology in the face of possible ecological, geopolitical and nuclear disaster while satisfying the era's taste for capsular cities and modular construction. Once again, this example demonstrates that in the cryosphere, architecture's relationship to site is often one of two extremes: either embeddedness—so much so that the landscape itself is used as building material—or total rejection, by hermetically sealing off from the harsh outside world. Much of the realised and imagined building in the cryosphere summons a schism between a so-called 'primitive' Arctic vernacular and Arctic high-tech aesthetic, reflecting the conflicting designs of architects and engineers and showcasing how the landscape has activated divergent desires between lost nostalgia and future unknowns.

Contemporary designs evoke references to some of the aforementioned projects yet largely avoid the pitfalls or unfulfilled promises of their predecessors. The Monte Rosa Hut near Zermatt is a telling example in this regard. While the structure bears noticeable aesthetic parallels with Perriand and Jeanneret's alpine refuge, this twenty-first century incarnation institutes a reciprocal relationship to its surroundings, eliminating interior mechanical heating in order to harness mountaintop sun to power thermal comfort. Excess solar energy is stored in lead-acid battery cells for future use and further warms interior spaces; water

10 AECOM & Hugh Broughton, Halley VI Antarctic research station, 2013.

from melting glaciers is stored in a nearby reservoir. The Hut marks a new path forward, showing that high-tech can also be 'regional' or at the very least regionally sensitive, benefitting from while respecting the local environment.

A similar approach can be detected in the most recent Antarctic research station, Halley VI (Figure 10). Although the design clearly harkens back to the era of Erskine's and Otto's megastructures, the primary reference is the 'Walking city' by Ron Herron of Archigram—and the inspiration is not only visual: Halley VI is the first fully relocatable polar station. A series of hydraulic legs outfitted with retractable giant skis enable the conjoined units to climb above rising snow levels and glide smoothly across icy terrain when travel is needed. The design aims for minimal environmental impact by independently sealing component chambers, thereby prohibiting the spread of fire ignited by static charge. This ensures that if a problem arises in one of the individual modules, it will not endanger the conjoined structure as a whole.

The future Ice Age

Building in ice-dominated environments should not only be viewed as a design challenge but as a field of possibility as well. The Svalbard Global Seed Vault, located on the Norwegian island of Spitsbergen in the Svalbard archipelago, is one example of an important resource that benefits from the dramatic cold and isolation to preserve the largest collection of agricultural biodiversity in the world (Figure 11). Far from geopolitical struggles and natural disasters that have led to the destruction of seed vaults elsewhere, the Svalbard vault crystallises the Expressionists' earlier dream of a pure and neutral setting, as well as the need to embrace building in Arctic environments to ensure our collective global future. Contemporary research projects by pioneering firms outline ways in which architecture and urbanism can thrive in such environments. Lateral Office's study of the Canadian Arctic, for example, makes clear the importance of granting equal value to Indigenous populations and vernacular architecture while remaining realistic about the future of development, resource extraction and territorial claims.[26] Arctic Design Group considers similar issues but with heightened attention to resilience and environmental impact by questioning the large-scale settlement potential of the Arctic and testing innovative design strategies in an age of new weather conditions and a human-led 'cold rush' to profit from and colonise this last remaining frontier.[27] Finally, Blouin Orzes have highlighted the need to align building and environmental cycles, attending to migration patterns, seasons and trade routes while demonstrating that both 'universal,' high-tech and 'vernacular,' local solutions are needed.[28]

11 Crop Trust, Svalbard Seed Vault, 2008, Svalbard.

Looking towards the future, the challenge for architecture will be to build with ice rather than against it. As receding ice shelves and thawing permafrost reveal novel plants, minerals and diseases, alongside desires to build off-land, architects will need to harness the resources of the cryosphere while simultaneously aiding its preservation. Resilient design methodologies will similarly have to account for ice, factoring in the consequences of frequent extreme weather events—not only the better-known fires, floods and earthquakes, but also increased sleet in winter and hailstorms during warmer months around the world.[29] Mirroring its own crystalline, layered form, ice architecture will have to be considered at every scale, from bolstered testing of shingle strength in the face of winter storms to building temporary refuges and off-world environments with frozen water. Despite the fact that the earth continues to warm, our next Ice Age may very well be on the horizon—but this time it will be at the hands and by the design of architects.

1 Stephen J. Pyne, 'The planet is burning,' AEON (November 2019), https://aeon.co/essays/the-planet-is-burning-around-us-is-it-time-to-declare-the-pyrocene.
2 Ibid.
3 On the Arctic's historical appeal see Christopher P. Heuer, *Into the white: the Renaissance Arctic and the end of the image* (Brooklyn: Zone Books, 2019), as well as Maggie Cao, 'The entropic history of ice,' in *Ecologies, agents, terrains*, eds. Christopher P. Heuer and Rebecca Zorach (New Haven: Yale University Press, 2018), 266–291.
4 Heuer, *Into the white*, 11–12.
5 Frank Lloyd Wright, *An autobiography* (London: Longmans, Greens & Company, 1932), 176. Wright writes: 'I wanted a home where icicles by invitation might beautify the eaves. So there were no gutters. And when the snow piled deep on the roofs and lay drifted in the courts, icicles came to hang staccato from the eaves. Prismatic crystal in pendants sometimes six feet [1.82 m] long, glittered, between the landscape and the eyes inside. Taliesin in winter was a frosted palace roofed and walled with snow, hung with iridescent fringes, the plate-glass of the windows delicately fantastic with frosted arabesques. A thing of winter beauty.'
6 Robert Hooke, *Micrographia: or some physiological descriptions of minute bodies made by magnifying glasses with observations and inquiries thereupon* (London: Printed by J. Martyn and J. Allestry, 1665). Quotations from Project Gutenberg e-book edition (29 March 2005).
7 Ibid.
8 Ibid.
9 Nakaya's research was instrumental in developing the Snow, Ice and Permafrost Research Establishment (SIPRE), which is now known as the Cold Regions Research and Engineering Laboratory of the U.S. Army Corps of Engineers. For more on Nakaya's work see Ukichiro Nakaya, 'The formation of ice crystals,' in *Compendium of meteorology*, ed. T. F. Malone (Boston American Meteorological Society, 1951), 207–220; Ukichiro Nakaya, *Snow crystals: natural and artificial* (Cambridge: Harvard University Press, 1954).
10 David Dernie and Jacopo Gaspari, 'Crystal utopias,' in *Material imagination in architecture* (Abingdon: Routledge, 2016), 123–172.
11 *Bruno Taut: Alpine Architektur*, ed. Matthias Schirren (Munich: Prestel, 2004).
12 The use of such materials also invites visual interplay in terms of layering and arrangement, juxtaposing literal and phenomenal transparency as defined by Colin Rowe and Robert Slutzky. See Colin Rowe and Robert Slutzky, 'Transparency: literal and phenomenal,' *Perspecta* 8 (1963): 45–54.
13 On Inuit construction, see Jeffrey Cook, 'Architecture indigenous to extreme climates,' *Energy & buildings*, 23.3 (March 1996): 277–291; Nelson H. H. Graburn, 'Authentic Inuit art: creation and exclusion in the Canadian North,' *Journal of material culture* (1 July 2004), https://doi.org/10.1177/1359183504044369; P. Hemmersam, 'Arctic architectures,' *Polar record*, 52.4 (2016): 412–422.
14 A catenoid section is defined as a space derived from an inverted catenary arch (or curve), with 'catenary' describing 'the shape of a flexible hanging chain or cable [in which] any freely hanging cable or string assumes this shape if the body is of uniform mass per unit of length and is acted upon solely by gravity.' See Stephan C. Carlson, 'Catenary,' *Encyclopaedia Britannica* (published 3 February 2017), https://www.britannica.com/science/catenary.
15 In the 1964 exhibition held at the Museum of Modern Art in New York, Rudofsky argued for the artistic, functional and cultural riches of vernacular architecture. See Bernard Rudofsky and Museum of Modern Art, *Architecture without architects: a short introduction to non-pedigreed architecture* (Albuquerque: University of New Mexico Press, 1987).
16 We might also mention the Sapporo and Tokamachi Snow Festivals in Japan, as well as ice sculpture competitions in Latvia and Russia.
17 Quoted in: Alla Aronova, 'The post-Petrine metamorphosis of triumphant military celebrations,' in *A history of Russian exposition and festival architecture: 1700–2014*, eds. Alla Aronova and Alexander Ortenberg (London: Routledge, 2019), 84.
18 As Clouds Office explains in their project brief, 'water ice is abundant in the northern latitudes and easily extracted as it's covered by only 30 centimeters of loose regolith.' See https://cloudsao.com/MARS-ICE-HOUSE.
19 http://www.maparchitects.dk/portfolio/item/iceberg-living-station-animation-made-for-icelab-exhibition/ with projections taken from 'Trends in Antarctic Tourism,' https://www.grida.no/resources/5245.
20 For additional reading on planned obsolescence, sustainability and adaptive architectures in response to climate change see Daniel M. Abramson, *Obsolescence: an architectural history* (Chicago: University of Chicago Press, 2016).
21 Defined by the National Ocean Service as 'the frozen water part of the Earth system.' More information can be found at https://oceanservice.noaa.gov/facts/cryosphere.html.
22 On tree migration: https://www.americanforests.org/magazine/article/trees-on-the-move/ and Sally N. Aitken et al., 'Adaptation, migration or extirpation: climate change outcomes for tree populations,' *Evolutionary applications* 1.1 (February 2008): 95–111.
23 See Georgina A. Davis, 'A history of McMurdo Station through its architecture,' *Polar Record*, 53.2 (March 2017): 167–185.

24 The importation of recognisably 'nationalist' styles to Antarctica during this period may also be a reflection of political debates and posturing concerning claims to and ownership of stretches of Antarctic territory and mineral resources. A concise history of this episode may be found in Kieran Mulvaney, *At the ends of the earth: a history of the polar regions* (Washington, D.C.: Island Press/ Shearwater Books, 2001). For more on the pitched roof's nationalism and nostalgia, see Bart Lootsma, 'The Tyrolean house: invented tradition or simulacrum?' *Volume #41*, 'How to build a nation' (2014): 118–125.
25 Ralph Erskine, 'Architecture and town planning in the north,' *Polar Record*, 14 (1968): 165–171, 167; see also Ralph Erskine, 'Building in the Arctic,' *Ekistics*, 10:59 (1960): 152–155.
26 Lola Sheppard and Mason White, *Many norths: spatial practice in a polar territory* (New York: Actar, 2017).
27 Leena Cho and Matthew Jull, 'Arctic paradox: apocalypse or Eden?' *uncube* 5, 'Apocalypse soon!' 48–52, http://www.uncubemagazine.com/sixcms/detail.php?id=8098347&articleid=art-1355158191204#!/page48.
28 'Arctic architecture,' The architectural league NY, 18 March 2020, https://archleague.org/article/arctic-architecture/.
29 The financial and structural costs of not doing so are already clear, as when Colorado filed for the state's costliest disaster following a hailstorm in 2017. Dean Vlahos and Rose Grant, 'How building science and research can help avert disaster,' AIA (27 March 2018), https://www.aia.org/articles/185061-how-building-science-and-research-can-help-:56.

HOT

Revealing fire

1 John Martin, *The great day of his wrath*, 1851–1853, Tate Gallery, London.

Fire in the age of the Anthropocene remains a representational challenge for architecture. It can inform both speculative and analytical studies. It can also confront tensions between continuity and renewal. In Western culture, its imagery has been closely shaped by early nineteenth-century British art. Those images, by artists such as John Martin or Francis Danby, mixed architectural fantasies with hellscapes featuring molten lava, tumbling rocks and crumbling cities. Yet rather than try to titillate an audience, Martin's images of fire shocks us into noticing their settings. Indirectly, the feeling the work evokes, an apocalyptic sublime, can inform more speculative architectural proposals. However, this is not the case for many kinds of representations dealing with fire and climate change. Instead, in the drier, more analytical studies that enable risk perception and decision-making, the assumption that fire is a hazard remains. Drawing fire can also be political. By foregrounding First Nations perspectives, we can also frame fire in terms of land management and cultural renewal, a form of truth-telling about the past that traces alternative trajectories into the future.

John Martin and the apocalyptic sublime

The images of the 2019–2020 East Coast Australian bushfires of charred-out houses or children sheltering on boats against a bloody sky invoked ancient biblical themes of the end of the earth. Our interpretation of such images as apocalyptic draws on artists like John Martin, from an earlier age of anxiety—the start of the Industrial

Revolution in Britain. Today, Martin is thought of more as an inspiration for Hollywood disaster movies.[1] Yet architects could do with looking at them again. These works place nature at its most violent in dialogue with buildings of near-infinite scale. Nature is not tamed by buildings but runs wild beside them. And while the intended effect may be to provoke awe in the viewer, it is a reminder that architects try to tame the image of nature to accommodate their buildings. However, Martin shows this need not be the case.

Martin's paintings reimagined biblical scenes in ever more dramatic settings (Figure 1). Few painters were so concerned with turning popular anxieties into visual form. They appealed to popular interest in Millennialism, a belief that the world was doomed until the occurrence of divine intervention, after which a long period of peace would follow.[2] Where earlier painters such as Rembrandt might have considered the psychological torment in the main protagonists, Martin created feelings of awe and terror through his staging of each scene.

It was an approach indebted to the philosopher Edmund Burke. Burke's formulation of the sublime—terror mediated by astonishment—evoked feelings of danger in the face of nature or God's power.[3] This approach shifted ideas of the sublime away from a classical emphasis on beauty, towards one that 'taught his contemporaries to snatch a fearful joy from the experience of art.'[4] For Burke, beauty was founded on pleasure and could be discovered in small things that were smooth, light or delicate. In contrast, the sublime evoked danger and was encountered in the qualities of vastness, ruggedness, darkness and gloom.[5]

2 Joseph Wright of Derby, *Vesuvius in eruption, with a view over the islands in the Bay of Naples*, c. 1776–1780, Tate Gallery, London.

This distinction challenged artists to seek out different landscapes, both real and imagined, to visualise the sublime. Painters, from J. M. W. Turner to Joseph Wright of Derby, searched for the weird and wondrous in the natural world, depicting waterfalls, caves, volcanoes and sea storms. Indeed, Wright of Derby became renowned for his paintings of Mount Vesuvius erupting, creating over 30 images of the volcano over his lifetime (Figure 2). Lava spouted straight up in many of his paintings, illuminating an otherwise dark canvas, creating an aura around the top of volcanoes. Wright had travelled to Naples in 1774, but it seems highly likely that he never witnessed much volcanic activity first-hand. His rendering of dramatic eruptions was more speculative than based in reality. Dividing the canvas between firelight from the volcano and moonlight by the sea, Wright set the stage for a shift from depictions of the natural sublime as emphasising the power of nature towards what Morton D. Paley has termed the 'apocalyptic sublime.'

Architecture featured in this new variation on the sublime, which considered the end of the earth and revelation before God.[6] With an

emphasis on biblical scenes of prophecy, such as *Belshazzar's Feast* or *The deluge*, Martin situated these events in strange, dreamlike reconstructions of Assyrian cities, whose perspectival vanishing points often landed beyond the frame of the image. Images of hell also received architectural form, often with a nod to French visionary architect Étienne-Louis Boullée, in Martin's many paintings and etchings of Pandemonium, the capital of Hell, in John Milton's *Paradise Lost*.[7] Very few human figures occupied Martin's canvases. Instead, landscape and buildings were stretched and fragmented to unsettle the viewer, creating a sense of danger which neither the protagonists in them nor the viewer could avoid.

And while the natural world in all its strangeness inspired artists, so, too, did the industrial world. The scale of new infrastructure, such as tunnels and docks, astonished viewers as much as any cave. This was a world that depended on fire—to light the new spaces to ignite engines. Fire during the eighteenth century was both industrialised and tamed.

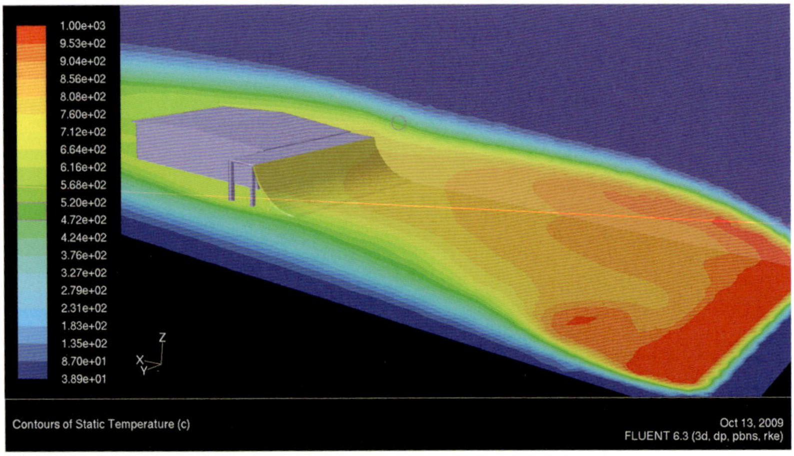

Martin's paintings reflect both the emergence of new lighting technologies and a wariness of both wildfire and industrial fire. Night light at the end of the eighteenth century was still considered a luxury, a symbol of decent comfort on the one hand, but one that created smoky, putrid atmospheres from burning animal fats.[8] In public, candles were used for festivities and carefully rationed for workplaces. This changed with the advent of gas lighting in the early nineteenth century, with towns and cities in Europe and the USA gaining gas streetlights. At the same time, the growth of cities brought along increased risks of urban fire. Cities were as much an accumulation of fuel as they were an accumulation of people. The avoidance of fire was largely dependent on the maintenance of social order.[9] Fire, therefore, in the European imagination, could highlight industrial productivity, but when uncontrolled, implied the breakdown of society. It seems apt then that Martin, one of the nineteenth century's most imaginative painters, used flickering gaslight and lava-strewn landscapes to depict hell and the end of the earth.

3 Nigel Bertram, Jordi Beneyto-Ferre, Laura Harper, David E. Mainwaring, Victoria Smith, SueAnne Ware, CFD analysis of fire break, Winning entry for *Design Challenge 09: Fire* organised by RMIT Design Research Institute, 2009, Polytactics, RMIT, Melbourne.

Fire and depicting risk

Fire as both a natural and a man-made hazard may be considered a risk when it is probable but not immediate.[10] Images depicting fire risks tell us much about how society manages and mitigates risk. Indeed, the proliferation of fire risks suggests a future-oriented society, one more concerned with controlling what comes next than understanding what has happened.[11] In contrast, apocalyptic imagery portends the imminent

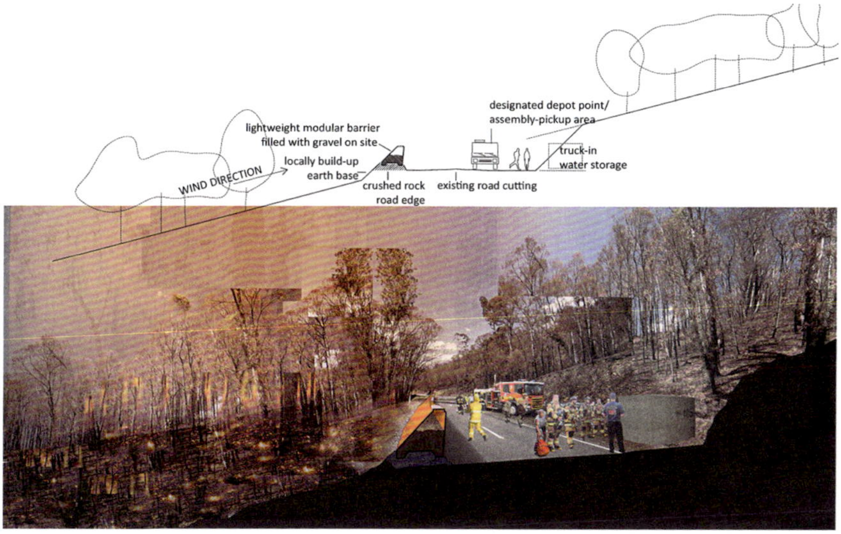

4 Nigel Bertram, Jordi Beneyto-Ferre, Laura Harper, David E. Mainwaring, Victoria Smith, SueAnne Ware, Perspective of fire break, Winning entry for *Design Challenge 09: Fire* organised by RMIT Design Research Institute, 2009, Polytactics, RMIT, Melbourne.

arrival of some form of divine intervention, one that people can do little to overcome. As such, these images suggest an acceleration of decline. On the other hand, today's mappings of drought-stricken rivers and probability assessments of wildfire spread indicate how fire risk is increasing. This is not used to suggest an inevitability to the outcome, but on the contrary to enable decision-making in the spirit of the future-oriented modernity that seeks to understand and control risks.[12]

So it is perhaps telling to compare two different competition entries to an ideas competition in 2009 for the Black Saturday Bushfires. These bushfires in communities north of Melbourne occurred in January and February 2009, after temperatures in preceding weeks had reached 46 °C. Over 2000 homes were lost and 173 people died.[13] In the, aftermath RMIT's annual transdisciplinary design challenge focused on fire. It was won by the *Polytactics* project team led by Nigel Bertram and Jordi Beneyto-Ferre, while another entry called *Smarter Stay, Smarter Go* in a team led by Stuart Harrison received attention.[14] Both designs translated some of the measures used to prevent flooding—sandbagging and flood warning systems—to prevent fire. However, the imagery in the two proposals differed greatly. Bertram's proposal showed a mixture of Computational Fluid Dynamic airflow simulations (Figure 3), crisp diagrammatic sections and plans, alongside more atmospheric renderings of the system in use during a fire event (Figure 4). Images of smiling families taking shelter from the sun were interspersed with more dramatic scenes of fire crews assembling beside a spot-fired forest. It is a reminder that no one representational trope works for fire but rather fire is multifaceted.

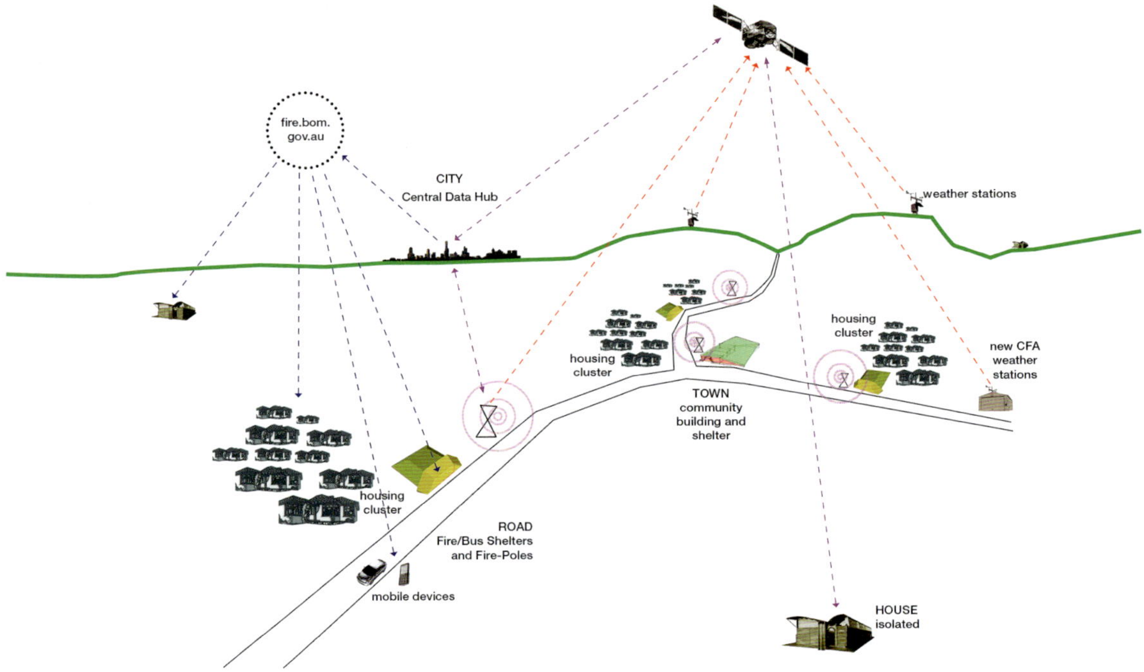

5 Stuart Harrison et al., Network diagram, 2009, Smarter Stay Smarter Go, RMIT, Melbourne.

The *Polytactics* team emphasised adaptation to fire ecologies and resilient thinking, a new concept in 2009 (almost 12 years ago at the time of writing, so climate models/adaptations have since changed radically). A range of tactics were to be considered—hence the project title—and these ranged from fire breaks around a community and movable barriers to protect firefighters, to local fire protection infrastructure for homes such as water tanks, assembly points and additional escape paths. The project generally conceived of fire as a regular occurrence, an event for the community to adapt to, manage and prepare for over a number of years.

In contrast, the project designed by the *Smarter Stay, Smarter Go* team considered community safety during a major fire event. The premise was that better and more up-to-date information would save lives. Familiar public utilities such as bus stops could be adapted to offer emergency shelter from fire. Looked at from the perspective of 12 years and one major fire season later, it is clear that both designs have merit and predicted an increased reliance on data and community preparation.

Yet it is telling that the renderings for only one of the projects showed any fire. Alongside more traditional plans and sections, the *Polytactics* team included a long section showing their polymer break in use during what might be a controlled forest burn,[15] or a fire crew about to stamp out a spot fire (Figure 4). The image splits in two, maroon and

6 Stuart Harrison et al., Fire pole mock-up, 2009, Smarter Stay Smarter Go, RMIT, Melbourne.

burnt umber smoke engulfs the forest on one side, while on the other, a distant steel-blue sky can be glimpsed beyond burnt-out trees. Colours are largely muted, save for some highlights where spot fires smoulder around the base of tree trunks. While less dramatic than Wright of Derby's studies of Vesuvius, the splitting of the image into red and blue halves is continued, with spot illumination provided by flames on the forest floor.

Architects can move the representation of fire in architecture and landscape beyond the fire itself, to how its emergence is communicated. The *Smarter Stay, Smarter Go* proposal sought to reinvent roadside warning signs and incorporate recommendations from the Victorian Bushfires Royal Commission for more consistent communications about fire risk.[16] The team considered fire not in terms of ecology but in terms of information and diagrams (Figure 5). They looked at how best to help residents to decide whether to stay or go in the event of a fire. While Harrison and his team acknowledged this could be done using more intrusive visual and aural aids such as alarms and flashing lights, they settled on rethinking the most common indicator of fire-prone land in Australia—the 'Fire Danger Today' sign. Instead of a sign meant to warn passing motorists of fire danger, the entry tried to warn pedestrians, public transport users and motorists of danger by turning a bus stop into a fire pole (Figure 6). Relative danger continues to be signified by a green to red colour scheme, but text and warning sirens are also considered possible. As images, Harrison's team's diagrams and renders are simple and often sketchy, as much to test an early idea rather than a finessed product.

Both projects were immediate attempts in the wake of a bushfire to rethink how to better prepare for a future event. They also look at fire differently, using two different fire paradigms, one physical and the other cultural. The cultural paradigm, as Stephen J. Pyne notes, considers fire only in terms of how it affects humanity, whereas the physical paradigm emphasises the effects of fire on the landscape. For the *Polytactics* team, fire was largely a physical paradigm, with many drawings considering how barriers can control the physical spread of fire for both people and trees. For the *Smarter Stay, Smarter* Go team, with the emphasis on communications and community shelter, fire was cultural. Still both addressed a broader range of concerns than most climate-responsive designs emphasise, going far beyond questions of thermal comfort to consider resilience and communication. With this came a wider range of representational challenges that highlight tensions between the physical, social and temporal nature of fire.

There is a difference between representing fire for thrills and representing fire for community resilience. Paintings of volcanic eruptions could evoke terror and delight, but viewers' lives were not under threat, when contemplating the scene in a darkened room. The protagonists in each image were at risk but not the audience.

I was reminded of this when thinking about the East Australian bushfires of 2019–2020. From October 2019 to March 2020, most of the East Coast of Australia was on fire. More than 17 million hectares of land burned in Australia—more than the area of England and Wales combined. One billion mammals, birds and reptiles perished.[17] Conservatively assessed, climate change increased the risk of this event by 30%.[18] This is the extreme weather event that experts had warned would come, but this time it came earlier than expected.

Although safe from the fires in Sydney, I was not safe from its effects, as visibility plummeted during the day and air quality in the city was the worst in the world. Images of out-of-control wildfires certainly evoked sympathy and solidarity with nearby communities, but they were not the images I relied on to make decisions. Instead, it was the combination of real-time weather warnings, *Fires Near Me* app and local air quality indices that helped me decide where to travel, how to move about and when to stay home.

Travelling with fire, denying fire and revealing fire

When Europeans invaded Australia, they altered the fire regimes of the continent. For thousands of years before, as Bruce Pascoe highlights, Aboriginal and Torres Strait Islander peoples skilfully controlled fire to increase the productivity of the land. They practised low-level burning as a form of land management, creating careful and flexible associations between peoples, plains, forests and copses.[19] Europeans, however, were terrified of fire and sought to suppress its spread across the continent. The system of settlement imposed on Australia, with its reliance on fencing to define territory, obsession with private property and introduction of a whole new range of animals, transformed the ecology of the continent and made fires larger and more unpredictable.[20] 'Fire,' as Stephen J. Pyne notes, 'went feral.'[21]

After invasion, two different kinds of fire emerged, the contained fire of the city and the wildfire of the countryside or Bush. The ecological transformation of the Bush meant that woodland returned where once there was productive grassland, while the reluctance to use controlled burns meant that when burning happened, fires were greater in size and harder to manage. Cities such as Sydney or Melbourne saw themselves as safe havens from fire—stripped of forests, fire was driven into combustion engines of motor cars, diesel generators, boilers, lawnmowers.[22] From the 1870s, gas was piped into homes, and with it heating and cooking were transformed, with flames ever more domesticated.[23] While some houses up to the mid-twentieth century had hearths, the only naked flame found today is on the gas cooktop. Cities largely extinguished fire, even if its evidence is everywhere from the suburban home to the myriad fire escape doors and sprinkler systems of apartment blocks.

The suburban home that emerged during the early twentieth century assumed that fire would occur within the home due to a faulty appliance or a mistended fire. There was little acknowledgement that wildfires continued to burn through many parts of the world. Homes might relate to climate with verandahs to shade the sun or breezeways to stay cool in the afternoon but, building suburban homes in areas prone to wildfires required a different approach. Marketers trumpeted the fire resistance of cladding materials, such as asbestos cement sheets, during the 1930s but gave few other recommendations. It was only at the end of the twentieth century that designers and housebuilders had access to clear, detailed information for building in bushfire sensitive areas.

Melbourne architect, Lisle Rudolph's drawings from 2003 show how misconceptions about bushfires had to be addressed before providing

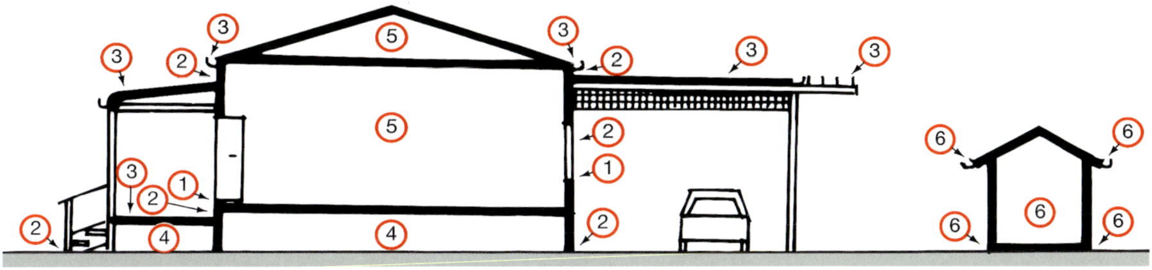

7 Above: Lisle Rudolph, Diagram of ignition of buildings by burning embers carried by the wind, 2003.
Middle: Lisle Rudolph, Diagram of ignition of buildings by heat radiation from the fire, 2003.
Below: Lisle Rudolph, Diagram of ignition of buildings by direct flame contact, 2003.

8 Lisle Rudolph, Kindling accumulation points, 2003.

any design advice. At this time, and to a certain extent still, most homeowners assumed that the main risk to a building in a bushfire is being engulfed by the fire itself.[24] Instead, Rudolph and his co-author, G. Caird Ramsay, showed that radiant heat and ember attack carried as much if not greater risk. The diagrams of ignition mechanisms presents small multiples of different fire risks to a simple pitched roof house, shown in section (Figure 7). In one image, low-level fire courses through the undergrowth while embers fly from a gum tree's canopy. In the next, heat radiates from the fire front. In the last image, flames spring towards the building. Rudolph's quasi-technical images allow a non-specialist audience to understand bushfire risk and take appropriate action. They continue the Olgyays' tradition of creating a new image economy to suggest new relationships between people and their environment.[25] Where the Olgyays sought to retrofit the modernist house for any climate, Rudolph and Caird retrofit the suburban house for bushfires.

The relationship between fire and home ownership is mediated through these images, suggesting courses of action to reduce bushfire risks. The single-storey, verandahed home with a covered garage is dissected for ignition risk and potential for accumulating kindling (Figure 8). Simple sections indicate standard details that need to be addressed, in the hope that homeowners and designers would rethink the way they design and build. And yet the drawings also suggest an endless array of DIY projects, of gutters to be unclogged, crawl spaces to be relined and outbuildings to be replaced. They suggest that fire is the unwelcome guest that residents are always preparing for.

Despite such preparations, new designs for buildings in bushfire-sensitive areas rarely show fire. Skies are blue and cloudless, an endless summer rather than an endless fire season. As Julie Firkin has noted, 'to encourage people to use a refuge, you should offer them a place that is safe and that looks safe.'[26] The house she designed, a speculative project for the bushfire homes service set up in the wake of the 2009 Black Saturday bushfires, used concrete, roller shutters and a large roof to protect against fire. The perspective emphasises the building's massing and large awning, conveying shelter. The shutters are downplayed, and instead distant views and still nature convey a sense of calm.

Of course, to show the landscape engulfed in flames, with families sheltering inside, might demonstrate the technical effectiveness of the design, but emotionally no resident would wish to go back to this time. Even when fire is shown, as in the *Polytactics* proposal, it is limited to showing firefighters in action, calmly undertaking a controlled burn rather than the last days of earth in John Martin's paintings. Instead, imagery of flames seems more appropriate when attempting to spring a homeowner into action, to suggest preparation for an inevitable event.

Both fire and people have the power to shape landscapes, often hand in hand. Climate change and current settlement patterns increase the risk of uncontrolled wildfires and negative community impacts. Part of the current problem is the lack of community understanding of how to live with fire. Fires are to be suppressed, rather than made an integral part of land management, as they have been and continue to be by First Nations peoples throughout Australia and the Torres Strait. Beneath every Australian city lies a landscape shaped by fire. Treating fire in militaristic terms, to be battled with and dominated, as a threat to property, misses its ecological, social and cultural role, its connection to people and place. Instead, Bruce Pascoe asks that we 'think differently about the country.'[27]

Settler Australia has valued land in terms of property, a tradable asset, a justification for invasion. On the other hand, the Aboriginal idea of Country, as Brisbane-based architect and descendent of the Kaurareg and Meriam peoples of the Torres Strait Islands, Kevin O'Brien notes, 'is an idea that binds groupings of aboriginal people to the place of their ancestors, past, current and future. It understands that every moment of the land, sea and sky, its particles, its prospects and its prompts, enables life.'[28] O'Brien's *Finding Country* project has, since 2012, used the investigation of fire to provoke non-Aboriginal architects to engage Country in their work (Figure 9).[29] In a series of workshops, exhibitions and publications, O'Brien challenges conventional roles of fire by asking participants at his workshops and exhibitions to consider the obligations and connections to Country within cities. Participants are asked to map a fragment of the existing city by creating figure-ground plans of one grid square of the city. Then they are asked to remove 50% of the built area by a variety of methods.

9 Kevin O'Brien, 'Finding Country: radical practice,' 2018, University of Sydney, Sydney.

Fire is used as an imaginative device to reveal Country, with participants asked to consider the effect of a controlled or free burn on

a part of the city. Instead of the appendages of Rowe's *Collage City*, which ask what parts of the city might be carefully replaced,[30] O'Brien's work asks what might be removed and revealed, in effect placing the discipline of drawing and Indigenous land management in tension to decolonise the city.

Whether as imagery of the apocalyptic sublime or attempts to find Country, drawings of fire reveal connections between our age and a much deeper sense of time. They can shock, or patiently address misconceptions to encourage action. Architecture has tended to supress fire, to deny its existence in most drawings. Yet rather than suppress fire, designers can reveal its impact. The most banal details can be shaped by fire. The most boring parts of suburbia can be animated. In essence there is an obligation on designers to confront the systems that have changed people's relationship with fire and to privilege deeper ways of understanding land and our collective place in it.

1 Julie Milne, 'The Abyss that abides,' in Martin Myrone, ed., *John Martin: Apocalypse* (London: Tate publishing, 2011), 54–55.
2 Stephen D. O'Leary suggests that the apocalypse was so woven into millennial rhetoric as it gave an explanation to the apparent growth of supposed evils, whose growth implied that divine intervention was imminent. Stephen D. O'Leary, *Arguing the apocalypse: a theory of millennial rhetoric* (Oxford: Oxford University Press, 1994), 6f.
3 Erika Goble, *Visual phenomenology: encountering the sublime through art* (New York: Routledge, 2016), 5f.
4 Morton D. Paley, *The apocalyptic sublime* (New Canaan: Yale University Press, 1986), 2.
5 Edmund Burke (1757), *A philosophical enquiry into our ideas of the sublime and beautiful* (New York: Harper and Brothers, 1844), 157–158.
6 Gavin Stamp has noted the influence of John Martin's work on the nineteenth century Scottish architect, Alexander 'Greek' Thomson. For a summary see Rory Olcayto, 'Apocalypse then: John Martin at Tate Britain,' *Architects' journal* 324:11 (13 October 2011): 41.
7 John Milton, *Paradise lost* (Minneapolis: First Avenue Editions 2014), 26. Citations refer to the First Avenue edition, which republished the 1674 second edition of the book.
8 John Crowley, *The invention of comfort* (Baltimore: Johns Hokpins University Press, 2000), 191f.
9 Stephen J. Pyne, *Fire: a brief history* (Sydney: New South Publishing, 2nd ed. 2019), 110.
10 Peter Itzen and Simone M. Müller, 'Risk as a category of analysis for a social history of the twentieth century: an introduction,' *Historical social research* 41:1 (2016): 7–29.
11 Ibid.
12 Anthony Giddens, *The consequences of modernity* (Oxford: Wiley, 2013), 177–178.
13 Australian institute for disaster resilience, 'Bushfire—Black Saturday, Victoria, 2009,' *Australian Disaster Resilience Knowledge Hub*, https://knowledge.aidr.org.au/resources/bush-fire-black-saturday-victoria-2009/.
14 Timberbiz, 'Latest designs in bush-fire prevention talked up' (3 February 2010), https://www.timberbiz.com.au/latest-designs-in-bushfire-prevention-talked-up/.
15 A controlled forest burn is an intentional fire prescribed to maintain forest health. It is undertaken when conditions pose little threat to the public or fire managers.
16 State Government of Victoria, *2009 Victorian bushfires royal commission interim report* (Melbourne: Government Printer, 2009), 154.
17 Lisa Richards, Nigel Brew and Lizzie Smith, '2019–20 Australian bushfires—frequently asked questions: a quick guide' (12 March 2019), https://www.aph.gov.au/About_Parliament/Parliamentary_Departments/Parliamentary_Library/pubs/rp/rp1920/Quick_Guides/AustralianBushfires.
18 Geert Jan van Oldenborgh et al., 'Attribution of the Australian bushfire risk to anthropogenic climate change', *Natural hazards and Earth system sciences* 21:3 (2021): 941–960, https://doi.org/10.5194/nhess-21-941-2021.
19 Bruce Pascoe, *Dark emu: black seeds: agriculture or accident?* (Broome: Magabala Books, 2014), 115–124.
20 Stephen J. Pyne, *Fire*, 143.
21 Ibid.
22 Ibid., 116–117.
23 Robin Boyd, *Australia's home* (Melbourne: Penguin Books, 2nd ed., 1978), 250–251.
24 G. Caird Ramsay and Lisle Rudolph, *Landscape and building design for bushfire areas* (Collingwood, Vic.: CSIRO Publishing 2003), 7.
25 Daniel A. Barber, 'The nature of the image: Olgyay and Olgyay's architectural-climatic diagrams in the 1950s,' *Public culture*, 29, no. 1 (2016): 131, https://doi.org/DOI: 10.1215/08992363-3644433.
26 Marg Hearn, 'Julie Firkin,' *Mark*, 52 (October 2014): 87.
27 Bruce Pascoe, *Dark Emu*, 123.
28 Kevin O'Brien, 'Sep yama: Finding Country Exhibition' (2012), http://www.findingcountry.com.au/.
29 Kevin O'Brien, 'Burning Country, finding Sydney,' in *Finding Country* (The University of Sydney: Faculty of Architecture, Design and Planning, 2015), 4.
30 Colin Rowe and Fred Koetter, *Collage city* (Cambridge: MIT Press, 1978).

CODA

Explorations: climatic design in the design studio

1 Serena Bomze, Emily Flanagan, Lucy Sharman, Ferry stations located along the Saen Saeb canal, Bangkok, 2020.

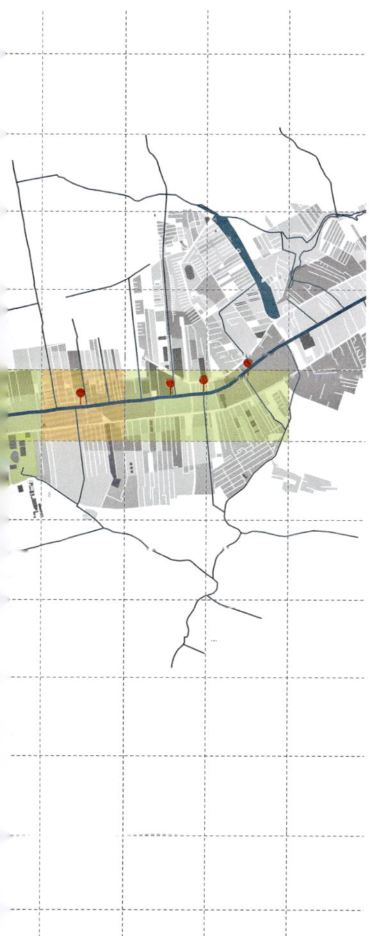

Around the world, visual histories of climatic representations contain rich references to disciplines that lie beyond the practice of architecture—anthropology, art history, art practices, ecology, geography, history of science, landscapes studies and urban planning. Some of these references have been explored in the previous chapters of this book: among others, nineteenth-century French caricatures created by Honoré Daumier; looming shadows cast by Hugh Ferriss' skyscrapers; fernery as a model of domestic architecture in nineteenth-century Queensland, Australia; cumulus clouds represented in Western art; Victor and Aladar Olgyay's wind studios; eighteenth-century micro-animals; region-wide dust storms that have paralysed China and South Korea; Simryn Gill's photographs; ice palaces in midwestern Minnesota, USA, and Harbin, China; and Antarctic scientific laboratories. Such references, though sometimes located far from the conventional purview of architecture, continue to serve as important examples for emerging designers as climate change becomes more pressing over the next few decades.

Using postgraduate projects from the Master of Architecture (M.Arch) sustainable studios at the University of Sydney and the National University of Singapore (NUS), this coda explores climates and their visual representations as core concerns of architecture embedded in the design studio. Highlighting how these concepts of climate could be translated into architectural design and their attendant representational techniques emphasises that the transition to the built environment remains a complex endeavour. These student projects not only experiment with representations of climate but attempt to rethink climatic design for building components such as atria, courtyards, envelopes and screens. We bring together a diverse set of student projects developed in Sydney and Singapore to illustrate how climatic design might be implemented and visualised in architectural practice. These postgraduate projects demonstrate a few of the considerable challenges involved in incorporating sustainable design into smaller structures and full-scale buildings. Both practical exercises in the architecture studio and professional buildings require different considerations of climatic design when transferred to the exigencies of the real world. We examine how some of the climatic phenomena proposed in earlier chapters may be applied as design propositions in the built environment.

Passive design in public shelters

The first section discusses four student projects from the University of Sydney which address the effects of climate change in Southeast Asia in the cities of Bangkok, Jakarta and Singapore. These projects concentrate on the role of passive design in a public shelter meant for the urban context of Asian cities. Student teams were also asked about how they would alleviate the high levels of heat and humidity generated by urban heat island effect in these three cities. All four projects attempt to address local conditions impacted by climate change as well as regional and territorial fluctuations manifested at state and national levels.

Downpour in Bangkok, Thailand

Bangkok's informal economies of street markets and canal waterways underscore a chaotic approach to Asian urbanism that merges residential density with cultural landmarks. Buddhist temples are interspersed with food stalls, contemporary skyscrapers and abandoned ghost buildings. Situated on a river delta, Bangkok, known as Krung Thep, brims with vibrant street life and ornate traditional temples scattered throughout the city. The Chao Praya River winds its way through the city, feeding into numerous canals. Longtail boats dot the waterways, and local residents often use these boats to traverse the length of the canal system. Comparable to many other cities in Southeast Asia, Bangkok suffers from low wind velocity, and monsoon season often brings extreme wind gusts that can blow from underneath, causing roof structures to crack. As illustrated, the Chao Praya streams through the historic quarters of Bangkok and makes its way into suburban neighbourhoods connected by the city's metro system.

Serena Bomze, Emily Flanagan and Lucy Sharman's project focuses on a particular strand of the Chao Praya river system, specifically the Khlong Saen Saeb canal that services a number of outlying neighbourhoods in Bangkok (Figure 1 and Figure 2). Their architectural design addresses several environmental variables related to climate change in Bangkok: the river's rising flood levels; hotter temperatures in the city due to urban heat island effect; increasing humidity levels; and the climatic effects of monsoon season. Their cantilevered roof repeats the design of a simple gutter—multiple gutters spread across the surface of the shelter's roof, with each component funnelling rainwater straight back into the canal (Figure 3). Any imminent deluge of rainfall also acts as a transparent wall that separates portions of the accessibility ramp leading to the canal's edge. The cleared walkway underneath the roof also acts as an open corridor for the public to access opposite ends of the station (Figure 4 and Figure 5). Here, the ferry station is reconfigured to become more accessible for the area's elderly residents, who can easily employ the ramp to step onto any boat. Clustered gutters, pinned into the narrow alley, lead straight out to the canal, filtering out over the waterway. Arrayed into five separate tiers, the gutters themselves are designed from a combination of teakwood for the joists in the roof and steel for the columns. The underside of each gutter is painted a lighter colour to reflect any residual heat from the sun as well as to maintain cooler temperatures for the open spaces underneath.

The ferry station's nighttime view illustrates its responsiveness to the urban environment: multiple gutters that comprise the roof are equipped with lighting, making the station a beacon for nocturnal transportation (Figure 6). Old tyres used to line the station's landing keep any boat from crashing against the canal's edge. The downpour during monsoon season in Bangkok transforms from being an ephemeral element of climate to an active component of the station's design.

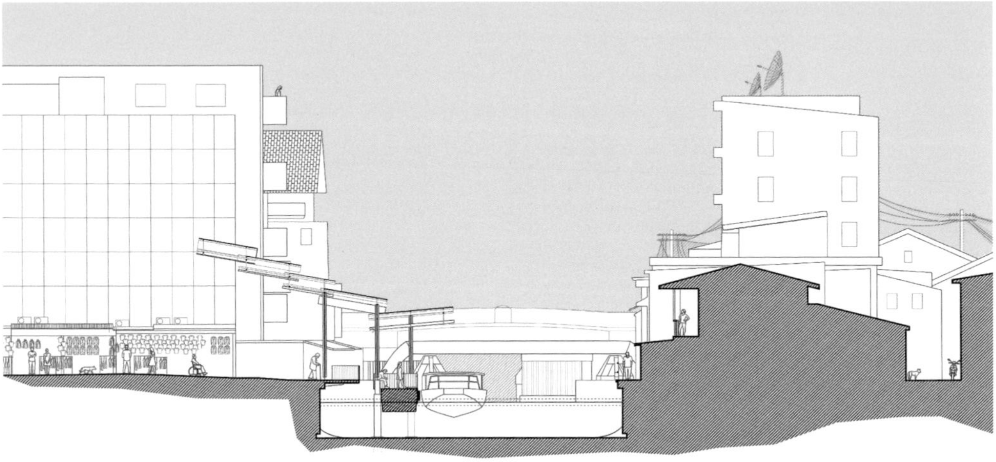

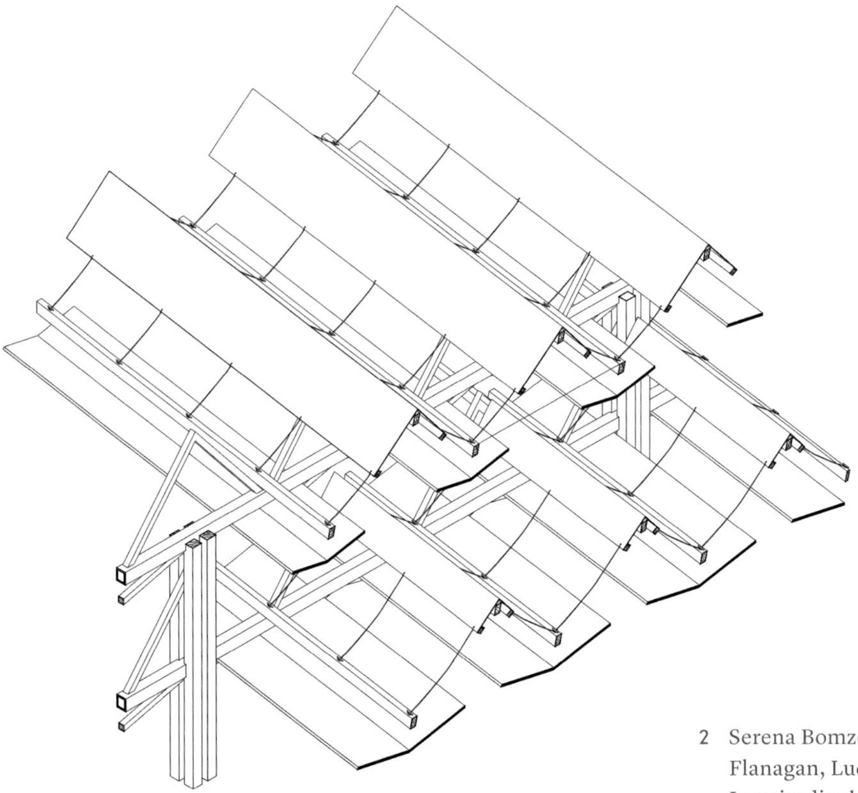

2 Serena Bomze, Emily Flanagan, Lucy Sharman, Longitudinal section through the Saen Saeb canal, 2020.

3 Serena Bomze, Emily Flanagan, Lucy Sharman, Construction detail of the roof serving as part of a proposed ferry station, 2020.

4 Serena Bomze, Emily Flanagan, Lucy Sharman, 3D rendering of the gutter roof looking out towards the Saen Saeb canal, 2020.

5 Serena Bomze, Emily Flanagan, Lucy Sharman, Rendering of rainfall streaming down back into the canal, 2020.

6 Serena Bomze, Emily Flanagan, Lucy Sharman, Nighttime view of the ferry station on the Saen Saeb canal, 2020.

Monsoon farming in Bangkok, Thailand

Monsoon season in Southeast Asia plays an important role in determining how agricultural crops like rice are planted and rotated throughout the year in Ayutthaya, Thailand. Ayutthaya has long been a traditional centre for the Siamese kingdom, from 1350 to 1767. Its fecund paddy fields often experience flooding from the Chao Phraya River at regular intervals (Figure 7). One of the dangers of such climatic changes is that rice must be harvested rather quickly during flooding conditions, or crops tend to become severely damaged. Similarly to the previous project, this proposed shelter takes into account the seasonal rainfall along the Chao Phraya River as well as the low-velocity winds in Bangkok. Careful attention is also paid to the economic cycles experienced by rice farmers, who must directly mill and store their own crops. They also must directly sell their rice through to the marketplace—the proposed school and shelter features a display of sustainable agricultural practices as well as potential job opportunities for those who live near the site (Figure 8). Taking a cue from Thai vernacular architecture, the building provides an overhanging roof constructed from bamboo timber, with deep eaves covering an open floor plan below (Figure 9). The use of recycled materials to reduce heat—such as compressed earth and communal timber—contributes to comfortable spaces during humid weather (Figure 10). Airflow from the outdoors is guided into the building through the strategic positioning of timber louvres (Figure 11). Minimal openings in the timber walls also ensure minimal heat gain over the course of the day and provide a modular system for long-term maintenance.

7 Mai Alarilla, Anthony Bucciarelli, Max Cha, Approximate flood-level projections on site, 2020.

Approximate Flooding Projection

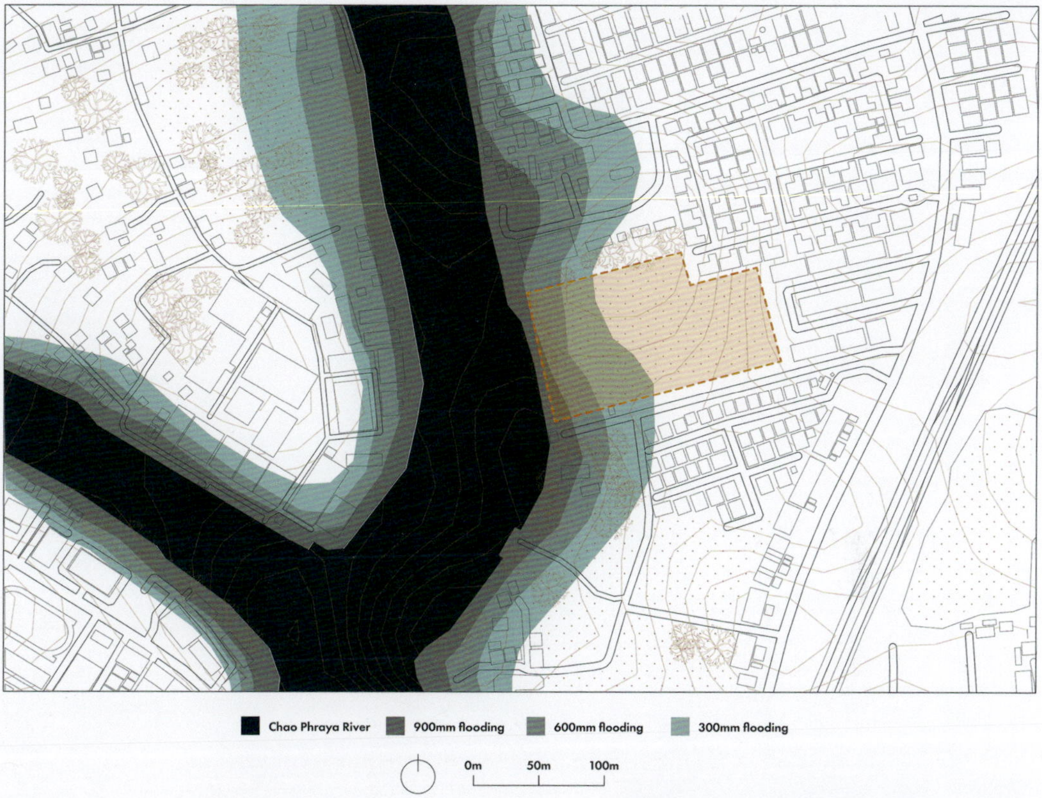

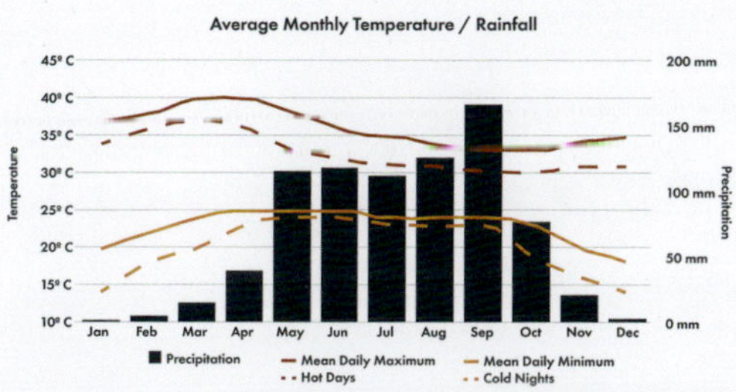

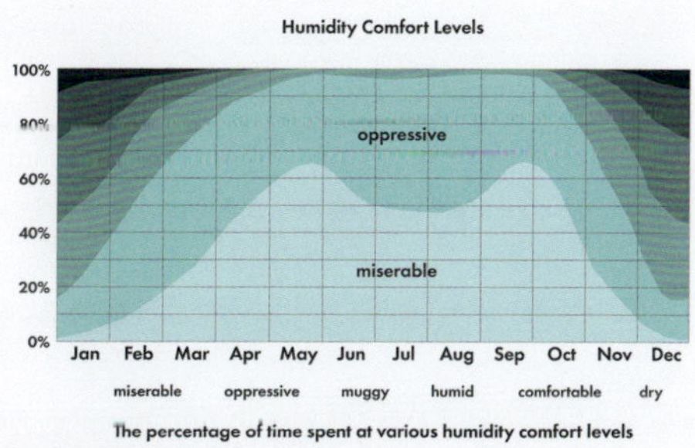

Flooding

The chosen site benefits from optimal access via water, however consequently suffers from flooding, particularly in the rainy season (May - September). The site floods by a maximum of 1m, a factor which must carefully considered.

Temperature

Ayutthaya is classified under the tropical savanna climate, and is warm every month of the year. The average annual temperature is 33ºC, minimum is 13ºC and maximum is 40ºC. This hot climate will be key to the project's design.

Rainfall

The year is divided into a distinct wet and dry season. Wet season (May - September) experiences 8x as much precipitation as the dry. This immense rainfall and the proximity to the river exposes the site to flooding.

Humidity

Being a tropical climate, Ayutthaya experiences high levels of humidity. 70% of the year is spent in 'oppressive' or 'miserable' levels of humidity. For this reason, ventilation strategies are extremely important in this site.

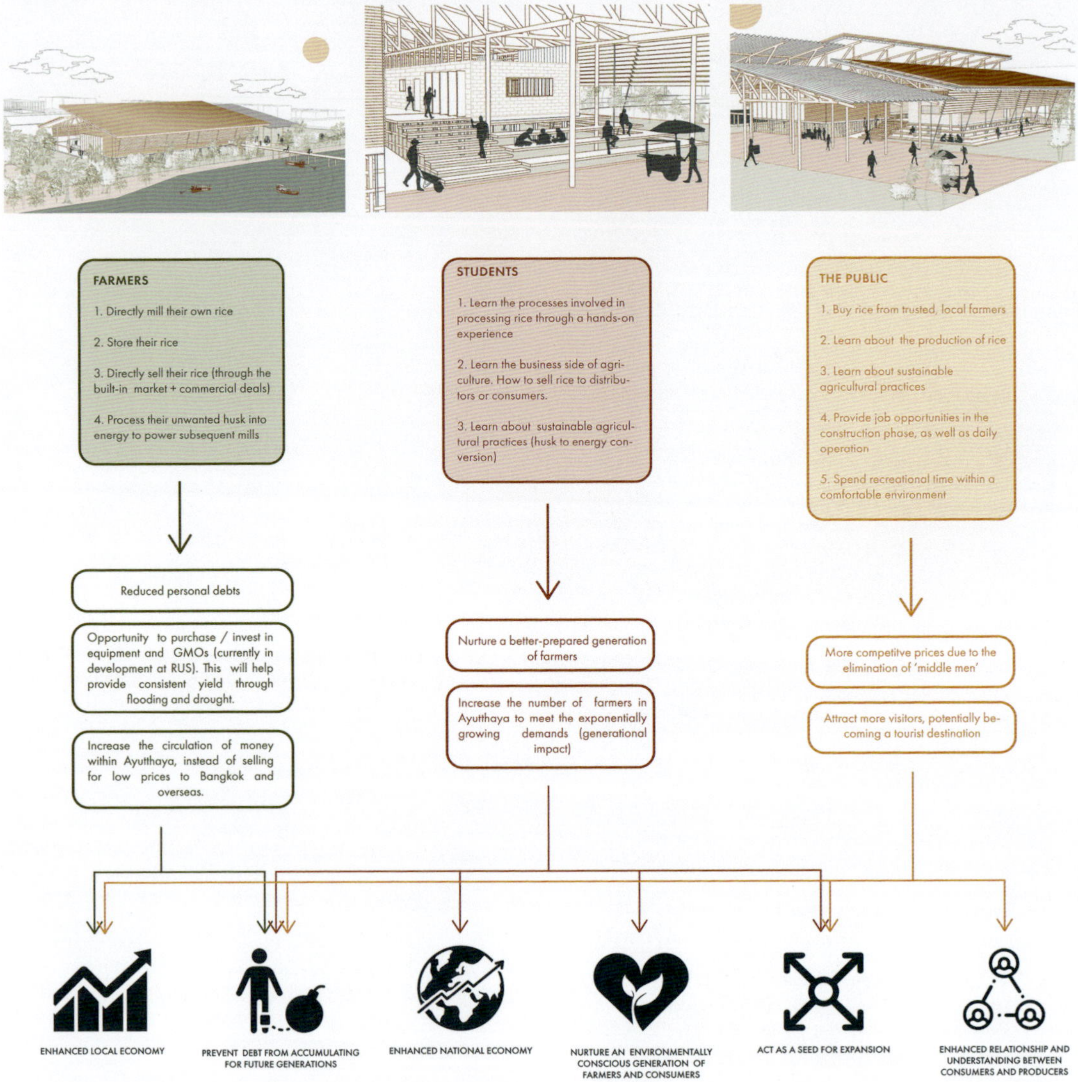

8 Mai Alarilla, Anthony Bucciarelli, Max Cha, Outline for user interaction, 2020.

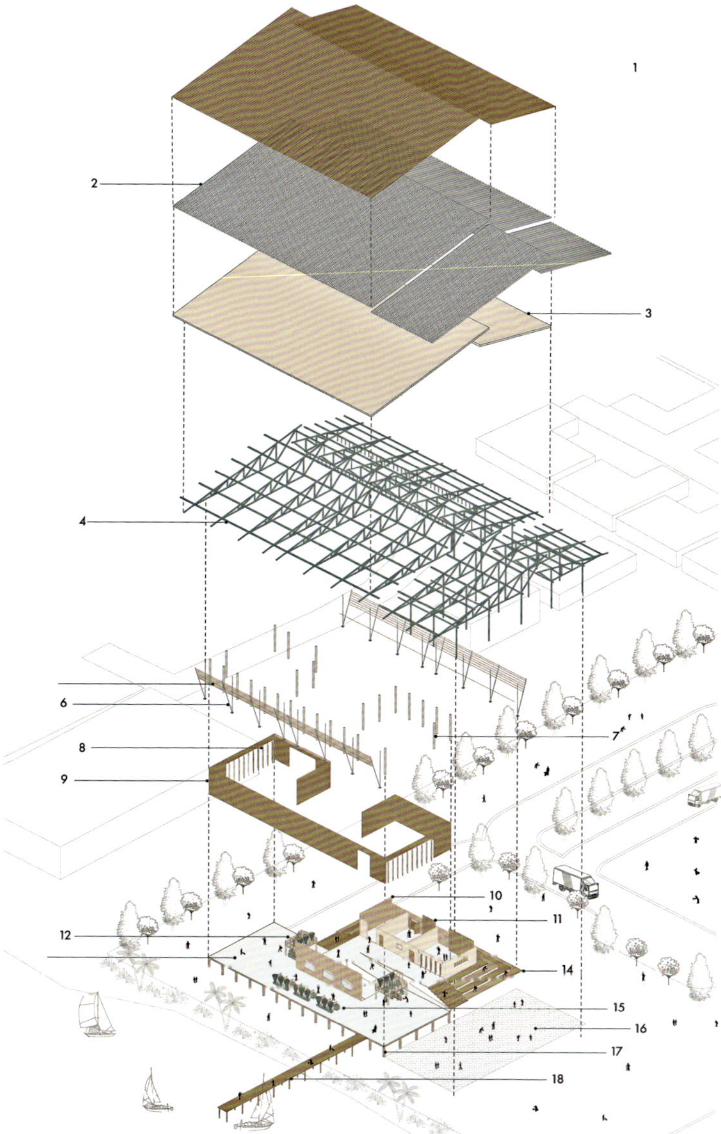

1	*bamboo timber roof slats*
2	*corrugated metal roofing*
3	*insulation*
4	*steel section roof truss*
5	*external timber louvres*
6	*steel support posts with 300mm x 300mm concrete pile*
7	*steel framework made of square hollow sections*
8	*operable timber louvres*
9	*horizontal bamboo slat wall*
10	*compressed earth ventilation brick*
11	*operable pull-out screens*
12	*automatic rice mill system*
13	*300mm reinforced concrete slab*
14	*communal timber seating and stairs*
15	*husk regeneration system*
16	*paved courtyard*
17	*300mm x 300mm concrete piers*
18	*boat jetty with bamboo structure*

9 Mai Alarilla, Anthony Bucciarelli, Max Cha, Exploded axonometric drawing, 2020.

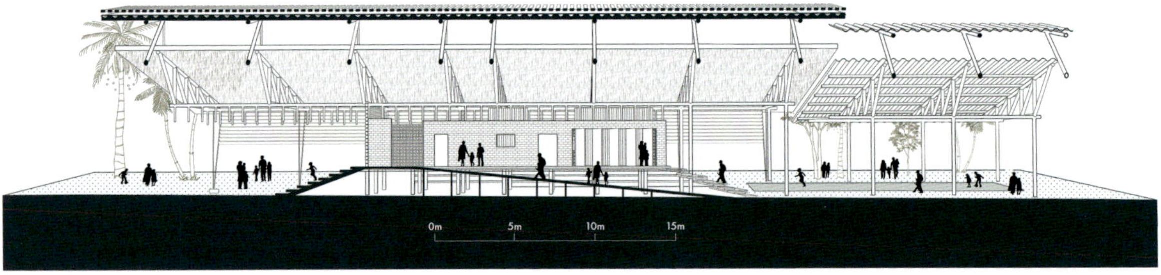

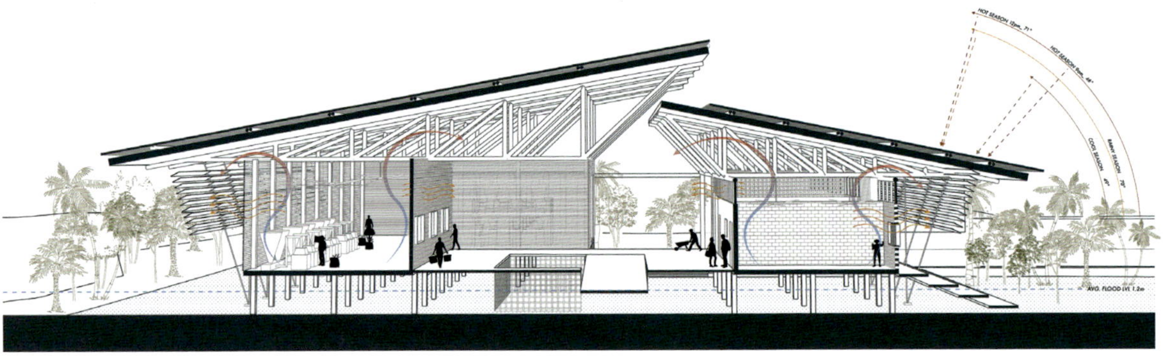

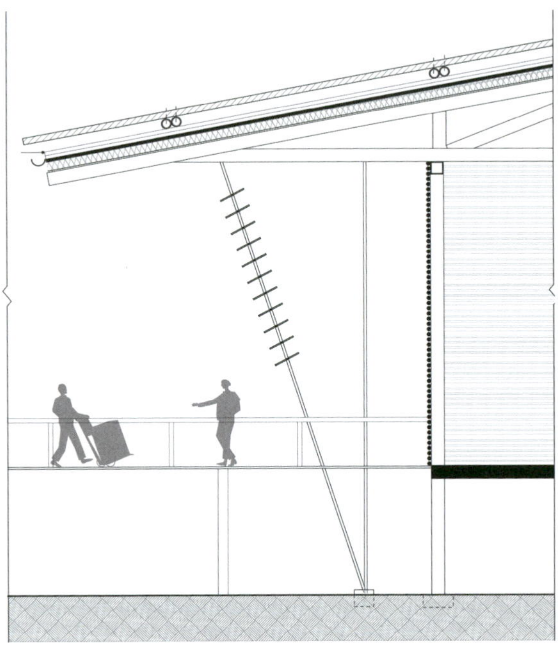

10/11 Mai Alarilla, Anthony Bucciarelli, Max Cha, Building sections and detailed section, 2020.

Shade in Singapore

The agricultural tower designed by Jeffrey Liu, Ali Megahed and Alexander Prichard is positioned as a transparent, faceted silo located in the middle of a busy Singaporean square (Figure 12). Each silo contains a ground-level marketplace as well as upper floors for the most popular foods consumed by Singaporean residents. The silo's interior is divided into fruits, herbs and vegetables that require variable hours of sunlight and humidity. This technocratic proposition is designed as three variations for diverse urban sites: infill, park and reservoir. The silo's exterior is marked by hexagonal clear panels, some of which are fixed and others which are able to be partially opened. These hexagonal panels possess an applied film, which imbues them with degrees of opacity to block out direct sunlight (Figure 13). Such opacity patterns can be programmed and mapped directly onto the types of fruits and vegetables being grown indoors (Figure 14 and Figure 15). Opacity levels can be set at custom levels measuring approximately 20% to 80%. Some panels can be opened manually for better local control. Open ventilation systems—such as a floor-sized fan positioned above the lobby and stack tower structure—allow air to move quickly through each floor, exiting through the top of the building (Figure 16).

12 Jeffrey Liu, Ali Megahed, Alexander Prichard, Aquafarm external visualisation during monsoon season, 2020.

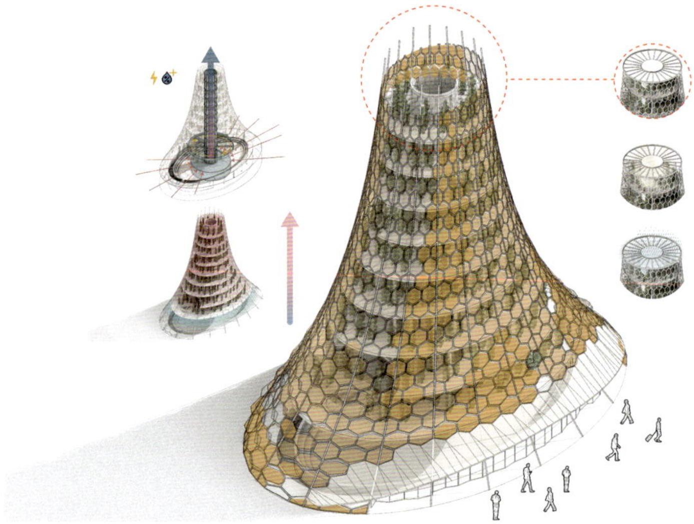

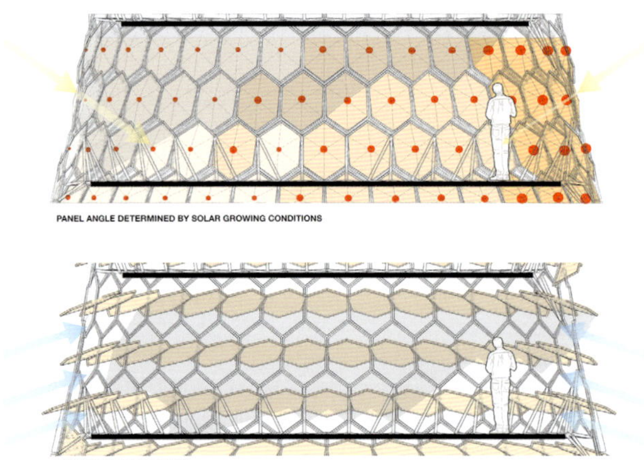

13 Jeffrey Liu, Ali Megahed, Alexander Prichard, Climatic strategy, 2020.

14 Jeffrey Liu, Ali Megahed, Alexander Prichard, Operable panels (blue) and fixed panels (orange), 2020.

15 Jeffrey Liu, Ali Megahed, Alexander Prichard, Opacity and operability of panels, 2020.

16 Jeffrey Liu, Ali Megahed, Alexander Prichard, Interior and exterior visualisations of the park typology, canal typology and city typology, 2020 (left to right).

17 Left: Kexin He, Rebecca Kwok, Spiros Spyrou, 3D rendering of *lumbung padi* and diagrammatic section, 2020.

18 Right: Kexin He, Rebecca Kwok, Spiros Spyrou, Elevation and axonometric drawing depicting flooding levels shown against the side of the building, 2020.

Monsoon season in Jakarta, Indonesia

Jakarta's monsoon flooding and Indonesia's vernacular architecture inspired the design of a riverside granary by Kexin He, Rebecca Kwok and Spiros Spyrou. The vernacular *lumbung padi*, or rice granary, served as a model, in particular for the sectional profile of their shelter (Figure 17). The original example possesses a thatched roof but is raised off the ground on simple columns, with space for storage located in the heart of the structure. The outer edge of this community storehouse/ granary dips into the Ciliwung River, allowing Indonesian fishermen to dock alongside the building in order to unload provisions. The warehouse/ granary acts as a community centre for storing supplies, vegetables and rice for the neighbourhood's families. As the water level rises, provisions and rice remain dry-stored in the upper levels of the granary (Figure 18). The outer panels are marked in Bahasa Indonesia to indicate the height of the water level rising from the Ciliwung River; these panels also serve as a public notice for community members. Constructed from bamboo and lightweight timber, this granary is intended to be a gathering place during non-monsoon seasons. It operates with open airflow and substantial shading devices: perforated screens, a scoop roof marked with vents and movable louvres all contribute to lowering indoor heat and humidity during hot weather (Figure 19). Woven bamboo bifolds doubling as operable screens in the interior allow users to control the amount of sunlight entering the granary. With the first floor lifted from ground level, increased airflow can circulate throughout the entire structure.

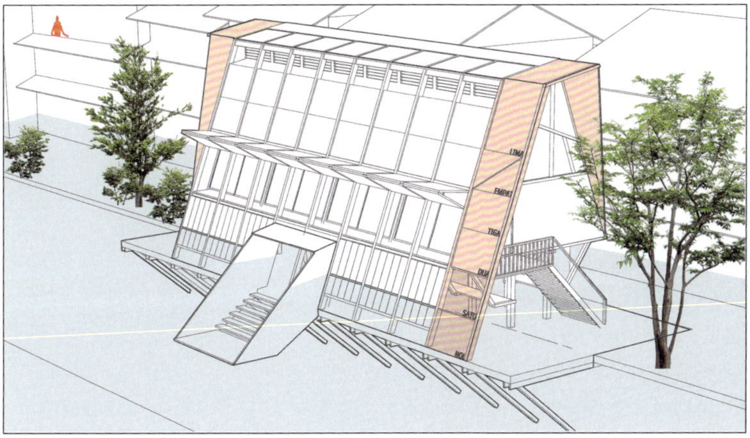

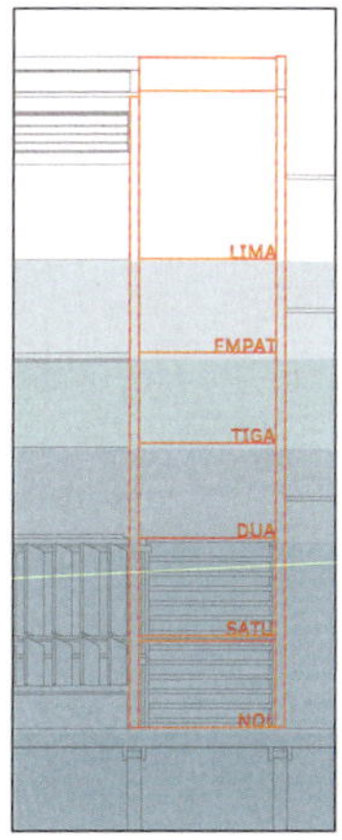

19 Kexin He, Rebecca Kwok, Spiros Spyrou, Balsa wood models illustrating operable louvres and panels, 2020.

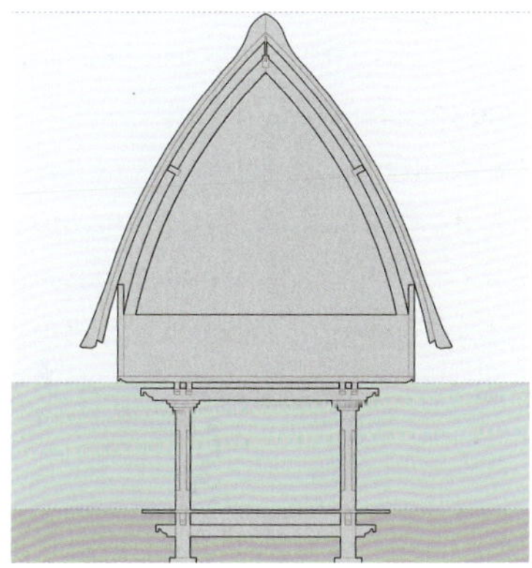

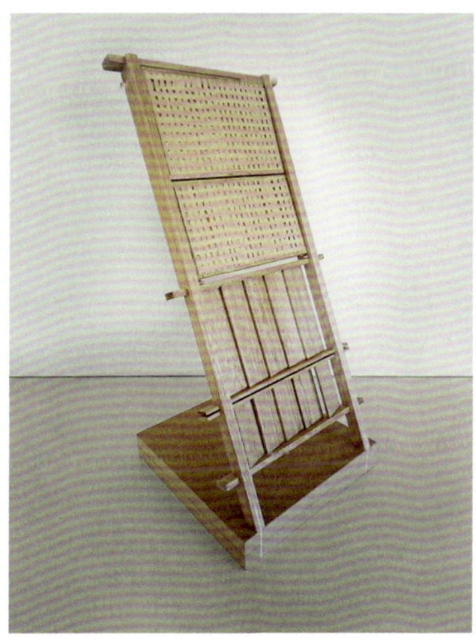

Methods of visual representation of climates

The second section of this coda surveys a selection of student projects from the National University of Singapore (NUS) which explore different methods of visual representation to describe the climates of real-world sites and theoretical premises. Visualising, drawing and modelling remain key currencies in the architecture discipline and practice. Through drawing and modelling, intangible mental images and concepts are allowed to materialise into tangible designs. More than a mechanical skill, drawing resonates as a critical tool of creativity that involves not only processes of depiction, but also extraction, manipulation, imposition, and so on. It enables the physical representation of our world—what it was, what it is and what it could be, and allows architects to speculate, invent and project. The act of drawing and the drawing itself can hence be used as a trigger to advance the intellectual capacity to design and further the development of architecture. Likewise, models are both generators for ideas as well as reflexive communication tools. They are not only a prototype, but serve as an important method of seeing, visualising and analysing architecture.

Alberti's treatise on architecture, *De re aedificatoria* (On building), was such a prototype for Renaissance architecture. Learning from classical models, Alberti placed an emphasis on precise geometry, proportions, symmetry and regularity in form through the primacy of the line. He used lines and geometry as a framework for architectural thinking. These architectural lines served to visualise, but also to control and to censor. They represented *graphesis*—or visual forms of knowledge production. His perspective line drawings prompted a novel three-dimensional way of viewing architecture, and as a result, these ideas influenced much of architecture, art and even computer modelling today. However, in the predilection for the line as an organising device, it was ill equipped to represent climate, ecology, weather including clouds, fire, snow, ice, dust, etc. However, in the face of the growing climate crises that affect us in very real and tangible ways, we realise that architecture must formulate strategies that incorporate climate, rather than separate it from the architectural repertoire.

Extending to, and inverting Alberti's insistence on the line, this section showcases drawings and models from students representing architecture by prioritising its invisible inhabitants—air, atmosphere and climate. The novel construction of drawings purposefully indicates the architecture's conceptual and physical interaction with these elements of the built environment.

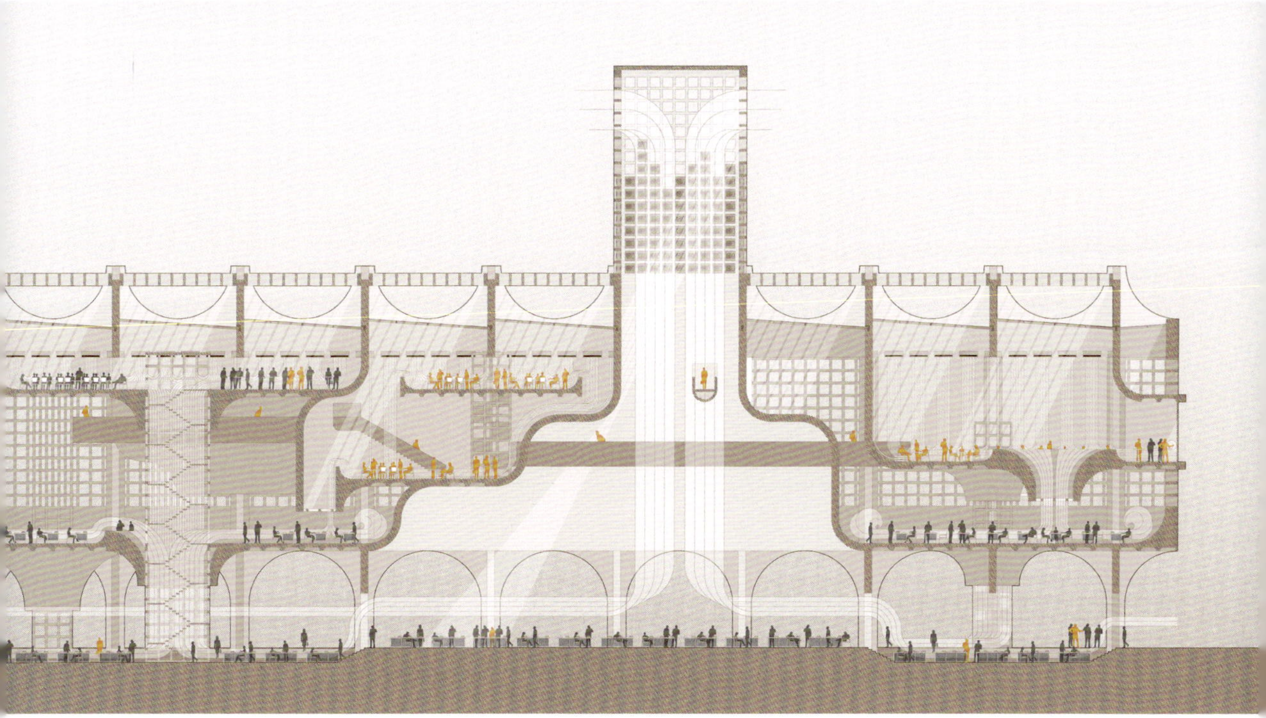

Badabing Badaboom— The politics of conditioned air in a goldrush boomtown and 'Thick walls, thin air'

20 Jason Tan, Section, Badabing Badaboom, 2015, Thesis studio.

In the Badabing Badaboom project, the section is employed to impose the visualisation of air as an indicator of politics and a determinant of hierarchy in the architecture. The convention of lines is used to define the climatic and political scenarios of the architectural body. Lines of air—natural and artificial—infiltrate and inhabit the politically programmed spaces, creating a quiet but powerful political commentary on the power relations between Chinese immigrants and a rural Ghanaian community (Figure 20).

In 'Thick walls, thin air,' the axonometric and worm's eye drawings are similarly constructed to open up the architectural spaces to the external air; the porosity of the building is both metaphorically and literally represented as an interaction between internal microclimate and the external climate. In doing so, the drawings traverse between climate and geometry (Figure 21 and Figure 22).

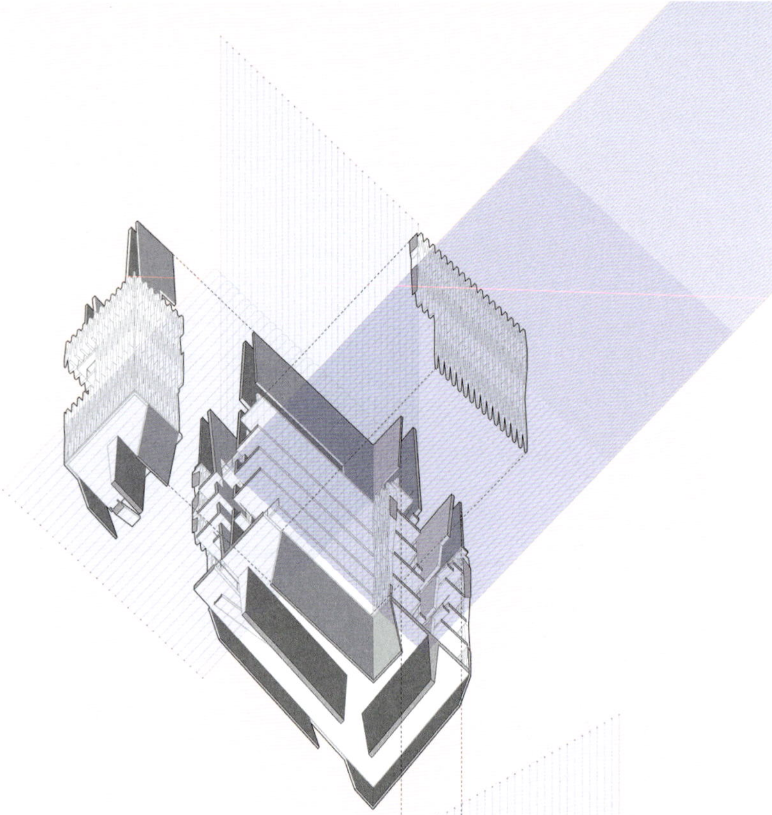

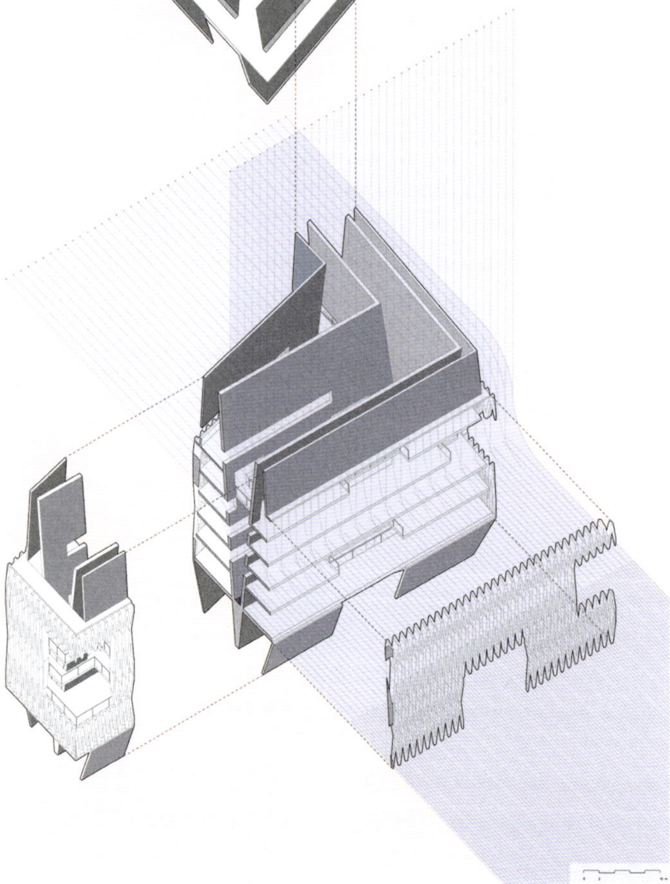

21 Nicholas Tai Han Vern, Luh Astrid Mayadinta, Axonometric drawing showing airflow from the south, 2019, Thick Walls, Thin Air, Seoul Biennale 2019 global studio: hot air of HCMC.

22 Nicholas Tai Han Vern, Luh Astrid Mayadinta, Worm's eye exploded axonometric from South side, 2019, Thick Walls, Thin Air, Seoul Biennale 2019 global studio: hot air of HCMC.

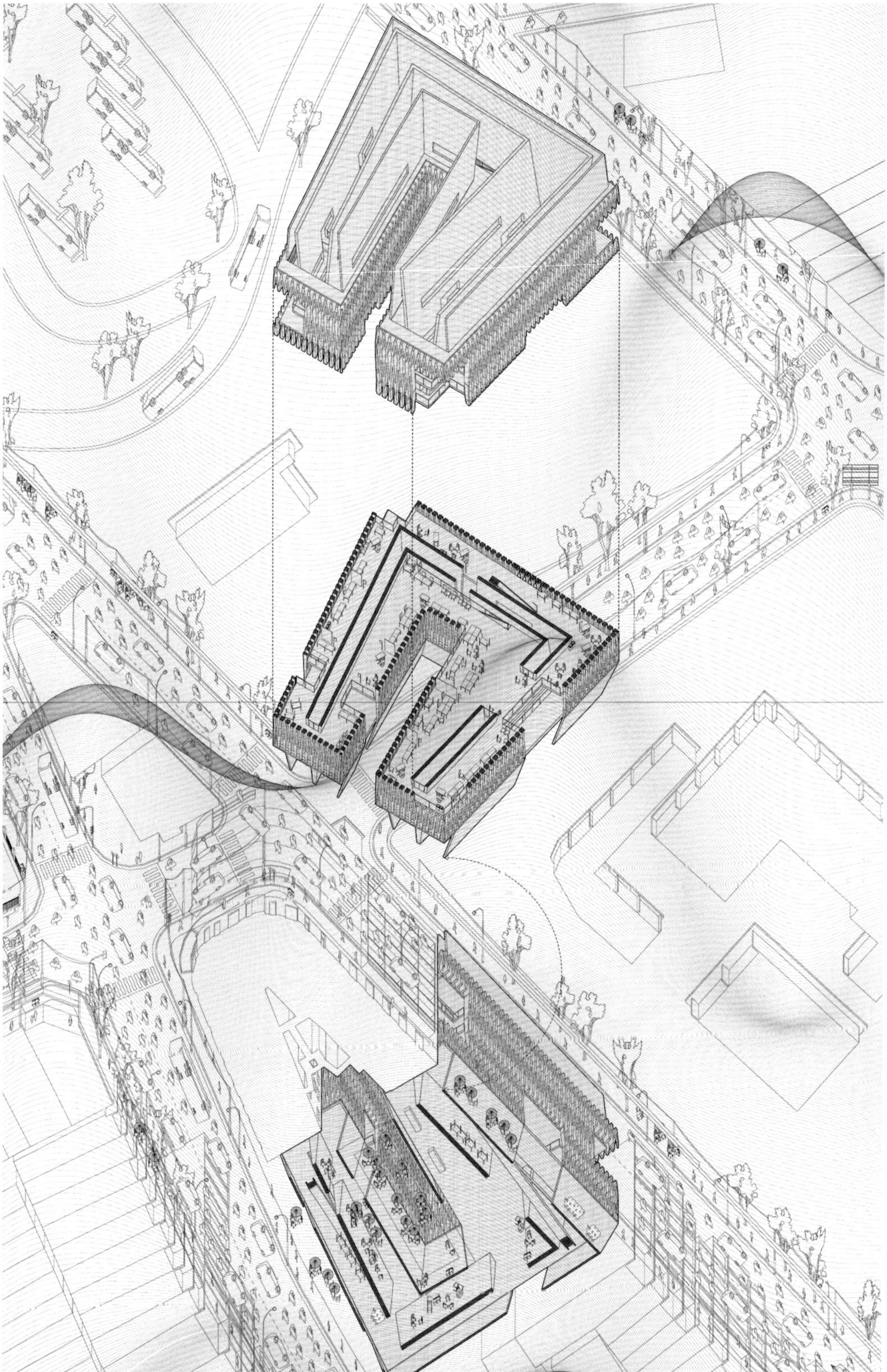

'Suaka' and 'Pasar Merah'

This technique of drawing is also developed to indicate a certain atmosphere and microclimate of the naturally ventilated spaces of the market in projects 'Suaka' and 'Pasar Merah.' In 'Suaka,' the tessellations of abstracted batik clouds in the exploded axonometric drawings mirror the stratified atmosphere of the tapered perimeter structure, moving visitors into the sanctuary of the *alun-alun* (Figure 24). Abstract batik cloud patterns that represent the air are reflected on the underside of the roof of the defensive perimeter in gold, echoing the bustling activities of informal traders and visitors. As suggested in the chapter 'Clouding architecture,' the sky here is intentionally represented as a washed-out background instead of an International Style sky, bringing to life the hazy, overcast Palembang air in the worm's eye sectional oblique drawing of 'Pasar Merah.' Through the use of the worm's eye view, the sky background is revealed through the architecture; in an attempt to create breathing space, a matrix of holes punched through the building contrasts with the typical filled-to-the-brim spaces of Palembang (Figure 23). Again, climate and geometry merge and separate fluidly, flowing between representation and reality to recreate the atmosphere of the architecture and the site.

23 Alexa Chia Yet Peng, Kok Shu Hui Lisa, Worm's eye sectional oblique, Pasar Merah, 2018, Hot air travelling studio.

24 Ulrich Chia, Jacelyn Pau, Haorong Lee, Exploded axonometric (left), The band of Wakafs urban worm's eye (right) Suaka, 2018, Hot air: the equatorial city & the architecture of atmosphere.

'Courtyard in a shell' and 'Breathe'

Modes of representation can significantly change the way we view climate and its interaction with architecture. In projects 'Courtyard in a shell' and 'Breathe,' climate simulations are carefully mixed into drawings, creating a type of pseudo-science where the architect can engage with the simulations not just as facts, but as aesthetic symbols. Climate here operates as a visual medium, just as architects would normatively represent structure or walls or windows. By delivering the very real climate implications of the built environment and showing the possibilities of designing microclimates within a building, embedding representations of climate into the architecture creates a tangible relationship between them. The result is a drawing that captures a moment in time of the interaction between climatic elements and the built structure.

In 'Courtyard in a shell,' the worm's eye exploded axonometric generates simulations of heat gain, airflow and drag into the drawing, integrating how we visualise the ecological relationship between climate and our built environment (Figure 25). Similarly, the wind drawing in 'Breathe' captures a frame in time and makes visible, air as an inhabitant moving within the city, changing the way we think about microclimates between buildings (Figure 26).

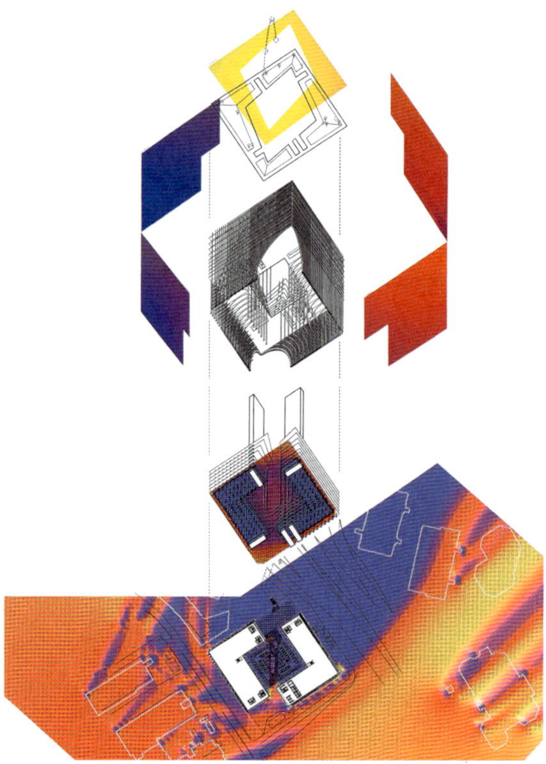

25 Yeow Bok Guan, Worm's eye exploded axonometric, block 47 & 51: Courtyard in a shell, 2018, JTC studio Hot, wet & breezy.

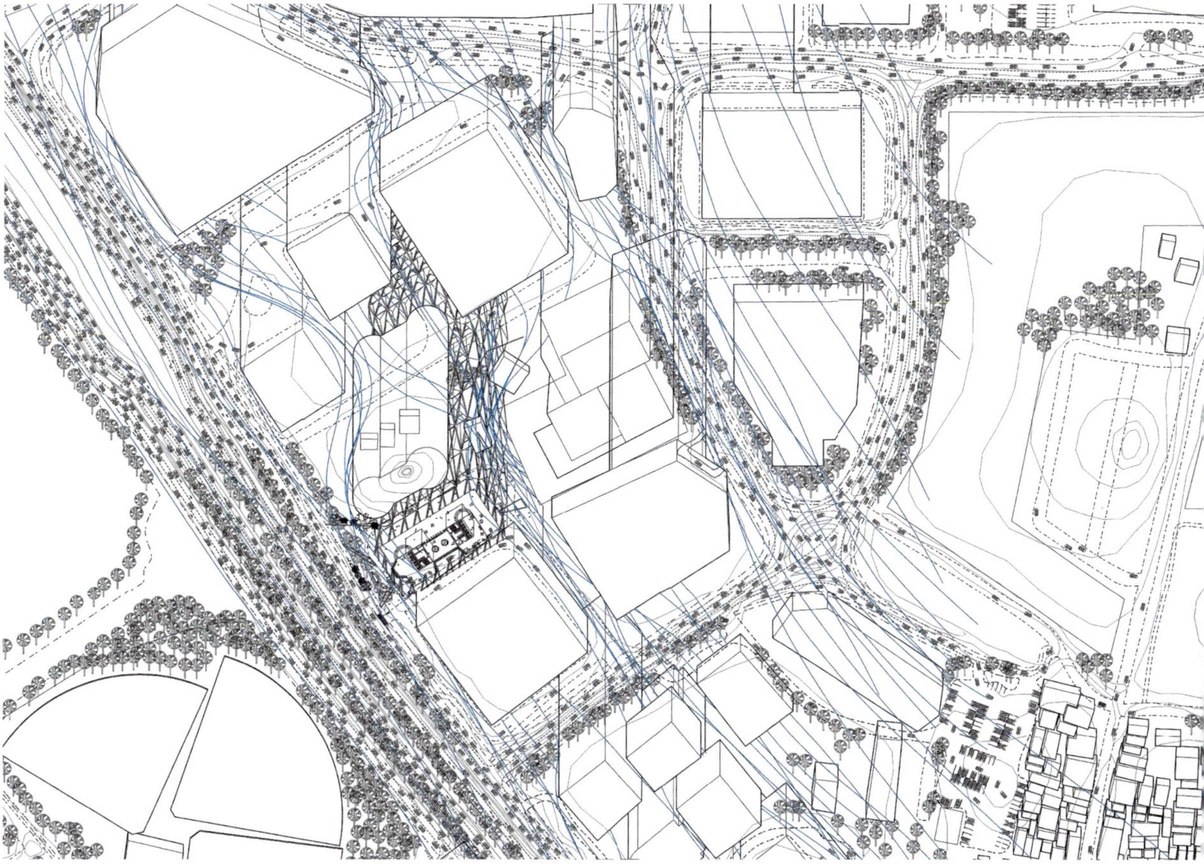

26 Sheila Ong, Tan Yuan Wei, Wind drawing, Breathe, 2015, Steam: The Equatorial City & The Architecture of Atmosphere.

'The veiled chamber'

The materialisation of air as a prioritised inhabitant in architecture is further shown through the isometric drawing and air model in 'The veiled chamber.' Like artist Rachel Whiteread, who creates sculptures by filling the void spaces of old buildings with concrete, these methods of representation use air as a solid material, filling the interior spaces of a building. As an inverted Nolli map, the isometric drawing and air model represent volumes and sections of air, not space, as the focal material of the architecture. Naturally ventilated and lit spaces slowly push back the need for stuffy air-conditioned ones (Figure 27 and Figure 28). Air in these models is understood as a material, with a physical presence that embodies the tangible qualities of living on the equator. Unlike the term 'space,' which implies the absence of material, the shift to working with 'air' affords the architect a way to visualise the invisible, taking custodianship of climate to use it as a fundamental component of architecture that requires care and careful consideration, even vision and speculation.

These explorations within the design studio emphasise the importance of acknowledging the intrinsic attributes of climates as physical forces and generative tools. They illustrate the possibilities of a fully embodied form of architecture that takes up climate as an inspiration for architectural design and an experimental tool for visual representation. Through the processes of drawing, modelling and visualising, climate can be increasingly recognised as a key architectural concern that unlocks the new potential of visible and invisible elements in architecture.

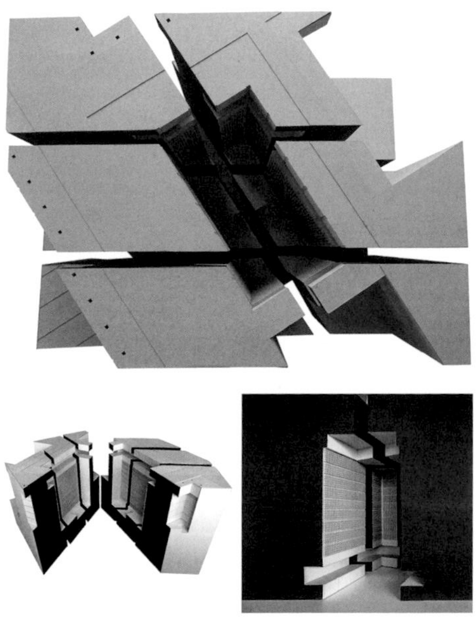

27 Jason Tan, Photographs of Air Model, The Veiled Chamber, 2014, Hot+Wet Studio.

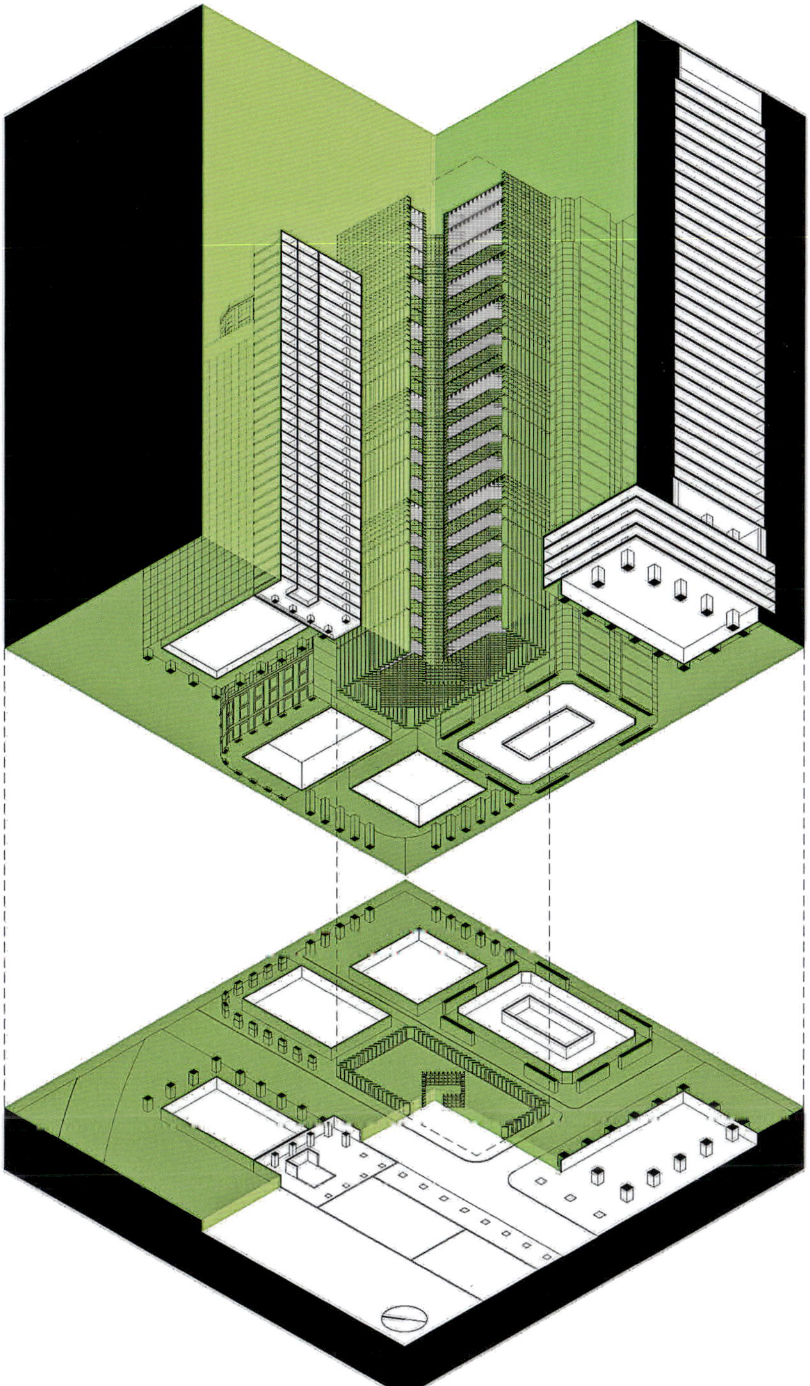

28 Jason Tan, Formal Reading Isometric drawing, The Veiled Chamber, 2014, Hot + Wet Studio.

About the editors and authors

DANIEL J. RYAN (PhD, University of Sydney) is Lecturer in Sustainable Design and Program Director of the Master of Architectural Science at the University of Sydney. His research explores the history of architectural science and architecture in the tropics, focusing on Australasia and the Pacific. He investigates the changing environmental role of domestic buildings and their technologies during the twentieth century. His work has appeared in Ėditions du Centre Pompidou, *Journal of Architectural Education, ABE Journal: Architecture beyond Europe, Architectural Theory Review,* among others.

JENNIFER FERNG (PhD, MIT) is Senior Lecturer in Architecture and Postgraduate Coordinator at the University of Sydney. Her research addresses environmental and humanitarian issues in Europe, Asia and Oceania from the eighteenth century onwards, and her articles have appeared in *Architectural Histories*, *Architectural Theory Review*, *Change Over Time*, *Fabrications*, and *Journal of the Society of Architectural Historians*. She was awarded a Transregional Research Junior Scholar Fellowship from the Social Science Research Council (SSRC). She was a visiting scholar at the Harvard Asia Center and visiting research fellow at University College London's Institute of Advanced Studies. She recently co-edited (together with Lauren R. Cannady) *Crafting Enlightenment. Artisanal Histories and Transnational Networks* (Oxford University Studies in the Enlightenment, 2021).

ERIK G. L'HEUREUX, FAIA is a Vice Dean, Master of Architecture Programme Director and Dean's Chair Associate Professor at the School of Design and Environment, National University of Singapore, teaching a new generation of architects to be committed to the complexities and potentials of architecture located along the equator. His design research combines passive performance, pattern and simplicity as a poetic response towards the equatorial hot, wet climate and a dense urban context, elaborated on in his architectural monograph *Deep Veils* (ORO Editions, 2014). His design work and contribution to the discipline has been recognised by the American Institute of Architects (AIA), being elevated to the College of Fellows, AIA in 2020, and his buildings have won several AIA New York and AIA National Design Awards. As Vice Dean, he leads the transformation of the School of Design and Environment at the National University of Singapore.

CHRISTHINA CANDIDO (PhD, Macquarie University/ UFSC) is an architect with a PhD in Civil Engineering from the Federal University of Santa Catarina (Brazil) and in Environmental Science from Macquarie University (Australia). Her research interest and expertise relate to design, experience and performance of spaces. Her projects and publications are related to the fields of Post-Occupancy Evaluation (POE), Indoor Environmental Quality (IEQ), new ways of working and learning, and climate-responsive design in tropical and subtropical climates. A/Prof Candido directs the SHE – Sustainable and Healthy Environments – Lab at the University of Melbourne. The SHE Lab develops a programme of applied research aimed at understanding how the built environment can improve sustainability and health. She works closely with the Green Building Council of Australia (GBCA), the National Australian Built Environment Rating System (NABERS) and the International WELL Building Institute. She is a WELL Faculty member.

LILIAN CHEE (PhD, UCL Bartlett) is Associate Professor at the Department of Architecture, National University of Singapore, where she co-leads the Research by Design Cluster. Her research connects embodied experience and affective evidence with architectural representation and feminist politics. Her award-winning film collaboration *03-FLATS* (2014) has screened in 16 major cities. She is on the editorial boards of *Architectural Theory Review*, *Australian Feminist Studies*, and the *idea journal* and is an advisor for the Bloomsbury Architecture Library. Her current book projects are *Architecture and Affect* (Routledge), *Remote Practices: Architecture at a Distance* (Lund Humphries), and *Art in Public Space* (URA, Singapore). Her forthcoming research explores the intersection of home-based work practices with domesticity through an affective-feminist perspective.

NATHAN ETHERINGTON is an architect and doctoral candidate at the University of Sydney. He is the founder and principal of NEA – Nathan Etherington Architect. He holds a Master in Architecture with Distinction from the Harvard Graduate School of Design for which he received the Kevin V. Kieran Prize for outstanding academic achievement. He has also received the Australian Institute of Architects' David Linder Prize. His current doctoral research considers the role of architecture and infrastructure in the projection of colonial governance through territorial transformation.

JOHANNA SLUITER is a doctoral candidate in Art History at the Institute of Fine Arts, New York University. She is a Chester Dale Fellow at the Center for Advanced Study in the Visual Arts at the National Gallery of Art, Washington, D.C. In her research, she focuses on postwar French architecture and exhibitions, with specific emphasis on issues of leisure, decolonisation and city planning. Her writing has appeared or is forthcoming in *Guernica: A Magazine of Art and Politics*, *The Street Art & Urban Creativity Scientific Journal* and The Museum of Modern Art's *Museum Research Consortium Dossier*.

NICOLE SULLY (PhD, UWA) is a Senior Lecturer in the School of Architecture at the University of Queensland, where she teaches History and Theory of Architecture, and Architectural Design. Her research focuses on architecture and memory, pathologies of place and critical reinterpretations of modern architecture. Publications include the co-edited books *Shifting Views: Selected Essays on the Architectural History of Australia and New Zealand* (University of Queensland Press, 2008) and *Out of Place (Gwalia): Occasional Essays on Australian Regional Communities and Built Environments in Transition* (University of Western Australia Press, 2014).

DEBORAH VAN DER PLAAT (PhD, UNSW) is a Senior Lecturer at the School of Architecture, The University of Queensland, Brisbane. Her research examines the intersection of climate, race, place and taste in nineteenth- and twentieth-century architecture, theory and criticism. She is co-editor of *Speaking of Buildings: Oral History In Architectural Research* (Princeton Architectural Press, 2019), *Hot Modernism: Queensland Architecture 1945–1975* (Artifice, 2015) and *Skyplane: what effect do towers have on urbanism, sustainability, the workplace and historic city centres?* (UNSW Press, 2009). Forthcoming publications include *The Architecture of Robin Gibson: Light Space Place* (URO Media, 2021) and *Karl Langer: Modern Architect and Migrant in the Australian Tropics* (Bloomsbury, 2022).

Acknowledgements

The editors would like to thank their respective institutions—the University of Sydney and National University of Singapore—for supporting this international collaboration. This design book represents a joint venture not only between our two universities but also between colleagues based in Australia, Singapore and the USA. We are grateful to our individual authors as well as architects for their contributions to this volume. We are thankful to our families and friends for all their support and encouragement.

This book is an outcome of a USyd-NUS Partnership Collaboration Award (2018–2019). Robyn Dowling, Andrew Leach and Ho Puay Peng helped us acquire funding for the colour images in this book. Srilakshmi Menon, Palak Mehta, Amanda Mo and Ong Chan Hao were instrumental throughout all stages of this project. Adrian Thai created the initial graphic design for this book, which served as inspiration for further design development. Lastly, Andreas Müller as editor for the publisher patiently guided this book to completion. Diethard Keppler created the book's final graphic design.

Illustration credits

Cover illustration
National Weather Service, College Park, Maryland, USA, public domain.

Introduction: redirecting the arrows of climatic design
DANIEL J. RYAN

1 Drawing by Russel Ball for Edward Mazria, 1979. Used with permission of Edward Mazria.
2 With permission of Rowman and Littlefield Publishing Group Inc. through PLSclear.
3 © 2018 Routledge. Reproduced by permission of Taylor & Francis Group.

Particles to dust storms: seeing climates from below
JENNIFER FERNG

1, 8 NASA. Photo courtesy of Jeff Schmaltz, MODIS Rapid Response team.
2 Public domain.
3 © Michael Layefsky. Used with permission of the photographer and Eugene Tssui.
4–5 Bibliothèque nationale de France (BnF).
6 Photo by Stan Honda/AFP via Getty Images.
7 Wellcome Collection no. 38709i.
9 G. Tipene/Shutterstock.

Wind, making the invisible visible: design for and with natural ventilation
CHRISTHINA CANDIDO

1 Public domain.
2 Christhina Candido.
3 above Stewart McDowell/ Wikimedia Commons.
3 below, 4–6 Christhina Candido.

Weathering the monsoon: affective relations
LILIAN CHEE

1 Photograph by Ong Chan Hao.
2–4 Courtesy of Simryn Gill.
5–14 Photographs by Ong Chan Hao.

Clouding architecture
ERIK G. L'HEUREUX

1, 13 Photographs by Finbarr Fallon
2–7, 13 Public domain.
8 Courtesy of the Frank Lloyd Wright Foundation.
9 Image courtesy of Fonds de Dotation Denise & Yona Friedman.
10 Photograph by Fujiko Nakaya.
11 Photograph by Wolfgang Kessling.
12 Photograph by Kevin Scott.

90% chance of rain: downpour as event
NATHAN ETHERINGTON

1, 4 above and below
© Foundation Le Corbusier/ADAGP. Copyright Agency, 2021.
2 © 2021 Commonwealth of Australia. Used with permission of Bureau of Meteorology.
3 Photograph by Nathan Etherington.
5 Mitchell Library, State Library of New South Wales and courtesy Glenn Murcutt, PXD 728/Roll 182.
6 Mitchell Library, State Library of New South Wales and courtesy Glenn Murcutt, ON 559/Box 18/nos. 675–705.
7 Courtesy of FRAC.
8 Lars Spuybroek fonds, Canadian Centre for Architecture. Gift of Lars Spuybroek.
9–10 Courtesy of Philippe Rahm.
11–12 Image courtesy of Stoss.

Creating shadows and seeking shade
NICOLE SULLY / DEBORAH VAN DER PLAAT

1 Public domain. Engraving from the National Gallery of Art, Washington D.C., Nr. 1983.61.1.
2 Public Domain. Wellcome Library no. 32782i.
3 Public domain, Wikimedia Commons.
4 Public domain. Engraving from the Metropolitan Museum of Art, Nr. 62.650.455.
5 Public domain. The New York Public Library Digital Collections, https://digitalcollections.nypl.org/items/510d47d9-4f42-a3d9-e040-e00a18064a99.
6 Image courtesy of the National Archives at College Park, Maryland, Nr. 46740253.
7 Image courtesy of the National Gallery of Australia, Nr. NGA 1975.41.
8 Public domain. Image courtesy of the State Library of Victoria, Nr. H27482.
9 Public domain. Image courtesy of the State Library of Victoria, Nr. H2002.130/18.
10 Public domain. Image courtesy of the State Library of Victoria, Nr. H96.200/1208.
11 Public domain. Image courtesy of the State Library of Queensland, Nr. 224712.
12 Public domain. Image courtesy of the State Library of Queensland, Nr. 224860.
13 Image courtesy of Picture Sunshine Coast, Sunshine Coast Council, Nr. M862911.
14 Image courtesy of the State Library of Queensland, Nr. 200485.
15 John Oxley Library, State Library of Queensland, Nr. 29499-0001-0008. Used with permission of the Heathwood family.
16 Karl Langer Collection, Fryer Library, The University of Queensland, UQFL158, Box 37. Used with permission.
17 Karl Langer Collection, Fryer Library, The University of Queensland, UQFL158, Box 44. Used with permission.

From crystal to cryosphere: architecture for the future ice age
JOHANNA SLUITER

1 Public domain. Image courtesy of Library of Congress, Washington, DC, Nr. 2005691861.
2, 6 Public domain.
3 *Snow crystals: natural and artificial* by Ukichiro Nakaya, Cambridge, Mass.: Harvard University Press, Copyright © 1954 by the President and Fellows of Harvard College. Copyright © renewed 1982 by Mrs. Ukichiro Nakaya.
4 Department of Image Collections, National Gallery of Art Library, Washington, DC.
5 © Minnesota Historical Society.
7 Courtesy of SEArch.
8 Courtesy of MAP Architects.
9 Courtesy of ArkDes.
10 Courtesy of HB Architects.
11 above Svalbard Globale Seed Vault/Mari Tefre, Creative Commons Attribution-No Derivs 2.0. https://flic.kr/p/7nYgQp.
11 below Svalbard Globale Seed Vault/Mari Tefre, Creative Commons Attribution-No Derivs 2.0. https://flic.kr/p/7nYgQr.

Revealing fire
DANIEL J. RYAN

1 Public domain.
2 Courtesy Tate Gallery, London.
3–4 Courtesy of Nigel Bertram SueAnne Ware and Letterbox Graphic Design Studio.
5–6 Courtesy of Stuart Harrison and Letterbox Graphic Design Studio.
7–8 Courtesy of Lisle Rudoph.
9 Image courtesy of Tin Sheds Gallery, University of Sydney. Used with permission of Kevin O'Brien.

Explorations: climatic design in the design studio
JENNIFER FERNG / ERIK G. L'HEUREUX

1–19 Courtesy of the University of Sydney.
20–28 Courtesy of the National University of Singapore.

Name index

Subject index

Support for this book provided by the University of Sydney
and the National University of Singapore

Graphic design, layout and typography:
Diethard Keppler, Marbach am Neckar,
and Philippa Walz, Stuttgart

Cover illustration by National Weather Service, USA

Editor for the publisher: Andreas Müller
Production: Heike Strempel
Paper: 135 g/m² Condat matt Perigord
Printing: Gutenberg Beuys Feindruckerei GmbH

Bibliographic information published by the
German National Library
The German National Library lists this publication in the
Deutsche Nationalbibliografie;
detailed bibliographic data are available on the Internet at
http://dnb.dnb.de.

Library of Congress Control Number: 2021944675

This work is subject to copyright. All rights are reserved,
whether the whole or part of the material is concerned,
specifically the rights of translation, reprinting, re-use
of illustrations, recitation, broadcasting, reproduction on
microfilms or in other ways, and storage in databases.
For any kind of use, permission of the copyright owner
must be obtained.

This publication is also available as an e-book
(ISBN PDF 978-3-0356-2361-1).

© 2022 Birkhäuser Verlag GmbH, Basel
P.O. Box 44, 4009 Basel, Switzerland
Part of Walter de Gruyter GmbH, Berlin/Boston

Printed on acid-free paper produced from chlorine-free pulp.
TCF ∞

Printed in Germany

ISBN 978-3-0356-2360-4

9 8 7 6 5 4 3 2 1

www.birkhauser.com